OUR RUNAWAY GLOBE

How To Restore Balance On Earth

The Rescue of Core Values and the Power of
Positive Change

Author:
Rafael Augusto Carreras

1st Edition -   June 2017 / Revised March 2018
Editorial: Dr. John McAllister
Cover Design & Illustration: Kristian Lehner
Author Photo: Cornelia Bujara

Issued in print, electronic and digital formats.
Paperback: ISBN 978-1547155668

For reference visit: http://www.collectionscanada.gc.ca/ciss-ssci/app/index.php?lang=eng

Publisher:
Carreras, Rafael Augusto. "Our Runaway Globe. Self-Published via Createspace, Charleston, 2018
www.createspace.com

Printed and bound in the United States
First printing: June 2017
10 9 8 7 6 5 4 3 2 1

IMPORTANT MESSAGES

I think the environment should be put in the category of our national security. Defense of our resource is just as important as defense abroad. Otherwise, what is there to defend?
- **Robert Redford**

We are living on this planet as if we had another one to go to.
- **Terri Swearingen**

Earth provides enough to satisfy every man's needs, but not every man's greed. - **Mahatma Gandhi**

It was not Exxon Valdez captain's driving that caused the Alaskan oil spill. It was yours. - **Greenpeace**

Plans to protect air and water, wilderness and wildlife are in fact plans to protect man. - **Stewart Udall**

-

THE RUNAWAY TRILOGY

Our Runaway Society

<u>Our Runaway Globe</u>

Our Runaway Rights

======================================

TABLE OF CONTENTS

DEDICATION

This book is dedicated to the only place we currently have to live in – our globe, that is, "Mother Earth," our planet.

It is also dedicated to the following people who are in desperate need of help but who either fail to see this or just do not want to accept it:

- Those whose over-optimism shadows and blurs their view of their surrounding reality and of what urgently needs doing to achieve a healthy balance of life on Mother Earth.

- Those who deny the facts because of political correctness.

- Those with blinkers on their eyes who believe that everything is fine and there is nothing to worry about. They think nature – or some celestial power – will always balance things at the end. But they refuse to see the one thing that is undeniable: the evidence of down-to-earth, mathematically proven science.

- Those whose greed and love of power keeps them prisoners in isolated, dark rooms surrounded by loneliness, mistrust, remorse, and a stupid pride that denies them the human ability to care and protect.

- Those who lack the humility, wisdom, and healthy heart and brain to realize that, on our globe, nothing is infinite.

- Those short-sighted individuals who need to break out of their cocoon, search for the truth, and fight for what is right.

I hope this book will help open the eyes and the hearts of all these people and enable them to confront the future with the courage that comes with accepting reality.

Finally, I dedicate this book to:

- Those who are truly interested in our environment and our ecosystem.

- Those who believe in the potential of new technologies and the infinite ability of the human imagination to adapt and survive.

- Those who understand that fresh water, clean air, and healthy soil are not just necessities but fundamental rights for every human being.

- Those who love nature because they understand that it is the most valuable and beautiful thing on our planet and needs nurturing and care.

- Those who not only believe in a better future but are willing to sacrifice time and effort to achieve it, not just tag along and do nothing.

- Those who understand that one day our planet will stop compromising with the increasing demands of an excruciating human footprint and who are not afraid of standing their ground firmly and proudly in defence of our common home.

I hope this book will strengthen the ability of these people to educate others, oppose attacks on our environment, and live more responsibly themselves.

Personal note:

When I was younger, I trusted in nature and in the "natural balance" of things. But as I grew older, I realized I had been daydreaming. I saw that what appears safe and positive on the surface is not always so nice when looked at more deeply.

For example, there are a lot of proverbs and sayings that mean well and are accepted at face value but are far from being true. They are meant to make us feel hopeful and satisfied, but in reality, they fog our vision, unfocus our minds, and obscure what is right. Here are three good examples of what I mean:

"What is coming is better than what is gone" (Arabic proverb).

Does this mean that our indiscriminate poaching and trophy-hunting of animal species is better than what is coming to them (and us) – their extinction?

"Be happy. Just because things are not good doesn't mean you can't see the good side of things" (popular Internet meme).

Tell that to the people of the Amazon and to the thousands of species who call the rainforest their home, where deforestation is rampant and becoming uncontrollable.

"Giving is better than receiving, because giving starts the receiving process" (Jim Rohn, motivational author).

Explain that to the proprietors of the tar sands in Alberta, to all the mining companies worldwide, and to all the oil rigs in every ocean, whose extraction and transportation of oil leaves nothing but contamination and destruction in their path. Would it not be enlightening to have a mathematical formula that would calculate what we humans take from our planet in relation to what we give back? Have we started the giving process, or are we just accelerating the depletion process? The end result will be alarming, no doubt!

A message and a question

Based on our daily behaviour, we all have a particular position in life within our countries' complex social, economic, and political networks. All these positions ultimately place us usually in one of the following four essential categories:

1. Those who think that confrontation, or even simply standing our ground, is aggressive and combative. These people tend to live in hesitation and doubt.

2. Those who regard denial as a sign of weakness and, in some circumstances, almost a crime (metaphorically speaking). These people will most likely engage themselves in doing something about a specific situation they might develop interest in.

3. Those who hold a legitimate, altruistic, and energetic interest with determined efforts to achieve change. These people are positive, progressive, and powerful.

4. Those who simply do not care about anything because they believe they cannot be part of a solution, so they remain completely passive.

The question is …. to which group of people do YOU belong?

INTRODUCTION

In general, a responsible person is a reliable individual – somebody you can trust and work with in good faith. The word "responsibility" has a strong relationship to authority, leadership, and power. When a person is keen on the concept of responsibility, they accept any liability, fault, or blame. Responsible people make their own decisions, usually based on proper research and planning.

Only responsible people have the burden of guilt and remorse; they accept accountability and bear the consequences of their previous actions. As well, they are also eager and willing to enjoy the positive aspects, rewards, and overall success of their actions.

Question: Is the majority of the human race honest and loyal, with a strong degree of integrity? Are we, in general, a responsible race on planet Earth?

Answer: Definitely not! We are not a responsible race overall. In fact, we are very far from it as a species. It appears that the great majority of people do not even care. They live in the moment without even considering the future. Their attitude is: Who cares? Life is short, so have fun, enjoy it, and whatever happens, just happens.

This is an absolutely, profoundly, and utterly wrong-headed, dangerous mistake. Being irresponsible is a short-sighted attitude and a seriously obtuse vision of life. It needs correcting immediately for the sake of both current and future generations. Those who think otherwise are either lying to themselves, absolutely biased, or simply disconnected from reality. Such people can never have taken or failed any sociology, geography, biology, history, or ethics courses.

Most humans are very far from being well-developed,

responsible individuals, but, luckily, there are exceptions, thanks to whom this world is still beautiful to live in. But for how long? The level of destruction and abuse of planet Earth is advancing faster than the cleaning and caring of the only world we have and that we call home.

Throughout history, it has been proven that human nature is mostly unstable and unreliable. The proof is easy to find. History shows clearly how humans continually make, if not precisely the same mistakes, at least very similar mistakes again and again. As a few examples, consider the following:

- Our relentless attempts to prove that any particular religion is better than all the others.

- Our reluctance to make local policies for the benefit of our communities and our environment instead of government or private economic interests (e.g. Alberta's oil sands or the Keystone Pipeline project).

- Our propensity to invade other countries in the vain attempt to stop terrorism or to promote fairness and freedom (e.g. the invasion of Iraq, the Russian takeover of Crimea, etc.).

The human race has always been involved in wars, killings, betrayals, and much more. Yet it is still a wonderful and beautiful world. This is only because there have also been enough individuals with positive and civilized attitudes who have helped to rebuild nations and advance human development.

Nevertheless, we humans continue to commit atrocities and, unfortunately, on a daily basis. At this moment, everywhere in the world, something nasty and absolutely irresponsible is going on, but we always seem to have a reason for why it is being done. We have behaved this way throughout history, and we never seem to learn from our own or others' mistakes. We keep on making the same mistakes and, trust me, there are lots more to come.

I am not being negative. Just pick up your local newspaper and check out what is happening in the world and even within your own community. Negative news is what the average person loves to read.

However, there are also beautiful, true stories that do not seem to reach the pages of the newspapers and magazines. Good news does not sell as many copies as bad news. Sad but true.

Luckily, everything tends to balance out. As I said before, there are also very good people with upright morals, sound ethics and a profound sense of responsibility. Moreover, humans in general are also afraid of what will happen to them if they get caught either when doing something wrong or even after they die. Therefore, many people make an effort to control their actions as much as they can. In their weak minds, they believe they will be punished in the next life, that Satan is waiting to punish them as soon as their last breath is exhaled.

I am not a religious person. I accept the existence of various religions and respect them, but I believe in science and in moral, ethical behaviour motivated by reason. I have to admit that, thanks to religion, this world is a little bit more civilized (regardless of the atrocities different religions have caused and keep on causing), because people are afraid of divine punishment if they do bad things.

In general, humans do not really feel guilty or even responsible for wrongdoing until they get caught. Otherwise, they would not act wrongly to start with. In fact, a well-known saying tells us: "You can do it; just don't get caught." That is, you are only guilty if you get caught. But let's face it. Only responsible people feel guilty about their wrongdoings regardless of whether they were forced to commit them, did them by accident, or got caught. Irresponsible people don't care about the effects of their actions on others. They will never feel guilty or at fault, or even under pressure, unless they are caught. To me, such people are like the rotten fruit on a tree.

Goals of this book

Very few people seem to be fully conscious of the fact that we humans depend 100 per cent on the planet's flora and fauna to survive, and not just on technology. If you ask people, almost everybody will say they are "aware" of this, but are they really, fully aware? What are they doing personally and on a daily basis to preserve the fine and delicate balance between humans and the environment?

What are we doing in Canada, and in North America as a whole, to preserve this peaceful, intricate, fragile, and exquisite balance? In this important matter, the great majority of us want to believe we are responsible people with the right attitude, but how many of us are acting accordingly?

As independent individuals in society, we all need to possess and master two crucial traits, responsibility and attitude. We need to embody these traits not just with respect to ourselves and our society but, most importantly, in our interactions with the environment and our planet's long-term needs.

Acting responsibly requires honesty, integrity, and loyalty, while the right attitude requires strength, ability, perseverance, and tenacity. Not everybody can have all these qualities at the same time, but we can at least try to achieve them as best as we can.

The aim of this book is to assist readers to develop their sense of responsibility and achieve the best attitude for the benefit of themselves, their families, and their communities, whether they are conscious of the need for this or not. To illustrate my intentions, allow me to provide a very short example and formulate a naïve but important question on just one of the many subjects this book will cover.

Example: Most North Americans (Canada, United States, and Mexico) think that fresh drinking water is not just their right, but that it can be used and exploited indiscriminately; as per their actions demonstrate. This is also true in many other countries around the world, but it is a sad and alarming phenomenon. What is worse is that the majority of those people wasting fresh water are not even conscious that they are abusing this vital resource. They do not have a guilty conscience or any remorse about it. In the meantime, others around the world do not even have a decent glass of water to drink, much less to brush their teeth or shower with. Few of us do anything on a daily basis to protect our watersheds and conserve this limited resource, rightly called "blue gold" by many.

Question: What do you think will happen if some cities or states in the United States run out of water (as is now happening at an alarming rate in California)? Water will be more important than oil, gas, and (yellow) gold in the not-too-distant future. Water is life, and without it, we all die. Simple as that. Anyone will cross frontiers to get water if it means the difference between life and death. In such a situation, do you really think that the United States will be as friendly to Canada as it currently is?

We Canadians have an abundance of accessible fresh water, but we cannot take this for granted. We certainly can't give it away for nothing as we are doing right now in the small town of Hope in British Columbia to the Nestlé consortium.

We are all integral parts of our society. Our daily impact, our influence, and our voices are a lot more powerful than we normally think. We have the solutions at our fingertips, but first we need to sincerely acknowledge the problems. In keeping with the Hindu and Buddhist idea of karma, it has been proven, socially and scientifically, that all our actions have consequences. There is definitely a balance that governs the universe all the way down to the communities we live in.

A good definition of *karma* can be found at: *thetreeofawakening.com/karma/*, where it is very accurately defined as follows:

> Your actions have consequences. They create a ripple in the universe. Karma is the invisible power that teaches you. Your life today is just a reflection of your past. You created your destiny. For every action, there will always be a reaction. Your thoughts and actions are powerful. They carry energy. They are like an echo. We have all taken a different path in life, but somehow, we are all linked. Whatever you do will always come back to you.

As I understand this, it means that our bad actions will always come back to haunt us in some form or other. It is not a matter of if, but when.

This book will be an eye opener to some and a confirmation to others. It is about what is really going on around us, within our borders and beyond, and how to cooperate to keep our world sane and healthy and ensure a decent, peaceful, and plentiful future for us and those we love.

We need to stop thinking that we all have the right to do whatever we please without considering the repercussions. We need to move beyond our greedy, limited, and short-sighted human perspective. This book is to create awareness and offers a critique, a vision, and a plan of action to enable us to do so. It provides ideas and proposes solutions that anybody can implement in their daily lives.

As human beings, we all want to improve our own lives while building a better future for ourselves and our families. We want to have everything we require to meet our essential needs and enjoy a few luxuries. We want to be pleased with ourselves, with the people around us, with the community where we live, and with what the future has to offer. This book will help you to achieve these goals, but only if you open your eyes, acknowledge the truth of what surrounds you, and are humble. Only when we fully and sincerely acknowledge what truly is happening around us will we be able to take appropriate action and, at a later date, feel good about ourselves and proud of our actions.

Above all, we all need to stop pretending not to see the imminent threats surrounding us and start taking the urgent and decisive actions our societies and our planet need. The main goal of this book is to create awareness in people of what in my view, is really happening in various areas. Hopefully, the reader can do his or her own research and develop a passion to ultimately do something about how to stop our "runaway globe" in an area that touches them the most. With this book, I am presenting a call to action. Every living soul on this globe must understand and implement the law of cause and effect that governs our destiny as a species. This requires immediate positive actions in our own lives to ensure a future world for all to enjoy.

Another goal of this book is to bring to the table information not only about the negative things happening around the world, but also about some of the beautiful and positive things people are doing to preserve or restore the delicate natural balance of their environments. The mass media only tells part of the story and only from the point of view authorized by governments and corporations trying to cover up the truth of what is really happening in order to serve their own interests.

As consumers, we must do our own research so that we can evaluate every product we consume and service we receive. It is our obligation to be selective and conscious in all our purchases, from those at our local grocery stores, to the best vehicle to buy and use, to the use of our natural resources, to the garbage we produce, to the pollution we generate, and so on. To illustrate this, five brief examples come to mind:

1. For many years, the tobacco companies said that smoking was not just cool but good for your health. They claimed that smoking helped reduce stress, for example, and therefore had a positive, healthy impact on people's lives. Government agencies did nothing until the link between smoking and tens of thousands of cases of lung cancer (and other cancers) became undeniable. Now everybody knows that smoking kills. They even used to advertise that the best cigars were rolled on women's thighs and that this made them taste better, but they failed to point out that they would have been rolled on sweaty, unhygienic women's thighs (if that was really ever the case). They didn't mention that smoking cigars (regardless of how and where they were rolled) caused tongue and mouth cancers. Personally, I have to admit that few things in life beat a good Cuban cigar (accompanied by a good cognac) at the right time and place. But ladies and gentlemen, moderation is the key to everything in life.

2. For many years, juice companies told us that drinking juice was equivalent to eating fresh fruit and that a glass of orange juice for your children in the morning was healthy. This was partly true. Juice provides vitamin C and also reduces inflammation, produces collagen (which protects

bones, ligaments, and other tissues), helps lower bad cholesterol in some people, and helps balance blood pressure in others. But the juice companies failed to add that their product also contained high concentrations of sugar that could lead to obesity and even diabetes.

Many people were deceived by advertising that claimed juice was 100 per cent "natural," unlike concentrated juice. It's true that the latter lacks fibre, which is vital for the digestive system, but so-called "natural juice" is often put into aseptic storage after it has been squeezed, pasteurized, and filtered, then stored for up to 12 months without oxygen. When finally ready to be packed and sold, something called "flavor-pack" is added for obvious reasons. What people end up drinking is definitely no longer "100 per cent natural." It will always lack the true natural properties of a fresh juice. Even juice from concentrate is better than these so-called natural juices, unless they really have been freshly squeezed.

3. Health is the most important treasure any human being can possess. But how many times have we gone to the doctor and unquestioningly taken what they say as the absolute truth. We need to keep in mind that there are good and bad doctors (and in-betweens) and be encouraged (even against our doctor's advice) to obtain second and third opinions from Dr Google and Dr Yahoo. They have impressive amounts of information, which also needs to be evaluated and used intelligently. None of this information is written in stone or should be swallowed uncritically (like many interpret the Bible), but it can at least assist us to ask our doctors the right questions and to make more informed decisions. Doctors should accept, not discourage, this and should help, not hinder, their patients to get more information and evaluate it in a balanced way.

4. Women's rights require deep and serious attention

everywhere, including throughout North America. The rape and the moral and physical abuse of women due to social misbehaviour, tradition, or religion is rampant in almost every corner of the world. Inequalities between women and men are still apparent even in the most modern and advanced societies, and urgently need attention and action. In particular, we need to teach our children from a very early age that we all are born equal and that respect for the opposite sex is not just fair and rational but mandatory, regardless of the country we live in or the traditions of any particular profession.

5. Thanks to our negligent and lax governments accepting everything for the sake of "political correctness," many immigrants in North America are not being properly integrated into their new societies. Regardless of country of origin or religion, many immigrants do adapt to North American ways of life. However, too many are not interested in adapting at all and are reshaping not just the overall mosaic of the country but are even creating segregated communities, which are being tolerated by our governments out of concern for "political correctness," "human rights," "freedom of religion," respect for "traditions," and "freedom of expression." These communities are not being properly monitored by the authorities or by the immigrants themselves. The result is abuse by both immigrants and average North American citizens.

This is not just a problem in North America but in most European countries too, where it is almost out of control. It has reached as far as Africa, Australia, and New Zealand and is expanding at an alarming rate. Regrettably, we are letting it happen throughout the world and are growing numb to these contrasting, divergent, and unfamiliar feelings, almost unaware of the problems it is causing –

until something slaps us on the face to remind us of the new reality, such as:

- The 2011 attacks in Norway perpetrated by what they called a "lone wolf terrorist" against the civilian population, the Norwegian government and, specifically, the Workers' Youth League. These attacks claimed the lives of more than 75 people, mainly young students.

- The attack on January 7, 2015, in Paris, on the French satirical newspaper *Charlie Hebdo*, where 12 people were shot dead and another 11 wounded.

These two examples of many such incidents show that we urgently need to redefine our concepts and practices of integration, monitoring, and enforcement with regard to immigration. We discuss these issues in more depth in the third book of The Runaway Trilogy, entitled "Our Runaway Rights."

CHAPTER ONE: RESPONSIBILITY

Responsibility and self-interest

The average human being does not necessarily act based on natural instincts, and we certainly do not act altruistically all the time. Most of us act according to self-interest, immediate gratification, and, unfortunately, often with little or no regret. We find ways to justify what we did or did not do regardless of whether it was right or wrong. Trying to always justify our actions is a horrible vice. It is a continuous cover-up and has turned into a serious disease in modern society. But the worst is that the majority lacks the courage to accept this.

A good example is how Wall Street – or any other stock market – is managed. Some business brokers hunt you down for your investments and when their vaults are full of money, manipulate the financial instruments or influence the market in such a way that there is suddenly a market crash in which average people lose their life savings and sometimes even their homes. The "lost" money does not just disappear, of course. It goes into the pockets of the privileged individuals who control the markets with the blessing of our governments. Whenever a dollar disappears, it goes somewhere. It does not just evaporate into thin air.

Perhaps some readers might not agree, but I am convinced that the average human being does not know how to be responsible for their own actions. Even when they know, they avoid responsibility or pretend not to fully understand the concept or its impact. They pretend to be unaware, or they ignore their responsibility or simply reject it.

The concept of responsibility is fading out in many societies. It is most certainly fading in North America. This is very sad and embarrassing. But "it is what it is, and we are who we are," right? I think lack of responsibility is wrong and totally unacceptable. I think we need to grow up and be responsible for our own actions. We need to acknowledge that everything we do has repercussions of the same, or even a larger, magnitude. A lot of politicians say they "take full responsibility," but how are they sanctioned? What penalty do they pay? Do they lose their jobs, or are they even demoted? Are their salaries reduced?

Of course, we all make mistakes and sometimes avoid some of our duties and responsibilities. This is just human nature, but we need to learn how to be more responsible and focus on good deeds. And if we make a mistake, we need to try not to make it again. We all need to strive and work hard to be responsible human beings. We certainly need to learn how to admit our guilt for our own actions. We definitely must learn how to live in peace and harmony, first with ourselves, and then we need to discover how to respect and protect others, our surroundings, environment, and our ecosystem overall. But I have to reiterate that there are many people, especially politicians, who, when they do something wrong and are caught, limit themselves to saying "I am so sorry. I made a mistake and accept full responsibility." The question remains, how does that fix the problem or help the rest of us?

Apologies are nice to hear, but what are the repercussions, the penalties, and the real liabilities? It is not just a matter of accepting wrongdoing but of paying for the consequences too. Otherwise the perpetrators will never learn their lesson and will end up doing it again. People refrain from doing things only if the consequences are as bad or worse. For example, imagine if a new law came out stating that whoever was found guilty, without a shred of doubt, of raping a woman or of being a pedophile would have his penis and testicles surgically removed? Do you think that the rates of rape or child molesting would reduce? You bet they would! Let's face it; what man in his right mind wants his "pride" cut off?

What is worse? A rapist or pedophile having his "masculine pride" removed, or a woman committing suicide because she cannot live with what happened to her? Or a child growing up frustrated and physiologically affected because he got betrayed and raped by the pastor of his neighbourhood church or his football or hockey coach or his own uncle?

Unless they are actually mentally ill, those who do not control their urges should pay serious consequences. For harsh problems, harsher solutions. Otherwise our legal system will be instigating, motivating, and assisting in the creation of hidden, vengeful, silent vigilantes, which the great majority might agree with, regardless of whether this is right or wrong.

As human beings, we need to make a daily effort to avoid arrogance, unhealthy pride, and anger. We need serenity, hope, and honest feelings. We alone choose what our dreams, goals, and destinies will be. Nobody else can do this for us. External forces influence all of us, but we ultimately select and control our own destiny. Time is a factor we need to be patient with. Opportunities are moments that we need to recognize and take advantage of. The selection of appropriate words is crucial to establish and maintain good relationships. But above all, self-esteem, family, friendship, and true, unrestricted love make the difference in our efforts to achieve a happier existence.

Now, let us come back to reality and to a more balanced world of action and of cause and effect. Almost everybody knows Sir Isaac Newton's Third Law: for every action, there is an equal and opposite reaction. What this means is that the specific size of the force in the first action should equal the size of force in the reaction. In every interaction, therefore, there are two forces of the same strength or magnitude acting against each other, that is, the second has the same intensity of force as the first, but in an opposite direction.

I have made mistakes in life like any other person, but I have sought assistance when I did not know how to solve them myself, and I have always tried to avoid making the same mistake again. People who can assist us are always at hand – family members, business associates, our lawyer, doctor, priest, professor, coach, or our close friends.

Definition of responsibility

Before we can evaluate our actions as human beings and who we really are, we need to define what responsibility really means. I believe that responsibility is simply the ability to judge for oneself, make independent decisions, and act, while being prepared to be held accountable for any actions that are done maliciously or incorrectly.

Responsibility is therefore the sense of real duty and the specific force of action in a civilized world that together guide people to achieve positive outcomes. To become a responsible human being, other characteristics also have to be present, for example, honesty, integrity, and loyalty. It is not easy to achieve the goal of being a truly responsible person, and only a small percentage of human beings do so.

Responsibility does not come easily, nor does it belong to any specific ethnic background, skin colour, religion, or geographic location. It comes from education, good will, trustworthy actions, and accountability, from noble, loyal, and honest feelings, and from the desire to respect yourself, to be reliable, and to respect others, the society you live in, and your environment.

True responsibility is hard to achieve, but I believe it is the ultimate goal in life for any human being. Those who achieve a high degree of responsibility also tend to get positive rewards, usually full of good will. Indeed, there seems to be, in general, a direct correlation between being responsible and achieving positive outcomes. But, to the eyes and experience of many it is often that the crooks succeed and the good guys appear "to lose".

I like to bring up the example of bullying. A bully is usually thought of as an aggressive, irresponsible, cowardly person who starts, joins, or continues an aggressive action against other human beings, but there are also passive bullies, those who see active bullying and do nothing about it. Passive bullies can be as aggressive as active bullies. They tend not to accept any kind of responsibility. They give many excuses – "I did not do anything," "It was not my fault," "I was afraid," "I could not do anything," "It was not my business," "I don't even know them," and so on. The list could go on forever, but the fact remains that they did nothing, then or later, to stop the bullying. Passive bullies are almost as guilty as active ones. They do not have any idea of what real responsibility means, so they need to be held accountable as well.

I found some fabulous quotes about responsibility on a well-known website called "Brainyquote.com," which are worth sharing:

- "No single drop of water thinks it is responsible for the flood" (author unknown).

- "No snowflake in the avalanche ever feels responsible" (poet Stanislaw Jerzy Lec).

- "If it is not us, then who? If it is not now, then when?" (poet and novelist John E. Lewis).

- "The accomplishment of your dreams requires personal sacrifice and hard work. May you have a determined spirit, willpower, and great passion for the accomplishment of your dreams" (poet and writer Lailah Gifty Akita).

- "The secret ingredients to true happiness? Decisive optimism and personal responsibility" (author and media relations expert Amy Leigh Mercree).

- "Attack the evil within yourself rather than attacking the evil that is in others" (philosopher, teacher, and politician Confucius).

- "The power behind taking responsibility for your actions lies in putting an end to negative thought patterns. You no longer dwell in what went wrong or focus on whom you are going to blame. You do not waste time building roadblocks to your success. Instead, you are set free and can now focus on succeeding" (author and business woman Lori Myers).

Responsibility and subtleness

To my mind, there are many factors outside the traditional definitions of responsibility that make a person responsible (or not). For example, it is our responsibility to realize that walls do not imprison us but that mental challenges do. Our imagination often stops us from doing achievable things. When a gorilla has been caged for a certain period of time and we remove the gate of the cage, the gorilla will stay inside for quite a while, until he realizes that what is stopping him is not the physical gate but only his mental conditioning. His imaginary barrier is in the shape of a gate. It is our responsibility to destroy the similar mental obstacles we have so that we can achieve greatness.

It is also our responsibility to realize that, if we hate something or somebody, the person who suffers is us, not the hated person in our minds. They may not even remember us, yet our hatred continues enslaving us. We need to let go and try to forget – not necessarily to forgive, but at least to let go! A good example was when a person asked his Jewish friend, who was a survivor of one of the concentration camps, if he still hated the Nazis? The friend's answer was: "Yes, I still do and with all my heart." "Oh, so you are still a prisoner," this person answered.

My grandfather said that, for him, a responsible person was someone who had stopped seeing the defects in others and instead focused on his own defects. He used to say: "There are people who see the straw in the eye of their neighbour, but fail to see the log in their own." When you start seeing the log in your own eyes and start doing something about it, you will be heading towards higher ground in matters of responsibility and honesty.

Not too long ago, an acquaintance of mine sent me three very interesting stories with very stimulating and refreshing morals. He did not remember how he got them, but they are worth sharing:

1. A caravan was stationed in the desert, when a plague rushed by, heading rapidly towards Damascus. The chief of the caravan asked the plague why he was in such a hurry. The plague answered that he wanted to take at least 100,000 lives in Damascus. Upon the plague's return, the chief stopped him and asked him how it had gone. The plague told him that he had only gotten 50,000 lives. The chief then asked him what had happened to the other 50,000 lives. The plague answered that the other 50,000 were taken away by fear.

The moral of this old Arabic story is that only responsible people are courageous enough to confront reality and have a better chance to be successful in their thoughts and actions. If fear invades our soul, the chances of survival are nil. The power of fear damages and distorts our self-confidence, which directly affects the level of responsibility we can achieve.

2. The Greek philosopher Diogenes was having lentils for supper. Aristippus, another philosopher, had created a new philosophy based on seeking pleasure throughout life by adapting to the circumstances around him. Therefore, he was used to being very submissive to the king, while flattering him constantly. Aristippus saw Diogenes eating the lentils and told him that he would not need to eat lentils if he learned how to be submissive to the king and flatter him when required. Diogenes answered that Aristippus did not need to be submissive and flatter the king if he learned to enjoy lentils.

The message here is that we need to be responsible for our own thoughts and actions as well as legitimate and honest with our convictions and feelings. By avoiding hypocrisy, we learn how to live and enjoy what we have.

3. An old man used to complain that he did not have shoes and had to walk barefoot, until he saw another man without feet, but who was grateful and happy just to be alive. On that day, the old man changed his attitude and sense of responsibility and was happier from there on.

No matter our beliefs or where we are from, we should always evaluate and properly consider our actions (or lack thereof). With a good sense of responsibility come healthy pride and honour. Unfortunately, for many, pride and honour are irrelevant and a thing of the past. In some cultures, people still acknowledge and even kill others for the sake of pride and honour. It is good, useful, and even powerful to have pride and honour in everything we do, but taken to an extreme, it can be detrimental. They are two totally misunderstood and sometimes forgotten traits, which many unfortunately take to extremes. Few people understand the delicate balance between pride and honour, much less how to successfully apply them properly in their lives, especially the younger generations. This is sad but true.

Responsibility and honesty

Honesty is a word that every human being knows and understands, but only a few speak and act according to honesty's true meaning. If we ask our neighbours if they are honest, they will all say "of course." But are they really honest people? Are we honest people ourselves?

Honesty means not to lie, to be loyal to your principles, and not to do or say things that are morally wrong. Honesty is to speak the truth and nothing but the truth. When you act, knowing that what you are doing is the right thing to do, you are being honest with yourself and others. But when you try to hide some of your actions, then you are not being an honest person, at least at that specific moment. This is deceitful, which is ethically and morally wrong. When people break the rules for their own advantage, then they are cheating. When people do not tell the truth, and take something that is not theirs, then they are lying and stealing. This is obviously not acceptable, yet many people turn a blind eye to avoid confrontations or repercussions.

When I was a young child, I was taught to tell the truth, and I give you my word that I tried hard. But, hey, I was just a kid. My grandfather used to say: "the child and the drunk always tell the truth," but the years have proven to me that this is not completely accurate. Approximate, perhaps, but far from accurate. All kids lie, and drunks are so out of it they will say anything without giving it serious thought and, therefore, are often far from truthful. Many people tell "white" lies to avoid hurting themselves or others.

It takes courage and a strong sense of responsibility to tell the truth consistently. In almost all cases, people tell "white" lies because they do not want to hurt or offend another person, and they foresee no serious consequences for not telling the truth. But I believe that being honest and telling the truth should always flourish above anything else and that the tone and "angle" with which we tell the truth can be used to avoid hurting somebody or creating conflict.

Many people do not want to accept their weaknesses or deficiencies, nor do they have the strength to overcome them. They lack sincerity and honesty with themselves and a proper sense of responsibility. Although this is not being taught or learned at home or at schools as it should be, I have often read and heard people saying that the average person is not always totally honest with themselves. Truly honest people are individuals who value, appreciate, and care about themselves. They have high self-esteem, a high sense of responsibility, and a strong desire to improve and better themselves. We all know it can be very difficult to face the consequences of our own actions, but we need to be sincere with ourselves if we want to develop, advance, and upgrade our quality as human beings. If people are not honest and sincere with themselves, do we really believe they can be honest and sincere with others? I personally doubt it.

When somebody acknowledges their lack of honesty and sincerity with themselves, this makes them vulnerable to criticism. This can make them feel insecure, uncomfortable, weak, susceptible to attack, and exposed to being hurt. But this is precisely where integrity and willpower kick in. If you are a determined person and accept yourself the way you are (with all your strengths and weaknesses), but at the same time also try to improve yourself, then you are being positive, productive, honest, and sincere with yourself. It does not matter how long it takes you, but you will reach higher levels in life.

When you just "accept" yourself with your deficiencies and

weaknesses but do nothing to improve, then you are not being proactive, positive, or honest with yourself. Every sane person wants to be a better person and have a better life, but those who lack the proper attitude and willpower always try to trick themselves by telling themselves they don't really care about the way they are and that it is okay to be passive and "stuck." They believe that happiness can be achieved through a life of conformism, and so they lack initiative to change. In my experience, this is simply a lie people tell themselves.

This is sad to see, yet there are many people all around us who are exactly as I just described. We interact with them on a daily basis wherever we go. Unfortunately, they insist, or falsely believe, that they are happy the way they are, and what is most alarming is that, if they deceive themselves long enough, they end up truly feeling that nothing needs changing. They separate themselves from reality and blind themselves to it. They will remain the same way for the rest of their lives (if they do not get even worse). They will remain unchanged and fixed in time as if sculpted in stone. To me, stagnation is destruction of the self. It is the perfect recipe for disaster, for falling deeper and deeper into the abyss of ignorance and self-destruction. People in this situation may say they are happy this way, but, deep within themselves, they know it's not true.

To my mind, people like these are either complacent, mediocre, or have given up on life, or they are legitimately mentally weak. They don't care about what's best for their own existence. This is the ultimate proof of lack of self-control, self-respect, self-esteem, and even of self-consciousness, which should reflect a true desire for becoming a better person. These people need help, and we should all strive to assist them if we can.

There is a well-known saying in many religions: "Help yourself and God will help you." The average person can find tons of excuses for why they fail to help themselves, but the truth lies in their conscience, which has become a silent partner in the crude reality of their existence. Let's face it; honesty leads to integrity, and this in turn leads to refinement, perfection, and success, which then bring a higher degree of happiness to ourselves and the people around us. This "virtuous circle" applies anywhere in the world. If there were an easier way for people to climb or spin out from their vortex of frustration, they would try harder to be positive in their efforts at self-improvement. If it were easy, they would all act differently and in their best interest, instead of accepting their "negative faith."

Oscar Wilde once said: "Be yourself, everyone else is taken." Yes, be original and true to yourself while never trying to be somebody else, because it all indicates you will fail profoundly in the medium or long term. Ken Keith wrote a book called *Silent Revolution: Dynamic Leadership in the Student Council.* In it, he wrote several things about honesty and about giving the best we have regardless of our circumstances. The four things that I liked the most and that I believe everyone should keep in mind are:

- Honesty and frankness make you vulnerable. Be honest and frank anyway.

- If you are successful, you will win false friends and true enemies. Succeed anyway.

- Give the world the best you have and you'll get kicked in the teeth. Give the world the best you have anyway.

- If you do good, people will accuse you of selfish ulterior motives. Do good anyway. (Source: goodreads.com)

Unfortunately, the philosophy of a good percentage of humankind is only to pretend to be honest and sincere.

Sooner or later, they get caught, but the problem, as they see it, is not their dishonesty and insincerity, only the fact of being caught lacking these positive traits. Everybody knows this, but almost nobody admits to it.

Honest people usually achieve happiness faster and to higher or deeper levels of satisfaction. Those who do not or cannot fully practice honesty, sincerity, and loyalty – due to their environment, outside pressures, or educational background – are sooner or later haunted by negative repercussions. Unfortunately, due to their intrinsic character, they usually don't care. They belong to a different breed, which, luckily, is not abundant in our societies. They are often people who care little about anything. When people lack principles, decency, willpower, character, strength, self-respect, and overall integrity, almost nothing bothers them. They are always "fresh as a lettuce." Go figure! They are like swine wallowing in mud and their own excrement, and they *feeel goood!* They are people with very low or no self-esteem and self-respect. They are individuals with nothing to lose and, therefore, they have total disregard for others' feelings and well-being and do whatever pleases them, and only them.

But we should ask:

- Are these people really happy?

- Do you rub shoulders with these types of people?

- Are you yourself one of these types, or are you surrounded by them?

- Do you like or do you avoid these types of people?

Before we continue, let's bring to the table four different definitions of the word "honesty":

1. According to the Merriam-Webster dictionary, honesty is "the quality of being fair and truthful."

2. According to dictionary.com, honesty is "freedom from deceit and fraud. It is truthfulness, sincerity, and frankness."

3. According to the Longman dictionary, honesty is "the fact or quality of being sincere and honest. Honesty is truthfulness and sincerity."

4. And finally, according to Wikipedia, "honesty refers to a facet of moral character and connotes positive and virtuous attributes such as fairness, integrity, truthfulness, and straightforwardness, including straightforwardness of conduct, along with the absence of lying, cheating, or theft." Honesty therefore implies being trustworthy, loyal, fair, and sincere.

Honesty is extremely valued in many ethnic and religious cultures. Honesty to these cultures is the best policy. It is a proverb of unknown provenance; however, the quote 'honesty is the first chapter in the book of wisdom' and is attributed to Thomas Jefferson, as used in a letter to Nathaniel Macon."

Even though Wikipedia is not considered by many to be very accurate or reliable, I like using it, because it helps confirm and broaden ideas, concepts, boundaries, and definitions. These then require corroboration and homework on my part, which I always proceed to do.

Honesty and the true meaning of sincerity

In addition to the above definitions of honesty, we need to include another important virtue related with the concept of honesty. This is sincerity. Honesty and sincerity go hand in hand, because sincerity means to be authentic and free of hypocrisy and deceit. Sincerity is generally seen as a sign of strength and integrity. But to some, it might also be a weakness – and the reason why some people tell the truth but not the whole truth! They say only what is convenient so as not to get into trouble or hurt somebody else's feelings. To my understanding, by avoiding the full truth they are not being sincere.

According to Aristotle, "sincerity or truthfulness is a desirable mean state between the deficiency of irony or self-deprecation and the excess of boastfulness." In the context of this book, sincerity is about being totally genuine, honest, loyal to your principles, and free from deceit, pretentions, and lies. It represents complete authenticity. Sincerity thus plays an integral part in the character of any honest person.

Again, white lies are statements that are not true but that are usually said to avoid hurting somebody's feelings. They are intended to avoid pain or harm. In my personal experience throughout life, I have found that women, in general, tend to tell more white lies than men. They tend to be more sensitive and compassionate than the average man, making them less honest than men. Women try not to hurt the feelings of others, while men tend to be more straightforward and less sensitive than the average woman, because we pay slightly less attention to the feelings of the other person, especially if we are speaking to another man.

A lot of men seem to think that, if they say something truthful that offends another man, too bad. Grow up, snap out of it, and smell the coffee. We are men, after all, so cope with it. But is that how it should be? It is hard to say, because every man (or woman) has a different level of sensitivity and, therefore, different capacities for accepting or denying the truth. Shouldn't we all try our best to be as sensitive and compassionate as possible without being construed as weak or naïve? Shouldn't we all be considerate but sincere, while always laying the truth on the table the best way possible?

The related concept of authenticity is very interesting and complex. According to Merriam-Webster, "to be authentic is to be real or genuine; not copied or false. It is to be true and accurate. It is to be original." For Wikipedia, authenticity is "the degree to which one is true to one's own personality, spirit, or character, despite external pressures." In this view, the self is seen as "coming to terms with being in a material world and with encountering external forces, pressures, and influences very different from, and other than, itself. A lack of authenticity is considered in existentialism to be bad faith." This is fascinating, because I believe this is where the great majority of the world population fails, and fails profoundly (including me sometimes).

Why? The answer is simple. We are supposed to be free in mind and spirit, but, in reality, we are not. It is just an illusion, so we act accordingly. If we were to be always 100 per cent honest and sincere, or if we were to be absolutely true in our interpretations and thoughts, and in our comments with others, we would constantly get into problems and conflicts. We would experience repercussions that could negatively affect us and push us further from the happiness we all seek. Nobody lives in a free country. We say "the truth will set you free," but the reality is that the truth can place you behind bars in many countries, and it can even get you killed in others.

Just take a look at what happened to 16-year-old Pakistani teen Malala Yousafzai, who was promoting a very noble and reasonable cause – education for young women. The Taliban shot her in the head. She survived, and I truly hope that "the truth will set her free forever." She deserves it more than almost anybody on this planet. She is a committed fighter for women's rights in a country where that can obliterate a woman's life in a second.

In my view, Malala is a true example of being "authentic to one's self-principles, thoughts, and actions." At 16 years old, she has shown more maturity, courage, balance, and vision than most politicians throughout the world and, above all, than those men and women who talk about women's rights but do and risk nothing for it. Malala has taught the world a very important and valuable lesson, which has not gone unnoticed; she earned the Nobel Peace Prize in 2014. Malala – and her father, who has supported her in her actions – fought against all odds by tackling head-on a system that discriminates against women's rights in a very cruel, abusive, and even cowardly manner. Clearly, Malala and her father have a high degree of honesty, integrity, and loyalty to their principles, thoughts, and ideas, as well as to themselves and the people who surround them. I have nothing but admiration for them and hope people around the world do too. Above all, I hope that more and more people learn to follow their passion for honesty, integrity, fairness, and loyalty in order to master that most valuable of human traits – responsibility.

Responsibility and integrity

Integrity is a concept that is difficult to explain and sometimes a little vague depending on the culture. In North American culture (and many others), integrity consists of a high degree of honesty, transparency, and decency regarding how respectfully you see yourself and how consistently you seek the truth. To live with integrity means to follow a perfect structure of morally accepted principles and values, the same as those that have been adopted and proven correct throughout generations.

To live with integrity means to live with truthfulness, wholeheartedness, straightforwardness, and seriousness. People who live like this tend to be strong believers in their principles and have amazing willpower, strength, and courage. A person who really values integrity and abides by its principles is always doing the right thing, even when nobody is watching and there is no reward on the horizon.

That is their natural way of being. Such people are valuable and magnificent examples to follow.

According to Merriam-Webster, integrity is "the state of being complete and whole. It is the quality of being honest and fair." For Wikipedia, it is "a concept of consistency of actions, values, methods, measures, principles, expectations, and outcomes. In ethics, integrity is regarded as the honesty and truthfulness or accuracy of one's actions. Integrity can be regarded as the opposite of hypocrisy, in that integrity regards internal consistency as a virtue, and suggests that parties holding apparently conflicting values should account for the discrepancy or alter their beliefs."

As the reader can perceive, integrity is a difficult concept to define, because everybody may have different values, methods, principles, expectations, standards, and even expected outcomes. However, nobody can deny that integrity is measured by the honesty, truthfulness, and accuracy of one's thoughts, goals, values, and overall actions. However, we need to keep in mind that our level of integrity is in direct correlation to how much we respect ourselves, the degree of our self-esteem, the society in which we live, and the degree of responsibility we have as a person. To be 100 per cent clear, integrity is the opposite of deceitfulness, insincerity, and falseness. These are the antitheses of the real meaning of integrity.

Honesty, sincerity, and authenticity (the essential parts of integrity) do not require justifications or long explanations. But let's face it; a few words can set us free, but they can equally make us prisoners. We need to remember that complete honesty and sincerity are often a double-edged sword in society, and there is sometimes a very fine line between doing the right or wrong thing. Here are some quotes relating to integrity that have caught my attention (source: goodreads.com/quotes/tag/integrity):

- "If you want to know what a man is like, take a good look at how he treats his inferiors, not his equals" (J.K. Rowling).

- "In the end, you should always do the right thing, even if it's hard" (Nicholas Sparks).

- "When you are content to be simply yourself and don't compare or compete, everyone will respect you" (Lao Tzu).

- "Leaders always choose the harder right rather than the easier wrong... Avoidance of self-deception is a matter of integrity not comfort" (Orrin Woodward).

- "Be happy, noble heart, be blessed for all the good thou hast done and wilt do hereafter, and let my gratitude remain in obscurity like your good deeds" (Alexandre Dumas).

- "As you change your point of view, your views bring about a change in you" (George Alexiou).

- "Too much honesty makes you sound insincere" (Patrick Rothfuss).

- "Politics is all about showing you have integrity – and hiding the fact that you really don't have any" (Jarod Knitz).

- "All things must be examined, debated, investigated without exception and without regard for anyone's feelings" (Denis Diderot).

- "Truth and integrity must be so rare these days that it confuses people when they hear it" (Donna Lynn-Hope).

- "Govern thy life and thy thoughts as if the whole world were to see the one and read the other" (Tom Fuller).

- "Dogs have more love than integrity. They've been true to us, yes, but they haven't been true to themselves" (Clarence Day).

- "Most Christians seem to have two kinds of lives, their so-called real life and their so-called religious one. Not [C. S.] Lewis. The barrier so many of us find between the visible and the invisible world was just not there for him. It had become natural for Lewis to live ordinary life in a supernatural way" (Walter Hooper).

- "Success follows those who champion a cause greater than themselves …. [and] The relationship you take for granted is the one that needs the greatest work" (George Alexiou).

- "Truth demands progress and change, and is always for the benefit of all souls—even if you must travel through a difficult learning process or make a shift as a result of facing the truth" (Molly Friedenfeld).

- "Wisdom is knowing the right path to take. Integrity is taking it" (M.H. McKee).

Responsibility and loyalty

To me, loyalty is one of the most important and sacred concepts human beings can achieve, possess, and follow throughout their lives. In my mind, the word "loyalty" means the sentiment, the support, the feeling, and the perception of an absolute devotion that anyone can feel and hold for their country, family, environment, friends, a group or party, a company, a religion, a movement or cause, and any other affiliation that a person considers important in his or her life. Loyalty means a high sense of faithfulness, commitment, duty, devotion, obedience, and integrity, which makes that person absolutely reliable, trustful, sincere, and supportive.

Unfortunately, no people I have ever known have acted with absolute loyalty for their whole lives. It is a very difficult thing to achieve. As human beings, we are weak and, even though we know right from wrong, we sometimes have a hard time making the right decisions. Loyalty demands continued strength, consistency, focus, and persistence. It is certainly not an easy task. I am surrounded by good people, yet it is difficult to achieve a total degree of loyalty and devotion among all of us.

What I believe we should always aim for is absolute loyalty to ourselves. The day we stop being loyal to ourselves and our principles is the day we start our descent from being a dignified human being. That sounds strong, but let us analyze and digest one question: What is the opposite of loyalty?

Allow me to name a few things that are the opposite of loyalty, so there is no chance of misunderstanding:

undependability	unfaithfulness
breach of trust	disloyalty
deceit	backstabbing
falsehood	trickery
fraud	two-facedness
snitching	desertion

and …

… worst of all, betrayal. Those who betray earn the title "traitor" — one of the strongest words there is. Those who deserve that appellation are considered to be one of the lowest kinds of human beings that can exist. Being a traitor is disparaging and denigrating.

Usually, people try their best to act morally and stay faithful to their beliefs. There is no doubt in my mind that most people try hard to be loyal to those around them, but unfortunately, while moving through life's complex jungle, the beliefs, morals, and values of a person can be influenced or distorted by their surroundings to such an extent that they fall over the edge into the abyss of treachery. Life pressures people to fight for themselves and disregard others and their own faith. This happens even more when economic pressures distort their attitudes and values.

The Merriam-Webster dictionary defines a traitor as "a person who is not loyal to his or her own country, friends, etc.: a person who betrays a country or group of people by helping or supporting an enemy." For Wikipedia, a traitor is anyone "who betrays (or is accused of betraying) their own political party, nation, family, friends, ethnic group, team, religion, social class, or other group to which they may belong."

Nobody wants to be a traitor, yet a great number of human beings do correspond to these definitions, whether they like it or not. Worst of all, they deny this to themselves even when examining themselves in the mirror. This is pitiful, but it is a reality. Such people will always try to justify their actions (or lack of action), but ultimately, they are guilty of not being loyal. With time, they lose sensitivity and truly do not care anymore about their disloyalty, a very painful and negative human trait that sometimes leads them into betraying their own Mother Earth.

There is a website called Values.com that includes inspirational quotes about loyalty. A few quotes from their site that I really liked are:

"Most important in a friendship? Tolerance and loyalty" (J.K. Rowling).

"You can buy a person's hands but you can't buy his heart. His heart is where his enthusiasm, his loyalty is" (Stephen R. Covey).

"Independence is loyalty to one's best self and principles, and this is often disloyalty to the general idols and fetishes" (Mark Twain).

"The scholar does not consider gold and jade to be precious treasures, but loyalty and good faith" (Confucius).

Some other excellent quotes about honesty can be found at pinterest.com:

"Speak your truth quietly and clearly" (Tammy Smith Designs).

"I do not want perfect; I want honest" (rainbow-arrows.tumir.com).

"Be truthful, gentle, and fearless" (theloveshop.etscy.com).

"Do not give me a pretty little lie; I prefer the ugly truth" (quotediary.me).

"I am not crying because of you; you are not worth it. I'm crying because my delusion of who you were was shattered by the truth of who you are" (Dr. Steve Maraboli).

"Respect is earned. Honesty is appreciated. Trust is gained. Loyalty is returned" (sphotos-cak.fbcdn.net).

"What I do not understand is how a person can tell you so many lies and never feel bad about it" (Narcissism).

"A real man will be honest no matter how painful the truth is. A coward always hides behind lies and deceit" (shynistarrlight.tumbir.com).

"Conscience is a man's compass" (Vincent Van Gogh).

"Be wise. Don't just take their word for it … Find out the truth for yourself" (Bravegirlsclub.com).

"The best people possess a feeling for beauty, the courage to take risks, the discipline to tell the truth, the capacity for sacrifice. Ironically, their virtues make them vulnerable; they are often wounded, sometimes destroyed" (Ernest Hemingway).

"Trust is like glass. Once broken, it will never be the same" (SydesJokes).

"People hate the truth. Luckily, the truth doesn't care" (Larry Winger).

"The further a society drifts from truth, the more it will hate those that speak it" (George Orwell).

"If I agree with you, we will both be wrong" (Unknown origin).

"It is better to be defeated on principle than to win on lies" (Lifequotesru.com).

"Always trust your guts and intuition" (Anonymous).

In my opinion, loyalty is one of the best attributes a person can possess. Dependability, honesty, and trust are the pillars of loyalty, with which people can dare to move mountains. Here are some of my personal thoughts about loyalty:

- Trust is earned with effort, sweat, and time, but it can be lost in a flash.

- If you lie, you better have the memory of an elephant, because the truth always floats and will come back to haunt you (pay-back-time).

- The truth is a must. It may set you free, but you risk repercussions.

- Never apologize for being honest and truthful to your principles, never!

- Be honest, loving, and truthful, and you will be powerful.

- Sometimes honesty can oppress you, and the truth can undermine or weaken you. But being honest and truthful with yourself should always justify the outcomes because, in the end, this will make you stronger.

Responsibility and hypocrisy

A responsible person is an individual who has a decent degree of honesty, integrity, and loyalty. In order to reach a higher plateau in life, we need to stop being hypocrites with ourselves. This does not come easily, but it is achievable!

Shouldn't we all do our best to stay away from hypocritical people? They tend to be false in almost everything they represent. They only waste people's time and are ultimately detrimental to their surroundings. Let me start by defining what hypocrisy means according to my upbringing. I was taught that hypocrisy is the action of pretending to have values, opinions, ethics, standards, virtues, beliefs, feelings, or other positive traits and qualities that, in reality, one does not possess. I was also instructed that hypocritical people tend to deceive others. They tend to lie and cheat with amazing ease, looking straight into the eyes of others. Such people are rarely happy, because they are very unsatisfied and some, deeply frustrated. More importantly, a dishonest person who lacks integrity and honesty inflicts this false pretense on others. These people tend to live in dissatisfaction and tend to suffer either in silence or to revel in a negative flow of feelings within their bitter beings. They are devastating for a healthy community.

A message for the rest of our lives

This message applies to everyone regardless of age. The younger you start learning responsibility, the better. My grandfather used to say that people should be able to walk with their heads high, proud of what they have done. Proud of having acted responsibly, honestly, ethically, with integrity and loyalty to themselves and the community they live in. My grandfather also said that, even when he was little, his parents taught him to tread in the correct lane in all his actions. He remembers doing that all his life, but at 50 years of age, he really began to focus and make a more conscious effort to live the rest of his life even better. Why? It was not just because it was the right thing to do, but also because he wanted to make sure that, when he died, he died a better human being, a better man.

He said that he belonged to a generation that had very clear and specific goals in mind. The main ones were to be the best son or daughter, the best husband or wife, the best professional, the best friend, the best parent, and, overall, the best human being that one could be, with a conscious mind and persistent, focused goals. All the while, he kept in mind the need for self-respect, a high sense of responsibility, and dignity in anything he did. To always honour your word!

He told me he always strived to accomplish the best he was able to do in his specific circumstances and surroundings, even when he was young. But after his fiftieth birthday, something very strong kicked in within him, something that made him value his life and his actions even more than before. His sense of responsibility grew stronger, deeper, and prouder. His determination to live more intensely in the present, and to let go of the past without worrying too much about the future, grew stronger and more focused. His respect for others grew deeper and more powerful as well, because he wanted to live in harmony with others, with less greed and with fewer desires, belongings, or high-flying dreams. He wanted to be more perceptive to reality, to the current moment, more accepting of what he could not change and more persistent about what he could change.

From then on, his level of satisfaction grew and his level of stress diminished. He told me how he had achieved more things with a better, more positive, more altruistic attitude than just by working harder and focusing. When he was 85 (a year before he passed away), he told me how he had achieved so much more happiness and peace from the day he decided to change his attitude at age 50. He then told me something I will never forget. He said, "Do not make the same mistake I did. I waited too long!" Unfortunately, I failed profoundly. It is only recently, during the past four years (starting at age 54), that I finally decided to try and emulate his attitude towards life. It has not been easy, but it is doable!

My grandfather's name was Daniel, but we all used to call him Papanel (short for Grandpa Daniel). The years have proved to me that he was, indeed, a very wise man. Papanel said he had done everything in the past as best he could, with the best of intentions, despite being pressured by the society in which he lived. He strived to live in a certain way and work at a certain time and speed, but after many years of hard work, he had grown tired of pleasing only others and of fulfilling his responsibilities only in order to be accepted as a productive person in society and bring the daily loaf of bread to the table.

Everybody needs to go through that stage while building a reputation and the foundation for a better future for self and family. Yes, he had responsibilities for his family, and he always tackled them with devotion, energy, and success. But although I agree with him regarding the overall day-to-day aspects of life, I also believe that, when somebody focuses and works hard to achieve a goal, an even higher degree of success and satisfaction can be achieved. The important thing is to develop the wisdom to define what is important and urgent and therefore needs immediate attention. As some friends have told me, "Do not sweat the small things; learn to choose your battles in life."

I have learned to live lighter, and I am trying to free myself from any excess moral (and physical) weight every day. It is not easy, but I am committed to it. I know that I need to be absolutely 100 per cent committed, or nothing will happen, and nothing will change. So I make a conscious effort every morning. It comes easier as the months and years go by. The earlier you start in life the better. I truly suggest you start today, and, if you do, I feel confident you will reap the benefits in the very near future. Life is already short enough. Enjoy it to the maximum within a responsible framework. Remember, you are not taking anything with you to your tomb except your memories, and those disappear and die with you forever.

Many of us get to a point in life where we want to live the rest of our days the way we want to live them and just enjoy whatever the future throws at us. However, living the way we want does not mean we have the right to forget our basic responsibilities, principles, and ethics. We need to care for and be respectful to others if we want to live in peace and harmony. Remember, we still live in society, and we are all bound by invisible civic rules. We do not live alone in a jungle, able to do completely as we please. Unfortunately, a lot of people do not know the difference, and so they completely let go. Their manners, level of education (or lack thereof), and their overall behaviour go haywire and seem to inhabit a different dimension from the one they were brought up in and the community where they live. That is when they get lost and become a detriment to themselves and to their society.

Yet we do get to a point in life where we want to live with freedom and more lightly in relation to our responsibilities and the physical things that surround us. We want to simplify our daily activities and be humble and realistic in our aspirations. In particular, it is perfectly understandable when some people want to stop living in the past, because this is like looking through the rear-view mirror without paying attention to where we are going. Others, as their age that is all they do. They live in the past only through their cherished memories.

Reliving our negative experiences is like texting and driving or drinking and driving. We will end up crashing and living with regrets for the rest of our days! Instead we should let go of the past that ties our forward strides with a shackle. To do so, we need to make a conscious and continuous effort to live in the present, free of old, futile memories. It should be forbidden to act in the present or for the future based on a framework of negative past experience.

My grandfather taught us to put more emphasis on learning something every day, loving our family and friends more, and spending more time with them. He advised us to appreciate nature to its fullest, from enjoying the sunrise until the moon takes its place in the infinite sky, to live without fear or regret, to acknowledge everybody around us, and to tell them something nice or simply remain quiet with a smile on our face, because to him, silence was golden too.

This reminds me of something Pablo Neruda once wrote. He was a Chilean poet, diplomat, and politician who won the Nobel Prize for Literature in 1971. The following lines from his poem *Queda Prohibido* (It is Forbidden) are from a translated version at smyln2big.blogspot.ca/2011/04/it-is-forbidden-pablo-neruda.html:

> It is forbidden to cry without learning
> to wake up one day not knowing what to do,
> to be afraid of your memories.
>
> It is forbidden not to smile at problems,
> not to fight for what you want,
> to abandon everything because of fear,
> not to transform your dreams into reality.
>
> It is forbidden not to show your love,
> to make someone pay for your bad humour.
> It is forbidden to leave your friends,
> to understand what you lived together,
> to call them only when you need them.
>
> It is forbidden not to be yourself in public,
> to be fake with people you don't care about,
> to feign being funny just to make them remember
> you. To forget all the people who love you.
>
> It is forbidden not to do things by yourself,
> not to believe in God and forget your fate,
> to be afraid of life and its engagements,
> not to live each day like it was a last sigh.
>
> It is forbidden to miss someone without
> cheering, to forget their eyes, their smile,
> just because your paths stopped being embraced,
> to forget their past and pay it with their present.

It is forbidden not to try to understand people,
to think that their lives are more valuable than yours,
not to know that each one has their way and their
happiness. It is forbidden not to create your history,
not to have a moment for the people who need you,
not to understand that whatever life gives to you,
it takes it away as well.

It is forbidden not to search for your happiness,
not to live your life with a positive attitude,
not to think that we can be better, not to feel that,
without you, this world wouldn't be the same.

I believe that we should be able to do whatever we desire as long as it is without selfishness, with respect, and with an absolute altruistic spirit. We need to evolve from where we have been in the past. We need to try hard to improve ourselves on a daily basis. Stagnation should be forbidden. We need to be dynamic, like a flowing river. Boredom and stasis are not good for our well-being and the well-being of our surroundings. Life throws us a lot of low balls, but we need to learn not to swing at them. They are just tests, and we have to learn to choose the ones we need to tackle and control. The ones worth swinging at.

Irresponsibility

To be irresponsible is to be thoughtless, careless, and reckless. An irresponsible person is someone who does not answer to any higher authorities, so they have no reason to care and can ignore consequences. Without venturing into the deeper meanings of being irresponsible, it is clear that it involves various negative attributes and unpredictable consequences. A lot of young people live irresponsibly or on the borderline, though it's not necessarily their own fault. Sometimes their upbringings, their families, particular situations, or the overall nature of the society they live in push them over the boundaries into irresponsibility.

In many countries outside North America, irresponsibility is sometimes a matter of survival. In North America, some people blame irresponsibility on distractions. They claim their irresponsible actions were an accident and that they did not mean them. Such people do not accept responsibility for their reckless actions. Everybody knows someone like that or at least has met someone like that during their lifetime.

Some thinkers put such unintentionally irresponsible people in the category of "scatterbrains" but, in my opinion, this gives them an escape route or an excuse. It excuses them for being inattentive and thoughtless or even just forgetful. But why give them any way to escape their responsibility? Although people like these do not necessarily act intentionally, they are still irresponsible, even if it's to a lesser degree than those who act irresponsibly while knowing the consequences. If somebody is forgetful or "scatterbrained," this does not mean they do bad things on purpose. However, that is not an excuse. People should always calculate and evaluate the likely outcomes before acting. That is the beginning of what enables an individual to act responsibly.

The sense of responsibility or irresponsibility is different in various countries. For example, Japan seems to have a more respectful attitude towards the land than other countries do. However, they do not seem to care as much about the oceans and the marine life within them. It seems they have grown immune to overfishing, pushing various species of fish, whales, and dolphins almost to extinction even against their own long-term benefit and to their own detriment (their own interests). Many countries are like this; they seem to suffer from some kind of long-term myopic syndrome. This subject will be dealt with in more detail later in this book. Why? Because it concerns two important related issues, responsibility, and the need for a change of attitude.

In relation to the environment, there is a very nice tradition that, whenever the Japanese have an important event in their lives, they plant a tree. They do this, for example, when they start at elementary school, when they win their first competition, when they graduate from high school or university, when they get married, when they have their first baby, etc. This culture seems to be very interested and fond of protecting their land environment at least. If the government had been the only one to have planted the trees, people would not necessarily want to care for them, but when they plant the trees themselves, they feel a personal responsibility, and they care for the future of those trees and the overall landscape. They feel attached to them because they planted the trees themselves, and therefore it means something special to them. Not surprisingly, some of the most amazing and beautiful gardens in the world are in Japan or have been inspired by Japanese style gardens.

The Japanese tradition of planting trees teaches us a lesson. If we do not take the initiative to do specific good deeds, we will never feel involved and, therefore, may more easily disregard many things that will have important consequences in this world. Imagine if everybody planted a tree or two on every important occasion in their lives. Wouldn't it be nice to plant a tree on those special moments that you want to remember forever? A beautiful tree symbolizes pride in our achievements and milestones. And it need not be limited to a tree, of course; it could be a bush, a flowering plant, or any other plant either for ornamental or agricultural use.

Yet how many people fail to realize, or have forgotten completely, that everything enjoyed in big cities comes from nature? This includes everything from the cement we walk on to the food and energy we consume. It all comes from our environment, either from flora, fauna or some other natural resource in our environment. If city people do not start caring and lobbying for environmental protection, we are all going to pay heavily in the future.

Unfortunately, many people seem to wear blinkers and suffer from the retrograde idea that an environmental disaster will never happen to them during their lifetime. This is an extremely ignorant, selfish, irresponsible, and even hypocritical attitude. Those of us who see the danger have a responsibility to help others open their eyes to reality. Again, this is also among the main motivations for writing this book.

Albert Einstein once said that "those who have the privilege to know have the duty to act". But I am convinced that knowledge, combined with true love and commitment, are better teachers than just the duty to act.

Responsible people, those who understand what is happening now and what will happen in the future if nothing is done, have a duty to educate others and, above all, to motivate others to take action for a better world. If we open the eyes of irresponsible people to how beautiful nature and Mother Earth are, these sceptical, dubious individuals might start developing some love for this planet and become, slowly but surely, engaged in the effort of saving it for countless future generations to enjoy.

CHAPTER TWO: PROTECTION OF FLORA AND FAUNA

There is a big difference between protecting flora and protecting fauna. They are two totally different matters, although they both need to be treated with the same respect, devotion, intensity, and, above all, absolute commitment. Whether some readers agree or not, by damaging the flora or fauna in our relentless pursuit of "growth" (more often, greed and economic gratification), our species is contributing to irreversible, long-term degradation of our ecosystem, which has supported and assisted human beings for thousands of years.

Careful, loving attention and dedication to our flora, fauna, and overall environment seem to be of secondary importance in most cultures and countries. Every country has its share of guilt for the damage to our planet. The following example is a worldwide problem to which the vast majority of the population has contributed. Please do not call me negative; I am simply being responsible, concerned, and realistic. Again, I want to create awareness and I will limit myself to offer the reader hard cold facts throughout this book.

The example: we all dispose of plastic in the form of bags, bottles, or whatever shape or form it comes in. The average human tends to dispose of plastic with absolute disregard for our environment. Into the garbage they go. Out of sight, out of mind. Therefore, we see plastic bags and bottles in our oceans, rivers, lakes, deserts, mountains, valleys, streets, cemeteries, job sites, parks, sanctuaries, and so on. But does the reader know what is even worse? That people keep on doing this on a daily basis even though we know it is dangerous and absolutely detrimental to the well-being of our flora and fauna, and human life as well. Some justify this in the name of economic development, progress, and the "evolution" of our planet.

It is evident that some countries do not seem to care deeply and genuinely for the protection of their flora or fauna as long as they attain economic benefits by exploiting nature commercially. Just take a look at the oil companies. They have caused serious environmental damage during and after the extraction of oil on both land and offshore. Just google "oil disasters," and you will understand perfectly what I mean. It is painful, but it is true. It is happening right now, somewhere on earth. It will continue to happen until we reduce our use of oil and find cleaner substitutes. I doubt that will happen anytime soon, if it ever does, but I truly hope it will.

And there is reason to hope. In 1963, a resolution was adopted by all members of the International Union for the Conservation of Nature (IUCN) to draft a multilateral treaty known as the Washington Convention or CITES (Convention of International Trade in Endangered Species of Wild Fauna and Flora), which came into force on July 1,1975. The main objective was to protect species in the wild by limiting and monitoring the international trade in wild animals and plants. Close to 34,000 species of animals and plants were listed for protection in conjunction with the General Agreement on Tariffs and Trade (GATT).

However, since the creation of CITES, the underworld of wild animal and plant trade has become more sophisticated. Although CITES exerts a certain degree of control, there are still many countries that do not pay enough attention to the protection of their environment and its natural beauty. They are more concerned with the economic bottom line and with political expediency. As a result, many species of plants and animals are on the verge of extinction, and, if we do not take drastic measures, our world is going to suffer a continuous, serious loss of both plant and animal species.

Please refer to Appendix 1 of this book for some alarming

examples of what is really going on around the world, including many cases the reader may find hard to believe. Fortunately, there is still something we can do to help preserve our environment, if we remember that we only have one world and that it does not negotiate with humans when we push it close to the edge or even in some situations over the cliff.

Case studies of irresponsible and responsible actions

So far, I have been talking mainly about honesty, integrity, and loyalty, and have related them to the overall concept of responsibility and irresponsibility. Now it's time to provide some specific examples of human beings acting either responsibly or irresponsibly. I will alternate these examples so as not to appear either too negative or too positive. I hope this will make the reading experience more interesting while bringing to your attention various true-life examples.

We all know that human beings have committed both irresponsible and responsible actions throughout history. I want to bring to the table just a few true and amazing stories, so that you can appreciate the significance of irresponsible actions and their pernicious consequences as well as the positive impacts of responsible actions.

Chevron vs. the Amazonians

There is a major oil company called Texaco, which is now owned by Chevron. This company constantly promotes its commitment to protect the environment by searching for renewable energy with the aim of achieving more efficient and smarter energy use.

Unfortunately, in their efforts to achieve this goal, they have caused immense damage to previously pristine lakes, rivers, and forests in several countries around the world. One country that fought fearlessly against this was Ecuador in South America. The exploitation of oil and its derivatives in this country caused a long list of serious health issues for local communities, due mainly to excessive amounts of toxic waste dumped in the areas where the oil was extracted or refined.

This damage occurred continuously between 1963 and 1992, but it was only after many years in court that Chevron accepted the fact that its subsidiary, Texaco, had dumped over 4,000,000 gallons of seriously toxic water into the beautiful and pristine Ecuadorian rainforest. They contaminated local water reservoirs and destroyed the health of many local people in the Amazon, while damaging many other species as well. Some of the Amazonian communities have been enduring various types of diseases such as lung problems, digestive complications, cancer, and serious skin infections that are difficult to treat.

Thanks to a group called *El Frente de Defensa de la Amazonia* (Front for the Defence of Amazonia) that rallied the fight against Texaco at the time, the case reached Ecuador's courts, which decided, after many years of judicial struggle, that Texaco was responsible and should pay damages of close to $10 billion USD. To date, Chevron has not accepted the court's decision or even made a public apology. Chevron is still trying to defend their case judicially and to avoid responsibility for Texaco's irresponsible actions committed purely in the search for profit rather than for a cleaner technology and the protection of the environment.

This was one of the worst disasters caused by the irresponsible actions of a large corporation with the power to extend their business activities into other countries while "holding hands" with local politicians and promising jobs and other economic benefits. It seems they do all this knowing very well that their activities will cause severe damage to both the economies and the health of local communities.

Unfortunately, when transnational companies do business in countries where government officials can be manipulated and corrupted, they have a serious competitive advantage and can implement very irresponsible actions while carrying out their exploration and production activities. For more information, please feel free to research this case on the Internet. You will find many sources of information that go into much more detail.

The Greenpeace Foundation vs. Climate Change

Greenpeace is an international environmental organization founded and incorporated as Don't Make a Wave Committee in 1970 by Dorothy Stowe, Irving Stowe, Paul Cote, Jim Bohlen, and Mary Bohlen. Two years later, their name was changed to the Greenpeace Foundation. Other sources also name Paul Watson as a founder and contributor.

Greenpeace was founded in Vancouver in 1971 as a non-governmental organization. Their head office is now located in Amsterdam in the Netherlands, and they have affiliate offices and hard-core supporters throughout the world. The foundation came about as a result of Canadian efforts to boycott and stop US nuclear testing on the island of Amchitka in Alaska. The US government had tested a nuclear weapon on Amchitka that did not cause major issues, but they were planning to test another nuclear weapon several times stronger. Many Canadians were very uncomfortable at the prospect and went to the border to march and complain, carrying protest signs, one of which read: "Don't Make A Wave. It's Your Fault If Our Fault Goes [i.e. the West Coast earthquake fault line]." As this suggests, Greenpeace has been focused from the beginning on promoting sustainable development. They have consistently raised public awareness about many environmental issues, such as global warming and the depletion of the ozone layer, which are two of the most important issues. Initially, nobody wanted to believe them. Not only did religious groups deny the importance of these issues, but initially many scientists were also deniers.

However, after many years of hard work, tenacity, and research, Greenpeace has demonstrated to the world that we are indeed, and without a doubt, undergoing global climate change due to "greenhouse gas" emissions from indiscriminate and irresponsible industrialization. Many countries around the world have had to accept this and are now building seawalls to protect cities like New York from being overwhelmed by the predicted rise in sea levels. However, if we continue ignoring and disrespecting the crystal clear and proven scientific recommendations, even these measures will not be enough, and many coastal cities will find themselves submerged sooner than expected.

It is impossible, and certainly not my intention in this book, to list all the reasons why Greenpeace, to my mind, is one of the most responsible organizations on the planet. They sometimes perform what seem to be short-term, irresponsible actions, but all their actions are meant to bring immediate, medium, or long-term positive results for the protection of our environment, ecosystem and, ultimately, for all human beings through the protection of our flora and fauna.

Greenpeace was the first organization to protect and work on mitigating the human impacts of climate change and to produce a sustainable development prospectus that has raised public awareness around the world. Among the most important areas of awareness and recommended solutions for which Greenpeace has fought relentlessly are:

- Global warming.
- Deforestation.
- Renewable energy.
- Anti-nuclear issues.

- GMOs.
- Arctic exploration.
- Extinction of species (land and water).
- Oil industries.
- Mining activities.
- Toxic waste.
- Fresh water conservation.
- Protection of oceans, rivers, and lakes.

… and the list could go on.

Each of these areas could be subdivided into a long list of specific subjects and problems that need urgent attention, and this is the reason Greenpeace needs your understanding and full attention. They want and need you to get involved and do something about these issues. This book is one of the ways that I currently have within my power to do something that may assist them in their efforts.

I encourage everybody to read and research more about Greenpeace and their truly amazing efforts and sacrifices in any of the various areas listed above. We should all try to make an effort to support this foundation in some way or other. We will be doing a favour to ourselves, our family, and to the future of humankind.

National Geographic produced a special issue in 2012 about "50 of the World's Last Great Places." According to Greenpeace, in a blog post by Andisheh Beiki (March 19, 2013), the Canadian Boreal Forest is highlighted in this special issue as "Earth's largest terrestrial biome teeming with coniferous evergreens and large mammals such as moose, caribou, elk, and bears." Unfortunately, as Beiki goes on to say:

The Canadian Boreal Forest is under threat from

industrial activities such as logging, mining, oil and gas development which require the destruction of vast forested landscapes. The majestic Boreal, while spanning an immense portion of the northern terrestrial hemisphere, is also relatively low in productivity due to nutrient-poor soils that limit growth to a short summer season. Because of its slow reproductive cycle, industrial activities in the region have a longer lasting impact if not managed in a sustainable manner. Iconic Canadian species such as the woodland caribou are at risk of extinction within less than a century. Today, with less than 10 per cent of earth's original forests remaining as intact landscapes, we are faced with the responsibility to protect and preserve what is left.

Now, please stop reading for a few seconds! Pause and reflect on what has been written above ….

Now please consider taking some much-needed and effective action in favour of Greenpeace and similar organizations. Feel good about yourself by acknowledging the value of your surroundings in a focused, determined, intelligent, and productive manner, regardless of whether you are part of a team or a lone ranger like myself. Leave a legacy of pride behind you that others can recognize, respect, and follow.

Remember that a lack of action can be as aggressive, damaging, and irresponsible as any actions meant to benefit only the minority and that end up doing more harm than good to most people and to our planet. It is often said that "people get the government they deserve." Doesn't this also apply to each one of us in relation to our planet? Our population on earth will soon reach 9.2 billion people (forecast for some time around 2050). We all need to work, eat, and do our best to survive, while demanding more of all the natural resources from our planet. Let's face it, until now (Feb of 2018), Mother

Earth has been very patient, plentiful, and good to us, but this cannot last forever! Mother Earth is getting tired, and this is starting to show. We all need to stop raping her or make an effort to stop corporations and countries from doing so: raping Mother Earth while destroying the precious life and beautiful environment of this planet to the detriment of all human beings. I encourage readers to make a good start by visiting Greenpeace Foundation's website at:

greenpeace.org/international/en/

Union Carbide vs. Bhopal

On December 3, 1984, a massive gas leak caused an unforgettable disaster in the city of Bhopal, India. This was a disaster that still remains under debate, even though the Indian courts ordered Union Carbide Corporation and Union Carbide India Limited to pay $470 million USD in settlement. What were the real causes of the disaster? There are several explanations, but the following two sources have been the most diligent in explaining the core cause of the disaster.

According to an article in Bhopal Medical Appeal entitled "Union Carbide's Disaster," the cause was poor maintenance:

> Regular maintenance had fallen into such disrepair that on the night of December 2, when an employee was flushing a corroded pipe, multiple stopcocks failed and allowed water to flow freely into the largest tank of methyl isocayanate (MIC). Exposure to this water soon led to an uncontrolled reaction; the tank was blown out of its concrete sarcophagus and spewed a deadly cloud of MIC, hydrogen cyanide, mono methylamine, and other chemicals that hugged the ground. Blown by the prevailing winds, this cloud settled over much of Bhopal. Soon after, people began to die.

Other sources cite two different main possibilities:

> The Indian government and local activists argue that slack management and deferred maintenance created a situation where routine pipe maintenance caused a backflow of water into a MIC tank, triggering the disaster. Union Carbide Corporation (UCC) contends that water entered the tank through an act of sabotage.

In any case, the horrible disaster killed about 8,000 people and seriously injured thousands more. It left a deep scar on the city of Bhopal, from which people are still struggling to recover. Dow Chemical bought out Union Carbide about 16 years after the disaster. With the disaster in mind, the chemical industry created what they call the Responsible Care Program, which focuses on emergency procedures, safety standards for employees, and community awareness.

It is sad to see, but it commonly happens: that new safety measures come about only *after* a disaster has already happened. After a disaster, the various industry players start working together and with more intensity. In their efforts to be a responsible participant in the well-being of the local communities where transnational companies operate, they work with local governments to develop new regulations to protect workers and communities. Performance and operational improvements are essential to avoid future disasters. For more information about the Bhopal tragedy and the responsible new safety measures and actions, please visit: unioncarbide.com/Bhopal

Svalbard Global Seed Vault

As previously mentioned, there are also many very positive and responsible individuals and companies. As another example, take conservationist Cary Fowler, who started a

"Seed Vault" to preserve as many varieties of seeds as possible from all over the world. He started this project in conjunction with the Consultative Group on International Agricultural Research (CGIAR). Their idea is to collect, with the help of people in many countries throughout the world, the largest possible variety of plant seeds that may be needed by gene banks around the world.

This is an extremely important and responsible project to preserve and protect the future of humans by ensuring, as much as possible, the preservation of all seeds and plants (our flora) for the benefit of human beings and all the animals that coexist on this beautiful planet of ours. According to various sources, the Seed Vault is a tripartite agreement between the Global Crop Diversity Trust (GCDT), the Norwegian government, and the Nordic Research Center (NordGen). It is located in a very remote area of the Arctic, the Svalbard Archipelago, on the island of Spitsbergen, and was constructed 120 meters inside a sandstone mountain in an area well known for permafrost (which aids in the preservation of the seeds) and lack of tectonic activity.

The idea is for these seeds to be preserved for thousands of years to come. A key player in the overall project is the Center for Genetic Resources of the Netherlands, which is part of the University of Wageningen. The Seed Vault is a very ambitious project whose mission is to preserve samples of seeds from all corners of our world. Why? Because as humans, we need to protect earth's delicate crop diversity. There are three good sources that explain the Svalbard Global Seed Vault's vital mission.

Crop Trust, an international organization working to safeguard crop diversity, wrote on their website (croptrust.org): "The purpose of the Svalbard Global Seed Vault is to provide insurance against both incremental and catastrophic loss of crop diversity held in traditional seed banks around the world.

The Seed Vault offers 'fail-safe' protection for one of the most important natural resources on earth."

Another source that accurately explains the Seed Vault's mission and long-term goals is Wikipedia, which gives the following interesting perspective and account:

> The Svalbard Global Seed Vault's mission is to provide a safety net against accidental loss of diversity in traditional gene banks. While the popular press has emphasized its possible utility in the event of a major regional or global catastrophe, it will be more frequently accessed when gene banks lose samples due to mismanagement, accident, equipment failures, funding cuts, and natural disasters. These events occur with some regularity. War and civil strife have a history of destroying some gene banks. The national seed bank of the Philippines was damaged by flooding and later destroyed by a fire; the seed banks of Afghanistan and Iraq have been lost completely.

As The Economist puts it, "the Svalbard vault is a backup for the world's 1,750 seed banks, storehouses of agricultural biodiversity."

There are only about 150 crops that are cultivated in the world, but each crop has many different varieties and specific forms. If we combine these forms, say beans and rice, we could have literally thousands of varieties just in the beans or rice category. Imagine if we were to do the same thing for every crop in its specific form. The combinations are literally infinite.

Many countries that are participating by sending seeds to this vault understandably call it the "Doomsday Seed Vault." Regardless of the name the vault receives, it is a very responsible project in which many institutions around the world have participated. The vault is a very good example of positive attitudes, actions, implementations, and plans for long-term protection of the seeds that secure our food supply.

Genetically modified organisms (GMOs)

There are various corporations out there that are gambling with the future health of the human race. These companies are big producers of pesticides and herbicides used to "protect" our plants and farms from insects and weeds. Unfortunately, the same crops they are meant to protect absorb these pesticides and herbicides, which are all manufactured using a variety of strong chemicals that have been proven detrimental to our health and are not meant for human consumption. When these crops, in the form of vegetables, fruits, or grains, end up on our plates, we consume various types of chemicals and modified engineered organisms in our foods without even knowing it. Among the main GMO producers in North America around the world are Syngenta, Monsanto, Dow Chemical Company, and DuPont.

Farmers certainly need to protect their crops from insect pests, fungal and viral pathogens, and other enemies such as weeds and invasive species. This is why pesticides and herbicides are relentlessly produced and marketed globally. Unfortunately, the trend in various markets, such as those in the United States and Great Britain, has been to increase the yields of the farming industry with GMOs. A good example is the explosion in the production of various types of tomatoes in Great Britain. GMO tomatoes were introduced in the 1990s with a huge success that appeared to justify their heavy research and production costs.

Tomato plants originated in South America and were brought to Europe in the mid-16th century. They were tiny and unappetizing at that time but very tasty and a good ingredient for various dishes. Thanks to hundreds of years of breeding, they now come in several varieties and, if grown organically, are very juicy, tasty, and healthy. An article of November 2, 2015, of Scientific America, states that genetically engineered tomatoes have *"potentially* health-boosting compounds", such as flavanols and anthocyanins. But other scientists and environmentalist have assured that tomatoes grown in organic soil are more nutritious because pesticides used in non-organic soils, negatively counteract the nutritional benefits of GMO tomatoes. More importantly, we have no idea what the DNA is of those GMO tomatoes we purchase. There are some environmental groups that claim GMO tomatoes contain scorpion DNA, which goes against nature itself, yet these tomatoes were supposed to be engineered not just for better yields, but to improve the nutritional value and even the taste. Sometimes the nutritional value of GMO foods is promoted through unreliable advertising. Is the real focus to achieve bigger and stronger yields or just for higher economic gains?

After researching further about the strange and unnatural DNA combinations (transgenic) in GMO foods, I found articles reporting on a venomous form of GMO cabbage in which scientists have inserted the gene that controls the poison in a scorpion's tail. In theory, they engineered the toxin to kill the bugs that eat cabbage leaves avoiding any harmful impact on humans consuming the leaves. Still, many avoid eating them.

Is this kind of genetic engineering appetizing? Are these the types of foods our children should have for dinner? Certainly not, although I'm glad we're all different in tastes and preferences and that we still have choices. Personally, I will stick with organically grown fruits and vegetables, not just for the taste but for their good nutritional value, with which human beings have grown up stronger and healthier through generations.

Engineering higher yields for the sake of profit at the expense of healthy nutrition is definitely not an action I would call responsible. Eating is not just a matter of filling up the stomach: the point is to fill it with nutritious foods that are healthy and tasty. According to many people, the GMO companies are "playing God" and going against nature. Is this a responsible or irresponsible action? This is something people need to research and think hard about before making a decision on what to serve on the table for their children and themselves to consume.

In the United States alone, over 85 per cent of sugar beets, corn, soy, canola, and cotton have been genetically modified to provide higher yields and better margins. The sad part is that GMO seed companies now control what the farmers can grow – and what we all have to eat. Did you know that over 80 per cent of processed foods now contain genetically modified organisms? After researching various articles, books, professional magazines, TED talks, and surfing the Internet for more information about these companies, I found something worth bringing to the reader's attention on the Dow Chemical Company website:

> Seed, Traits, & Oils: Our seeds and traits research is committed to increasing yields for farmers and growers worldwide by improving genetics and stress tolerance, and helping to ensure effective weed and insect control. New investment in research, in combination with strategic acquisitions, is resulting in more productive and resilient crops. Our innovations in conventional breeding and plant biotechnology lead to seed hybrids and varieties with greater yield potential. Through our healthier oils business, we develop seeds to produce canola and sunflower oils with zero trans-fat and lower saturated fat.

I personally feel confident they are trying to achieve the goals they describe, but I suspect they sometimes "go beyond the call of duty" and venture into areas that are risky, dangerous, and frankly unacceptable. For example, some readers will have heard about the Enviropig, but for those who have not, I would also like to quote the following from mnn.com:

> The Enviropig or "Frankenswine," as critics call it, is a pig that's been genetically altered to better digest and process phosphorus. Pig manure is high in phytate, a form of phosphorus, so when farmers use the manure as fertilizer, the chemical enters the watershed and causes algae blooms that deplete oxygen in the water and kill marine life. So scientists added an E. Coli bacteria and mouse DNA to a pig embryo. This modification decreases a pig's phosphorous output by as much as 70 percent – making the pig more environmentally friendly.

Guelph University and National Geographic published two interesting articles explaining in more detail the concept of the enviropig. Please refer to: uoguelph.ca/enviropig/ and: nationalgeographic.com/news/2010/03/100330-bacon-pigs-enviropig-dead-zones/

Now, for information about the 12 strangest and most abnormal cases of genetic engineering, please refer to Mother Nature Network and look for an article on their website entitled "12 Bizarre Examples of Genetic Engineering" written by Laura Moss and posted on Oct. 27, 2010 at: mnn.com/green-tech/research-innovations/photos/12-bizarre-examples-of-genetic-engineering/enviropig#ixzz3Km1xiLXC

An unsettling and weird example from the above source, which for me is difficult to fully understand and, above all, believe and trust, is the following:

> Medicinal Eggs: British scientists have created a breed of genetically modified hens that produce cancer-fighting medicines in their eggs. The animals have had

human genes added to their DNA so that human proteins are secreted into the whites of their eggs, along with complex medicinal proteins similar to drugs used to treat skin cancer and other diseases.

What exactly do these disease-fighting eggs contain? The hens lay eggs that have miR24, a molecule with potential for treating malignant melanoma and arthritis, and human interferon b-1a, an antiviral drug that resembles modern treatments for multiple sclerosis. Whether the report is scientifically accurate or just a marketing gimmick is irrelevant, but people need to know this and keep it in mind for future egg consumption.

The above text is difficult to believe. I am not saying that it is not true, but if it were a proven scientific discovery, they would be selling these eggs all over the world, in every supermarket, and everybody would have known about this from the day they were developed or invented. Perhaps it simply has not been tested extensively enough to be accepted by the proper authorities, health institutions, and drug administrations. But I have to admit that, if it were 100 per cent true, and even though it sounds freaky, I would seriously consider buying them for our family. But wait, that is just me. Others would not even contemplate the idea of having "Frankenstein eggs" in their fridge, much less eating them.

In the name of science, humans have tested and sometimes sacrificed animals such as rats and monkeys, as well as humans. This has been done since ancient times, and I guarantee you that the quest for new discoveries will never cease.

All research is supposed to be done for the benefit of the human race, but in reality, a great majority is done for the benefit of corporate bank accounts. I believe that most companies start by trying to achieve something good, but, in their quest to reach their goals, some lose track of what is right and what is wrong. If they are willing to correct themselves, then they are acting responsibly, but if they continue to be concerned only with their profit targets and higher returns for shareholders, they are definitely in the category of very irresponsible companies.

However, that is not for me to decide. It is for the reader to understand the difference between right and wrong and between a responsible or irresponsible action. It is for the reader to try and do something. We have to stop turning a blind eye and instead start making small but relentless efforts to contribute positively for the sake of our planet.

Is the worst of GMOs still to come?

According to Ramon J. Seidler (former Senior Scientist in the US Environmental Protection Agency) the situation is getting worse by the day due to the fact that weeds and insects are becoming stronger and more resistant. This is leading to the creation of "superweeds" and "superbugs" that need ever stronger and more dangerous pesticides and herbicides to stop them. These superweeds and superbugs have adapted their DNA and outgrown the damaging effects of glyphosate, a powerful chemical developed by Monsanto that constitutes the main ingredient in the herbicides sold by this company to control weeds. They have also adapted to the Bt (Bacillus Thurnigienesis), which is heavily used in insecticides.

Along with the superbugs caused by GMOs, there is also a serious worldwide problem of superbugs that are resistant to almost all antibiotics. Sabrina Tavernise and Denise Grady wrote an article for the New York Times (May 26, 2016) entitled "Infection Raises Specter of Superbugs Resistant to All Antibiotics". The article states that the United States military, has identified superbugs that can cause untreatable and deadly infections. Tavernise and Grady report that:

bacteria can easily transmit their resistance to other germs that are already resistant to additional antibiotics. The resistance can spread because it arises from loose genetic material that bacteria typically share with one another. The bacteria are resistant to a drug called colisitn, an old antibiotic that in the United States is held in reserve to treat especially dangerous infections that are resistant to a class of drugs called carbapenems. If carbapenem-resistant bacteria, called CRE, also pick up resistance to colistin, they will be unstoppable.

Therefore, the worst is yet to come, as more and more aggressive chemicals are required. One example is 2,4-D (Dichlorophenoxyacetic), an acidic ingredient used in-Agent Orange, which was widely handled as a defoliant during the Vietnam War. This is a seriously toxic chemical that, in conjunction with another extremely strong herbicide some call "Diablo" (devil in Spanish), is now ending up in the food we put on the table for our own children to eat. This herbicide is known in the chemical industry as Dicamba. It is a combination of organochlorine with benzoic acid, two deadly substances.

Regarding insecticides, Dr David Bronner (president of Dr Bronner's Magic Soaps and a microbiology graduate from Harvard University) stated:

The use of systemic insecticides, which coat GMO corn and soy seeds that are incorporated and expressed inside the entire plant, has skyrocketed in the last ten years. This includes the use of neonicotinoids (neonics), which are especially powerful neurotoxins that contaminate our food and water and destroy non-target pollinators and wildlife such as bees, butterflies, and birds. In fact, neonics in widespread use in the

United States are currently banned in the European Union because of their suspected link to Colony Collapse Disorder in bees, among other causes.

This is as fascinating as it is alarming. Readers should do their own research and analysis and come to their own conclusions about everything related to GMOs. Not everything you read is true, so I strongly recommend reading several sources from different authors. We need to be aware and proactive about anything used by farmers to increase the growth of the crops we consume.

Now, there is an amazing technological discovery achieved by two scientists at St. Boniface Hospital and the University of Manitoba in Winnipeg, Canada. Laura Glowacki, from CBC News published an article about the two researchers (Dr. Grant Pierce and Dr. Pavel Dibrov's) stating, "Canadian researchers discover a new drug to fight antibiotic-resistant infections." It is apparently a better way to kill invasive bacteria that are resistant to current antibiotics. Glowacki wrote that the new drug, called PEG-2S has been published in a study in the Canadian Journal of Physiology and Pharmacology. They claim it has little side effects and it worked efficiently in combating invasive bacteria without affecting healthy cells. Antimicrobials and antibiotics resistance to superbugs is a priority for every hospital, for the research direction in pharmacology, and for the World Health Organization. The PEG-2S drug proved to be effective against growth of chlamydia bacteria (sexually transmitted disease) and it can potentially have a wide positive impact in the protection against serious diseases like gonorrhea, wound infections, septicaemia and cholera. According to both scientists, this new drug successfully worked on pneumonia, Legionnaires' disease, periodontitis and gingivitis. This discovery is extremely important to the World Health Organization. Unfortunately, the approval of this drug could take ten years, and the reason why health officials are concerned over spread of resistance to last-resort antibiotics.

In defence of Monsanto and similar companies

GMO companies exist to make money like any other commercial enterprise, but at least they are also trying very hard to improve the dietary standards of many countries while doing their best to provide them with sustainable agriculture. By this, we mean agriculture that can sustain a better life for everyone involved. Companies like Monsanto are also trying to reduce world hunger, create more nutritional foods, and increase agricultural yields, while considering external factors such as climate change and renewable energy sources. Are they doing this for power and profit? Is their real goal to achieve worldwide control of farming while increasing the value of their shares?

According to a recent study by PG Economics, GM crops, by reducing fuel consumption, have helped reduce greenhouse gas emissions from many agricultural practices. GM technology has also enabled new plant varieties to tolerate insects and weeds that would otherwise destroy the crop and the well-being of the farmer. From my personal point of view, and putting aside for a moment the negative aspects of these companies and their GMOs, I have to agree that companies like Monsanto have contributed to improve agriculture by introducing crops that consume less water consumption and therefore require less irrigation.

GMOs: The good vs. the bad

It is hard to say whether companies like Monsanto are, on balance, detrimental to our society or are a stepping stone to progress and development. We all know that our population is bound to grow exponentially in the next 20 years and that we need to feed all these people. Do we have enough land and, above all, decent soil to grow healthy crops? Do all countries have the proper political structure to help improve ecologically their agriculture industry along with their farming yields? Do we have enough water for irrigation when the population is exploding? Can our future food demands be met by traditional agricultural methods and techniques? I doubt it. Therefore, the government should implement a very serious and meticulous monitoring programme for companies like Monsanto in relation to our real agricultural needs for specific products and for the benefit of farming communities. Moderation, honesty, and careful analysis are going to be the key elements in deciding which technological advances in the world of agriculture to accept or reject for the benefit of mankind. Personally, I do not fully trust GMOs, and I do my best to keep them off our dinner table.

Conservación Patagónica (Patagonia Natural Park)

An excellent example of hard honest work, integrity, and loyalty to sound human principles, and to the world that surrounds us, is the Patagonia Natural Park, which was started by conservationists Christine and Douglas Tompkins. From a young age, they wanted to establish new protected areas, and their goal has always been to protect agriculture, promote healthy communities, conserve local species, and generally safeguard ecosystems. The Tompkins family has done extensive work in the conservation of parks in South America, especially in Chile and Argentina. They pride themselves on being known around the world as protectors of wildlife, restorers of the landscape, and promoters of organic farming. Within their core principles, they always focused on sustainable and ecological agriculture.

The conservation groups with which they have worked for many years believe that all humans have an ethical obligation to share the planet with other species, and that everybody has the obligation to change their attitudes and actions for a better future in which all forms of life can flourish. The Tompkins have put special emphasis on improving all kinds of agricultural activities for the protection of the environment and all the species living in it. Doug Tompkins traveled extensively in South America and fell in love with the Patagonia region in the south of Chile and Argentina. Unfortunately, the beautiful grasslands, diverse landscapes, and bountiful wildlife that Patagonia has to offer were being threatened by mining, industrial aquaculture, deforestation, and the construction of hydro dams. The Tompkins responded by incorporating a nonprofit organization in California called Conservación Patagónica (CP), a conservation foundation called Conservation Land Trust (CLT) and a 760,000-acre nature sanctuary, Pumalin Park.

The mission of Conservación Patagónica is to "build new national parks in compelling ecologically critical areas of Patagonia" (read more at: conservacionpatagonica.org). Conservación Patagónica then had the opportunity to create the Patagonia National Park in Chile's Aysen Region. There is a beautiful valley in the heart of that region that forms part of a pass over the Andes. This represents a transition area between the grasslands of Patagonia in Argentina and the South Beech forest on the West coast towards Chile. Two Chilean National Reserves are on either side of that beautiful valley.

The Chilean Parks Service tried for many years to unite the reserves and create a large protected area, but they could not succeed due to lack of resources. Luckily, Christine Tompkins visited the area and noticed how for many years the grasslands had been "protected" from the guanaco (a species native to South America also known as Lama Guanicoe). Grazing competition from the livestock of local ranchers (cattle and sheep) has always been an issue. All this was happening in the Chabacano Valley. All the grassland looked patchy and in really bad condition. The local ranchers were using unsustainable ranching practices for their cattle and sheep industries.

This is how Patagonia National Park was born. The immediate objective was to protect 650,000 acres of grasslands, mountains, and lakes, but this has developed, over the years, into a long-lasting infrastructure that attracts tourism and promotes the economy of the area, now based on conservation of the ecosystem and wildlife.

There is another national park in Argentina called Perito Moreno. In May 2013, Conservación Patagónica donated an area called Estancia Rincón (37,000 acres of land) to Perito Moreno National Park. Estancia Rincon provides access to and from Perito Moreno to the impressive and dramatic south face of the second tallest peak in Patagonia, which had never been climbed at the time.

These accomplishments of Christine and Doug Tompkins are a formidable act of loyalty, honesty, integrity, and overall sense of high ethics and responsibility. A South American "aficionado," Jaime Bascunan Aldunate, once wrote: "Muchas gracias a la familia Tompkins por su generosidad y confianza en la Republica de Chile y Argentina." (Thank you to the Tompkins family for their generosity and trust in the Republics of Chile and Argentina)

Han sacado adelante estoicamente estos proyectos de conservación a pesar de tener a prácticamente toda la prensa y la opinión pública en contra, que nunca creyeron en sus reales intenciones de donar finalmente las tierras a los sistemas de parques nacionales. Es una pena que la misma publicidad que se utilizó para atacarlos no se utilice ahora para reconocer su generosidad. (You have stoically succeeded in these conservation projects against all the press and public opinion, which never believed in your true and real intentions of donating these lands to the national park system. It is a pity and great sadness that the same press that was used to attack you fearlessly is not used now to appreciate your generosity).

Espero que logremos conservar estas tierras en las mismas o mejores condiciones en que ustedes las entregan. Al ver el estado en que se encuentran algunos de nuestros parques nacionales, tengo dudas al respecto. (I truly hope we manage to conserve these lands in the same or better condition in which you gave them to us. As I observe some of our national parks, I have my doubts.)

I guess the validity of Bascunan's doubts will remain to be seen. When there is a will, there is a way, but our efforts, sacrifice, focus, and true spirit need to be present at all times. Best wishes for our brothers in Chile and Argentina and an eternal thank you to the Tompkins family!

Invasion of Iraq

Right after the 9/11 terrorist attack in New York, the then US President George W. Bush, received "confidential intelligence information" that Iraq had weapons of mass destruction. He made most people in the United States believe, through numerous public speeches and by taking advantage of their emotional state at the time, that Iraq was a hostile country with secret weapons of mass destruction and that they were getting ready to use them against the US at the first opportunity. Little did the US population know about President George W Bush's real intentions at the time.

China and many other countries have confirmed publicly that the United States presented false and inconclusive allegations as a pretext to invade Iraq. In fact, the US went to war against

Iraq before the United Nations inspectors had completed their investigations, much less published their conclusions and recommendations. Unfortunately, a number of other countries backed the US military intervention and joined the attack for obscure and shady reasons. The political ties among these countries were very strong, but history has proven George W. Bush wrong about the reasons he used to justify invading Iraq.

It may occur to some that perhaps George W. Bush and his close advisors had altogether different reasons for military action that were never publicly revealed, even though some politicians may have known but were unable to do anything about them. A similar situation may apply to other countries that may have known the real motives behind Bush's actions, but again felt there was nothing they could do.

Was this attack a responsible, justified one, or was it a self-interested action taken without any proper mandate from the United Nations and with hidden political, strategic, and economic motives? From my personal point of view, whoever believed George W Bush's justification for attacking Iraq was as ignorant, dumb, or dangerously deceptive and treacherous as their commander in chief himself. But again, that is just my personal opinion. What does the reader think now that the cards have been laid on the table?

Many countries were against the invasion of Iraq, and when it was executed, everybody around the world soon realized that the invaders never found one single weapon of mass destruction. In fact, Iraq's weaponry turned out to be very antiquated and weak compared to that of the USA and its allies. It seems that the motivation for war was either a problem between the Bush family and Saddam Hussein or an economic strategy.

In the aftermath, some American politicians became so

uncomfortable with the invasion that Democratic presidential contender Hillary Rodham Clinton at the time said:

> I think it's the height of irresponsibility and I really resent it. This was his decision to go to war, he went with an ill-conceived plan, an incompetently executed strategy, and we should expect him to extricate our country from this before he leaves office.

For more information, please see "Clinton attacks Bush's 'irresponsibility' on Iraq", by John Whiteside, Political Correspondent, Iowa Sun, Jan 28, 2007, at:

washingtonpost.com/wpdyn/content/article/2007/01/28/AR2007012800743.html

According to very interesting and well-researched sources such as the Paul Thompson website (pthompson.org.uk), the United States and the United Kingdom did not invade Iraq to uphold a decision of the United Nations or because of the rationale of resolution 1441. The US and the UK did not go to war to get rid of weapons of mass destruction nor in self-defence, much less for humanitarian reasons. As confirmed by the governments and political parties of various countries and many public media sources of information, the US and the UK went to war for oil and in order to boost the US economy through an active ongoing war (and all the associated expenditures). The war also benefited the economic interests of private suppliers who were paid to keep it going and later to participate in Iraq's reconstruction, all the while economically enslaving future generations through the massive debts that were incurred, just as has happened in many other countries around the world in the past. The way Paul Thompson described the build-up to the war on his website is interesting and worth quoting at length:

> US threats to go to war against Iraq are largely driven

by oil and empire – expanding US military and economic power. As these goals primarily benefit oil companies and the already rich and powerful, the Bush administration relies on fear to mobilize public support for war among ordinary Americans by linking Iraq falsely with the very real threat of terrorism and through rhetoric like 'axis of evil.'

Many top officials of the Bush administration come directly out of the oil industry. President Bush himself, as well as Vice-President Dick Cheney, National Security Adviser Condoleezza Rice, Secretary of Commerce Donald Evans and others all have strong ties to oil companies.

But the US isn't threatening an invasion simply to ensure its continued access to Iraqi oil. Rather, it is a much broader US play for control of the oil industry and the ability to set the price of oil on the world market. Iraq's oil reserves are second only to Saudi Arabia's. And with US-backed Saudi Arabia increasingly unstable, the question of which oil companies – French, Russian, or American – would control Iraq's rich but unexplored oil fields once sanctions are lifted, has moved to the top of Washington's agenda.

Many in the Bush administration believe that, in the long term, a post-war, US-dependent Iraq would supplant Saudi control of oil prices and marginalize the influence of the Saudi-led OPEC oil cartel. Iraq could replace Saudi Arabia, at least partially, at the centre of US oil and military strategy in the region, and the US would remain able to act as guarantor of oil for Japan, Germany, and other allies in Europe and around the world.

What happened in Iraq is in the past, but the damage that has been perpetrated is irreversible, and there is nothing anybody can now do about it. But the question remains: Should George W. Bush be considered a war criminal and be brought to justice as Saddam Hussein was?

War criminal or not, who am I to answer this question? Who am I to condone his actions or to hold him responsible? Should I judge whether the US and the UK performed a responsible or irresponsible act for or against humanity? I am just one lonely voice on this planet. Nevertheless, the questions remain, and they serve as good tests of what being responsible or irresponsible is. They certainly prove what Bill Gates once said: "Life is not fair, so get used to it."

Benefits of teaching people that food is everything

I once read an article in the May 2015 issue of National Geographic entitled "Food is Everything." It was written by a Spanish chef, José Andrés, who moved from Spain to the United States and currently has 20 restaurants. Andrés introduced tapas to the US and also founded a humanitarian organization called World Central Kitchen, focusing on the power of food and how to provide smart and efficient solutions to world hunger. He has traveled around the world to provide volunteer assistance in disaster zones.

In this article, Chef Andrés provides a wonderful angle on why food education is important. He brings to the table the following perspective, which every human being should listen to, understand, and apply as best they can for themselves and their families for the rest of their lives. Chef José Andrés says: "Food is national security. Food is economy. It is employment, energy, and history. Food is everything. I believe everybody should be aware not just of the food they eat, but of the implications of eating it."

According to Chef Andrés, if we are keen about eating locally and sustainably, great things can be achieved, but to do so, cities need to designate areas in their poorest communities and devote them to the expansion of farmland. This will provide accessible food at lower costs in these communities.

In the same issue of National Geographic, four examples that support Chef Andrés' point of view are highlighted by Kelsey Nowakowski. They concern corn in China, wheat in Russia, soybeans in Brazil, and rice in India and provide good, responsible examples for the rest of the world to follow.

Contrary to common belief, the consumption of corn in China has now outstripped the consumption of rice, increasing by 125 per cent in the past 25 years, while rice consumption has only increased by 7 per cent. This has happened thanks to government incentives and farmers' willingness to improve water quality in China. Apparently, corn uses a lot less water than rice while simultaneously creating less fertilizer runoff to pollute watersheds. As a result, the use of fertilizer has decreased tremendously, and this has had a significant positive impact on the quality of drinking water.

According to the Economist (May 16-22, 2015), the Organization of Economic Co-operation and Development (OECD) did some research and found that, in 2012, China's subsidies to farmers exceeded those of any other country by far. They were more than five times greater than subsidies in the United States ($30 billion compared to $165 billion). Japan was in second place with $65 billion in subsidies. But what it is very important, aside from subsidies, is the proper management of the food reserves each country has, and this is where China lacks an edge. Countries like Japan, South Korea, and Switzerland, where subsidies account for more than half the farmers' income, are doing better, according to this article.

As for wheat in Russia, according to the World Bank, Russia

is among the top five countries when it comes to conservation of agriculture. It has adapted its agricultural practices to compensate quickly for the sanctions imposed by the United States and its European allies, expanded its efforts to develop better agricultural technologies to increase production, and achieved great success, notably in wheat production.

In Brazil, the deforestation of the Amazon basin for cattle and soybean production is well known. The Amazon rainforest was seriously threatened between 1990 and 2005, when enormous quantities of forest were cleared to expand cattle and soya bean farming. However, thanks to the relentless efforts of farmers and activists, and government support for them, 33,000 square miles of rainforest were protected. As a result, the farmers had no choice but to increase their productivity and efficiency, and Brazil is now the second-largest producer of soybeans. This was achieved through better tools, more efficient machinery, and earlier-maturing seeds that yield faster crops. Nevertheless, we have to be honest with ourselves and ask whether Brazil has really *stopped* the deforestation of the Amazon rainforest. The answer can be found in the next section.

Meanwhile in India, with the support of the World Bank, a variety of hybrid rice has been developed that grows faster while using less water. Most Indian farmers rely on monsoons for their water supply but have recently suffered serious droughts. The government was forced to step in to educate their people on how to use water more efficiently while providing technical support. In the process, a new drought-resistant rice was developed. Known as Basmati, it matures 30 days sooner than other varieties of crossbred rice.

These examples from China, Russia, Brazil, and India clearly indicate that with proper scientific research, more food can be produced in a more harmonized and balanced fashion for the benefit of our environment and the overall well-being of our relentlessly growing world population. This is especially important in the poorest communities and in areas where droughts are known to be devastating.

An important method where more countries need to embrace is the practice of Aquaponics, which is the combination of hydroponics (soil-less growing of plants) and aquaculture (fish farming). It grows both, plants and fish in one cohesive and co-ordinated system. While the plants offer a natural filter for the water in which fish live, they, in return provide the plants with an organic food source, fish waste. There are also other members that thrive in the growing element. These are known as red worms and microbes. They convert the fish waste into nitrites and into nitrate, while the solids are converted into plant's food in the form of vermicompost. Aquaponics uses $1/10^{th}$ of that of solid-based garden and definitely less water than hydroponics or aquaculture recirculation. Gardening is almost eliminated and fertilizers only play a small, delicate, and more environmentally part of the process. The global Aquaponics industry is exploding mainly because of the use of LED lights, less water consumption (that circulates between plants and fish), and the production of cleaner and healthier products for human consumption.

Deforestation in Brazil and Indonesia

In an article in Scientific American in June 2015, Richard Schiffmann observes that, in the 20-year period from 1990 to 2010, there was a 62 per cent increase in deforestation of rainforests compared to the period between 2004 and 2011, when the rate of deforestation plummeted, mainly due to environmental regulations and prohibitions on the sale of soybeans that came from cleared rainforest lands. Unfortunately, according to Schiffmann, the tree cutting has doubled from earlier years since 2014. He says this has been corroborated by an independent research institution (via satellite imaging analysis) called "Imazon".

The main reasons for the Amazon deforestation are:

- The need for farmland to support cattle due to the worldwide increase in demand for beef, which mainly satisfies the increasing trend for fast-food burgers in North, Central, and South America.

- The demand for beautiful woods such as mahogany, which end up as flooring, doors, furniture, and many other luxury items throughout the American continent from Argentina to Alaska.

- The need for more hydroelectric dams and everything that is part of them.

- The desire for a transcontinental highway to connect east and west by cutting the Amazon Rainforest in half.

- Lack of commitment by Dilma Rousseff to rainforest protection policies at the time. Ms. Rousseff was the Brazilian president, but was removed from power in May of 2016 for alleged mismanagement of public affairs and lack of real concern for the well-being of the Brazilian population, environment, and ecosystem.

- At the time, pardons and reprieves offered by Ms. Rousseff to those who illegally cut down trees. It seems she was more concerned with economic growth than the well-being of the Brazilian population along with its flora and fauna. It is also imperative to mention that she never considered the rest of the population of the western hemisphere and the long-term impact in its environment, above and beyond the Brazilian territory. According to critics, she seemed to have had a very narrow minded vision for the environment and the ecosystem.

In Brazil, the authorities do not seem to understand or care that deforestation, as Richard Schiffmann and other researchers write, decreases the movement of atmospheric moisture, which then affects rain patterns in the southern hemisphere and beyond. The resulting lack of moisture brings droughts that, in turn, put at risk not only the new farmlands, but also cities such as São Paulo, which according to the Brazil Amazon Research Institute (INPA), will experience a permanent drought.

Just because we do not live in Brazil, we cannot turn a blind eye to an environment that is being raped for the sake of economics and so-called "progress." This is going to affect our own weather patterns, water supplies, and oxygen levels across the American continent. There is not a human being (scientist or not) who can accurately predict the "tipping point" when our atmospheric moisture will change forever, causing devastating effects from Canada and the United Sates all the way to Chile and Argentina (and beyond). Not even Malcolm Gladwell (author of *The Tipping Point*) can predict it. Schiffmann says that, according to Thomas Levjoy (an avid Amazon researcher), the Amazon is already 20 per cent deforested, and at any time "a perfect storm of deforestation, fire, and climate change could potentially transform vast swathes of the southern and eastern Amazon into a savanna."

The deforestation in Brazil and Indonesia (and in other countries) is motivated mainly by economic gain and private benefits for a few, while the rest of the population lives in poverty and with very low, or non-existent, levels of education. Isn't it time for everybody to ask themselves a very legitimate, important, and delicate question: Do these forests, regardless of where they are, ultimately belong only to the people of that country or to humanity as a whole? If countries invade other countries for various reasons, what stops them from invading a country that has no idea how to manage and protect its own forests or is mismanaging them for twisted economic interests and whose irresponsibility will ultimately affect every single life on Earth?

Aggressive tree cutting without proper management and control of the forests causes serious deforestation issues. This should be considered an act of aggression against humanity as well as against all the wildlife that call the forests home. It is leading to the extinction of many species, such as the Orangutan in Sumatra and Borneo. The word Orangutan comes from a Malay word that means 'person of the forest'. These wonderful and unique animals share 97 per cent of their DNA with humans, yet we are pushing them to extinction.

The rainforests are also the lungs of Mother Earth, and humans are destroying them purely for economic benefit, exploiting them without proper reforestation programs. Is this a responsible or irresponsible action? Even worse, what are we doing to stop it? Is our lack of action irresponsible or responsible? To pretend not to see the problem and to do nothing about it are, in my view, very irresponsible absences of action.

Shouldn't countries like the United States, Canada, Great Britain, Germany, and the rest of their European allies do something about deforestation by force if need be? They employ force to secure oil supplies and for strategic military reasons throughout the world, so why not for the water we drink and the air we breathe? Aren't these more important?

Personally, I believe that military interventions can be good to keep peace or restore justice in a country, but what about the protection of our forests, oceans, rivers, and the flora and fauna in them for the sake of our environment and for the future of humankind? Where do we need to draw the line and demand that countries take care of their forests and oceans or else risk invasion?

I could continue giving many more examples of irresponsible measures perpetrated by people or governments, but, luckily, everything tends to balance itself to keep coexisting on this wonderful marvel of planet Earth. But again, when and where will the tipping point take place?

Tomorrow's technology

Technology is advancing at an amazing pace in various industries, but the medical and pharmaceutical industries are advancing at a particularly impressive rate. There are four articles about specific, responsible advances for the benefit of humankind that I consider especially important. The first two were published by Scientific American in May 2012. The third and fourth were published in Canadian National Geographic in April 2015 and June 2013 and were written by Nick Walker and Sarah Hewitt, respectively.

The first article reports on some promising developments in medicine in the area of customized technology for genetics. In the future, people will be able to have their own unique physiology considered instead of averages from larger group trials. Their own genes and stem cells will be used to customize medical solutions at 100 per cent accuracy. In 2003, the first complete human genome sequence was announced. At that time, it was time-consuming and very costly to do and thus inaccessible to the average person, but now it can be done for any individual in a matter of hours for about $1,000 or less. According to the article, the advances in developing artificial eyes (bionic eyes) have been particularly impressive. A blind person can now be enabled to distinguish shapes and sizes at least. In 2008, a totally blind person had an electronic chip implanted in one eye. After a brief time, the patient managed to distinguish shapes and sizes. Though not totally perfected, this technology is here to stay and will no doubt be further improved.

Meanwhile, as the article reported, nanoparticle engineers have been assisting medical doctors by enabling nanoparticles to carry out tasks such as detecting tumours and malignant cancer cells. Before this, some molecules in a tumour could not be easily detected, putting the patient at risk. Nowadays, these nanoparticle minerals literally highlight the cancer cells, so that doctors can see them and aggressively treat immediately.

The second article described tornados, hurricanes, and cyclones, which currently cause much loss of life and considerable negative economic impacts across North America and in many other countries. In an article entitled "New Technology Allows Better Extreme Weather Forecasts," Jane Lubchenco and Jack Hayes report on how "new technology that increases the warning time for tornadoes and hurricanes could potentially save hundreds of lives every year." With serious and undeniable climate change getting worse, such improvements in weather forecasts and predictions are extremely important to save human lives.

As Lubchenco and Hayes say, engineers and researchers have developed new technologies at the National Oceanic and Atmospheric Administration that have greatly enhanced the capabilities of radars and satellites and also improved the ability of supercomputers to reduce warning times for thunderstorms, tornados, hurricanes, and floods, and more accurately predict the intensity of what is coming, so families can take shelter in appropriate places. Incredible amounts of data can be analyzed better and faster by these supercomputers. A new technology called dual-polarization can even assist researchers and scientists to detect tornados when they are still invisible to the human eye. We can also now detect and differentiate the various types of precipitation and their intensity and amounts, which will help people to plan accordingly.

The third article I want to highlight here talks about the technological revolution taking place in the way people farm. It talks in particular about "cubic" farming, as practiced by a Montreal-based company called Urban Barns, which, according to the article, "is leading a fresh-produce revolution." This method of farming capitalizes on space utilization, pest controls, water usage and maximization, nutrient controls, the total amounts to produce, and the ideal amounts to produce per square metre. It uses metal frames with metal trays and different pulley cables to move the trays up and down as the farmer is attending to a specific crop.

These modular machines are extremely flexible, adaptable, and easy to work with in an environment where temperature and light can be accurately controlled. The crops are seeded and grown in a soil substitute called rock wool, a fabric-like material made out of specific mineral fibres. The rock wool is not biodegradable, but McGill University researchers are now developing a biodegradable soil substitute made out of coconut.

One of the most important contributions of cubic farming is that it requires no pesticides, herbicides, or fungicides. This is extremely important to increase the nutritional value of the crops and for protecting our watersheds, which are currently being contaminated by chemicals manufactured to control weeds and pests. Cubic farming definitely provides safer food products, using very strict control standards before and after seeding and careful monitoring to ensure safer, tastier, and more nutritious food products.

Another very positive impact of cubic farming is that the water needed to irrigate these crops is nutrient rich and applied at a specific rate per minute to the crop. Any excess of water drains down and is collected and re-circulated across the system, so no water or nutrients are wasted. Farmers around the world are closely observing this method of farming, because it represents a huge improvement for future farming, especially for countries with water limitations and poor soil conditions.

The last article represents an interesting report about wildlife and, specifically, sea birds, in a group of small islands northwest of Vancouver Island called the Scott Island Archipelago. These islands, especially Lanz Island and Cox Island, support an amazing diversity and concentration of breeding sea birds, the most important being the Tufted Puffins and the Cassin's Auklets. These breeding grounds are vital for the Canadian Pacific ecosystem of the region and are therefore considered ecological reserves and are closed to the public. In any case, they are extremely difficult to reach due to strong currents, rocky shores, and high cliffs. The Canadian government needs to commit funds to protect these islands. According to the scientists and researchers that brought this to the attention of the government, the islands should be considered a national wildlife area for the benefit of the birds, the Canadian people, and the world.

However, the sea birds have shrunk in population by 40 per cent over the past 15 years. According to Hewitt's article, abnormal warm weather has affected the zooplankton bloom from which the seabirds feed, making their foraging grounds less nutritious. But even though the government cannot protect the seabirds from the warming of the planet, it can protect them from pollution threats such as oil spills, fishing nets, and plastic bottles in the oceans and on the shores. It can also protect them from fishermen who accidentally trap birds while fishing for sea-bird forage species.

According to Blair Hammond, the manager of ecosystem conservation for Environment Canada in Vancouver at the time, the government is not allowing new activities without permits, is carrying on more surveillance of already established regulations and more conservation, and is improving at-sea surveys. Behind these government efforts, there is an environmental group called the Canadian Parks and Wilderness Society, which insists that there should be minimum no-take zones for commercial and recreational fishing. This environmental group is also insisting that Environment Canada confine traffic to limited areas far enough from the boundaries in which the seabird coexist, feed, and reproduce.

Destruction of heritage sites during the Syrian civil war

Our irresponsibility does not only impact the environment and its flora and fauna. Warfare is another irresponsible human activity, and one that impacts humans and their own creations directly. Wars always bring with them destruction of countries and the sacrifice of human lives. In addition, the civil war in Syria has experienced the destruction of many ancient archeological sites considered world heritage sites. Shelling by the army, militias, and rebels has mainly contributed to the destruction of these sites. A major activity that takes place immediately after any occupation is looting. Archeological treasures thousands of years old then find their way into the international black market at very high prices that collectors do not think twice about paying. Over the past several years, virtually all the archaeological sites in Syria have been threatened by the civil war between government forces and rebels who oppose President Bashar al-Assad's regime. The area is so dangerous that the world can only watch what is going on from above via satellite technology.

In July 2013, Marissa Fressenden confirmed in Scientific American the destruction of the Citadel of Aleppo in northern Syria, which was constructed in the 12th century and is a UNESCO world heritage site. Meanwhile, the world worries that the civil war will completely destroy many more ancient palaces, mosques, bathhouses, and so on. The Battle of Aleppo in 2014 destroyed many historical sites, including the Palace of Justice, as well as the modern Carlton Hotel. Some ancient ruins have been used as military posts by the forces of the Assad regime, the main reason why the militia have destroyed the archeological sites in their efforts to capture or kill military opponents.

Some of the archeological sites that have been damaged include:

- The ancient Semitic city of Palmyra.
- The ancient villages of northern Syria, which were also a world heritage site.
- Citadel Aleppo, a fortified palace in the city of Aleppo, once occupied by Greeks and Byzantines, among others.
- The Mosque of Sermin and the Mar Elias Monastery.
- The city of Bosra, which is located in southern Syria and was a prosperous provincial capital in the time of the Romans.

The destruction and looting of these sites are very damaging for our human history. For many years, UNESCO has considered Syria a very important contributor of world heritage sites, which justifies and explains a vital and paramount part of our human history. All these sites and more are being monitored daily using modern satellite technology and imagery analysis, which unfortunately shows that most of the damage has been substantial and irreversible.

I do not expect everybody to be familiar with the Syrian archeological sites listed above. Therefore, let's imagine for a moment that we were to suffer similar losses in North America. Let's assume, for a brief moment, that Mexico, the

United States, or Canada were involved in a civil war.

Regarding Mexico, imagine if the archeological sites at Tulum, Palenque, Chichen Itzá, Teotihuacán, the Museum of National History in Mexico City, the Castillo of Chapultepec, Bonampak, Balcón de Montezuma, La Basílica de Guadalupe, Chiapa de Corso, Cholula, La Catedral Nacional, El Palacio de Iturbide, el Palacio de Cortéz, Tenochtitlán, Uxmal, and similar treasures were totally destroyed.

In the United States, due to the young age of this country, we cannot focus on ancient archeological sites, but imagine the destruction of places such as Mount Rushmore National Memorial, the Statue of Liberty, the New York Public Library, the Golden Gate Bridge, the National Mall in downtown Washington, the United States Capitol, the Library of Congress, the National Air and Space Museum, the Liberty Bell, the Lincoln Memorial, the National Museum of Natural History and the Washington Monument, Cathedral of St. John the Baptist, among many others.

Canada is also a young country, but imagine the destruction of such national landmarks as Parliament Hill in Ottawa, the CN Tower in Toronto, the Saint Joseph Oratory and Notre Dame Cathedral in Montreal, the Vancouver Library, or the Lions Gate Bridge or Port Mann Bridge in the same city, the legislative buildings in Alberta, Manitoba, Ontario, Saskatchewan, or New Brunswick, the Banff Hotel and Chateau Lake Louise in Alberta, Niagara Falls in Ontario, the provincial parliament building in British Columbia or in Quebec, the Confederation Building in Newfoundland and Labrador, Province House in Nova Scotia, and so on.

We all remember the terrible loss of the Twin Towers in New York City. Aside from the loss of life, what was the reaction and feeling of people across the United States to the destruction of this famous landmark? Now imagine if the

Statue of Liberty were to be destroyed by another "act of war" tomorrow? Wouldn't that have a huge impact on the psyche of the people of New York and across the US? What if Mount Rushmore was the casualty? What about the magnificent historical memories that those places represent to the American people? What about the concept of the "American Dream" and the security and freedom immigrants from all over the world have come to seek in the United States?

Last but not least, imagine if the Neuschwanstein Castle in southern Germany, which was built during the reign of Ludwig II of Bavaria (during the 19th century), was destroyed prior to Walt Disney's inspiration for Disneyland's Sleeping Beauty Castle.

With all the previous examples, I trust the reader can now fathom the serious extent of the destruction of the archeological sites in Syria.

Global warming debate

Is the global warming a result of the earth's normal life cycle or is it due to human activity? There is a big debate worldwide to find out what the real cause is. Different scientists have different points of view, but some things are crystal clear to some well renowned scientists:

- The earth is (and always will be) going through its own natural life cycle (currently a warming cycle).

- Scientists like Professor Judith Curry (head of climate science department at Georgia Tech University) have insisted that the models to predict future warming have been extremely flawed, so the data is unreliable.

- Other scientists (like Professor Phil Jones, director of Climate Research Unit at the University of East Anglia,

UK) predict a warmer decade than the previous two or three decades.

- Some scientists even argue that the world stopped getting warmer almost 17 years ago and that, in fact, it is now cooling down.

- Many scientists worldwide insist that human activity is directly responsible for the excess yearly marginal increases of carbon dioxide in the atmosphere, which assists in the acceleration of global warming beyond and above its natural cycle.

- Maclean's magazine acknowledges Professor Mike Flannigan, from the University of Alberta and director of Western Partnership for Wildland Fire Science, as a worldwide expert in wild forest fires. Flannigan confirms, through a study published in the Proceedings of the National Academy of Science, that boreal forests are burning a lot more frequently than in the past 10,000 years. In Canada alone, the areas burned each year (i.e.: The Fort McMurray area in Alberta) have risen alarmingly, and according to him, this is "due to human caused climate change".

Whatever the case might be and the complexities of the situation, for many people around the world it is an undeniable fact that humans are leaving behind a negative and damaging footprint on our environment worldwide that is accelerating the natural cycle of global warming.

Accepting that climate change is caused by human activity

It is a confirmed scientific fact that both natural forces and human activities have driven global warming since the mid-twentieth century. Natural forces have been responsible for climate changes in the past, but scientists have now proven that mankind has developed with such force and speed since the beginning of the industrial revolution that current global warming, along with many so-called natural disasters, are caused mainly by human activities. Overpopulation along with "development and progress", have certainly proven to be the tipping factor of our global warming problems.

Unfortunately, only a small percentage of the population is conscious and mature enough to accept responsibility for their participation in the acceleration of planetary warming. Yet a person has to be absolutely ignorant, naïve, or in a high degree of stubbornness and irrational denial, to believe that we humans go through life on earth without leaving behind a negative imprint. Just go to cities such as Kaohsiung and Pingtung in Taiwan, Chongqing, Guangzhou, and Linfen in China, or Mumbai, Sukinda, and Kanpur in India. Air contamination in many cities is so excessive that you will practically choke if you jog or even walk several blocks on the worst days of air pollution.

And guess what? Things are forecast to get even worse. Although other cities may not suffer the same degree of pollution and garbage accumulation, the problems are getting worse in every major city in the world. From Mexico City, to Dublin in Ireland, to Johannesburg in South Africa, to Brazzaville in Congo, to Dar Es Salaam in Tanzania, to Port-Au-Prince in Haiti, to La Oroya in Peru, and the list goes on.

Not every urban problem is a matter of air pollution and garbage, of course. What about old buildings, bridges, infrastructure, houses, and so on? What about the city of Detroit in the United States (just one example in North America), which has various areas that are abandoned and in ruins? It is full of old, decrepit buildings that are literally falling apart, houses in terrible condition, and lots of garbage as well. Yet this amazing city was vibrant once, full of life and energy 24/7, a leader in high tech, and with a fascinating North American cultural background. The city of Detroit is living proof that "growth and development" are not necessarily the best goals for a city to pursue, as former Uruguayan President Jose Mujíca has eloquently pointed out in the past.

In order to help readers understand and hopefully share some responsibility, let's go to another extreme and compare the cities we have mentioned with famously pristine places such as Bora Bora, Cozumel, Bali, Aruba, and Hawaii, among many others. What do all these places have in common that the big cities we have been discussing do not?

Please stop for a moment and perform this quick mental exercise. Imagine the differences between these latter places and the previously mentioned cities. The common denominator of the latter is a low population and a lack of industrial activity. We can try to deny that, with more people and industry, humans are not changing the balance between nature and us, but we would simply be deceiving ourselves. Whether we like it or not, the more people and industry, the more the human impact on our planet and the less time for recovery, if it does recover. Unfortunately, human activities are starting to grow exponentially in their impact on Mother Earth.

We can reduce the speed with which we are harming our planet, but we cannot stop the harm altogether unless we stop three very important aspects of human existence: our demographic explosion, our overproduction, and our uncontrollable greed and relentless desire for more and more things. We humans have the "right to reproduce" and the "right to make a dollar," but unfortunately, we take everything to extremes and with absolute disregard to "moderation". Yet we also have the right and obligation to protect our planet. Remember, we only have one planet. That is the reality, and we need to adapt to it …. or succumb and die.

What will happen 100, 300, or 500 years from now if we keep on reproducing like rabbits and not putting a stop to the continued exploitation of our natural resources in the name of jobs, growth, and development? We all know that only selected people and enterprises are benefiting financially from this uncontrollable greed and relentless desire to provide higher returns for their shareholders.

Once again, please stop for a moment. Imagine yourself 496 years ago, when the Spaniard Hernándo Cortés de Monroy y Pizarro first arrived on Mexico's virgin beaches, or position yourself 523 years ago when Christopher Columbus "discovered" America while landing in the Bahamas Archipelago that he later named San Salvador.

Seriously, *close your eyes* for a few seconds and imagine the new world as it was then. Cortés and Columbus found beauty and richness beyond their wildest imagination. They found gorgeous virgin beaches, wonderful forests, outstanding grasslands, impressive mountains, plentiful rivers, crystal-clear lakes and only a few, scattered inhabitants. The fauna and flora were so abundant that it was difficult for the Spaniards to truly grasp the extent and vastness of the beautiful new continent. They were surrounded by impressive, plentiful, and "endless" natural resources in a pristine natural environment untouched by human greed.

Keep your eyes closed and now imagine what there is today along the coasts of California, Mexico, and all the way down to the south of Argentina. Imagine also the east coast of the United States and Canada. They have all developed and grown into hundreds of cities covered with asphalt and concrete where millions and millions of people live and interact on a daily basis. We have created devastating concrete jungles that depend on exploiting natural resources for all their needs on a daily and growing basis. Unfortunately, most people living there do not see it that way, not yet at least, despite the obvious contamination and pollution of our environment and its damage to our ecosystem.

Now open your eyes and refresh your mind. Do you actually see the difference from 500 years ago? Do you understand where we are all heading in the next 100, 300, or 500 years and at a much faster rate of growth than ever? I do not believe the average person fully understands the severity of our problem. If they do, they certainly do not seem to care. Honestly, I am glad I will not be here to see the future! Why? Because many resources and species have disappeared already or are disappearing as I write, and many more will be gone forever, reshaping the world as we know it for the worse.

Due to these trends, the main issues in the future will be more closely related to security, freedom, power, and totally controlled societies. Let's forget what the explorers discovered about 500 years ago. Much of it is far gone and lost, and what is left is being destroyed in the same manner. I am being as absolutely realistic as I can. I do not want to be negative nor blindly optimistic, just realistic, basing my view simply on the past 500 years of human history. We humans, unfortunately, do not seem to change.

With advances in technology, population growth, industrial expansion, economic "development" and so-called progress, the human population will explode in the next 50 years to over nine billion people (from about seven billion in 2015). Our need to squeeze natural resources from this earth will grow exponentially because of this demographic explosion and the greed of some groups. Unfortunately, we can seriously start saying good-bye to the Arctic and much of the Antarctic as well, where Chinese interests are already lurking and therefore, threatening the pristine environment and ecosystem of the Antarctic.

Unfortunately, the people who should reproduce the least are the ones reproducing the most. The average, educated, middle-class couple in North America and Europe is opting to have few, or no, babies, but the average, uneducated, poor couple, not to mention religious fanatics, in many other countries around the world are having more and more (for example, in Somalia, India, Bangladesh, Zimbabwe, Nigeria, Iraq, Kuwait, Philippines, Vietnam, Afghanistan, Belize, Liberia, and in many others).

Thus, it appears that the average family in this world is not properly planning the size of their family in direct correlation with their real needs, their habitat, a comfortable spacing for their children, and their proper support. It is important to keep in mind that the factors that ultimately influence the size of families are responsibility, religion, human rights, and individual choices. These four factors operate very differently in different parts of the world, making it extremely complicated and close to impossible to control or guide how many children couples should have per family in relation to their ability to sustain them and provide for their needs, while still trying to protect our planet.

Already, the one-child policy in China has had a negative impact on that country, with 54 per cent of newborns now being boys and only 46 per cent girls. The policy has had a very unfavourable effect on social relations; many men have to go abroad to find a wife, while women have the upper hand in choosing whom, how, and when to marry. Having a job and owning a car or an apartment carries a lot of weight in women's choice of a husband. A funny belief, but accurate nevertheless, is that many men try to buy a BMW, not because it is a better car, but because, for a lot of men, the letters BMW now stand for "Be My Wife." Since many men are very superstitious, this is without a doubt the car of first choice for many of them.

We need to do something to control population growth in poor countries, but imagine if we were to apply the same philosophy of only one child per family worldwide? What a disaster! First, we need to have equality between men and women, but, in many countries or cultures, this is close to impossible for the present. There also need to be social or economic benefits that will motivate people to comply for the sake of their own future well-being and that of their children.

Natural cooling and warming of the planet

There is no doubt that planet Earth has undergone, and will continue to undergo, natural cooling and warming cycles as it has done for millions of years. This is simply the natural evolution of our planet. However, scientists have been telling us for many years, that aside from any natural change process, earth is now being pushed more quickly and more strongly toward climate change by all the activities humans are engaged in on a daily basis.

There are various natural events and cycles that influence the planet's climate and overall environment that are beyond human control, according to the Intergovernmental Panel on Climate Change (IPCC), a group that has been organized by the United Nations and works in close collaboration with the United Nations Framework Convention on Climate Change (UNFCCC). Together the IPCC and UNFCCC focus on how to stabilize greenhouse gas density in the atmosphere, among other issues. They analyze the different patterns and causes of planetary warming and determine whether these have been induced by human activities. They then prepare a report for the UNFCCC on the social, economic, and environmental impacts and how to deal with them. They evaluate how the main culprits can mitigate the concentrations of greenhouse gases in the atmosphere by applying specific policies within their countries that will strictly adhere to UNFCCC guidelines and recommendations. The IPCC evaluates situations that cannot be explained by natural causes. They concentrate on events that are human-induced.

Therefore, to fully understand the climate changes our planet is going through, the IPCC studies how greenhouse gas (GHG) emissions are created by human activity, while pointing out the main nations at fault. They have concluded that the greenhouse gases emitted by humans result mainly from the combustion of fossil fuels. The main offenders are electricity production, manufacturing, and the constantly increasing use of cars as our main means of transportation.

Different greenhouse gases have different heat-trapping properties. The molecules of carbon dioxide (CO2) trap heat, but the molecules of methane exhibit 20 times the heat-storing capacity, making it a far more dangerous contributor to planetary warming. Meanwhile, there are many other elements that are far worse than methane. One example is nitrous oxide, which is close to 300 times stronger than CO2 in trapping heat. However, nothing traps more heat overall than CO2 due to its high concentrations in our atmosphere compared to any other element. Therefore, scientists mainly mean CO_2 when they refer to "greenhouse gases" in our atmosphere. According to the government of Canada (climatechange.gc.ca), the natural causes of climate change are mainly solar outputs and volcanic activity, although the latter is short-lived compared to the continuous solar output that increases the amount of incoming energy and, therefore, the amount of heat in our atmosphere.

However, the Canadian government also acknowledges that humans are the main contributors to climate change through burning of fossil fuels, conversion of forest land for agriculture, and economic exploitation of forests. In fact, like many other governments around the world, the Canadian government acknowledges publicly that "human activity has now become the main cause of recent climate change" and also confirms that climate change is now a trend, not a cycle. Although the depletion of the ozone hole is not the main cause of global warming, stratospheric ozone depletion (ozone hole) has been caused mainly by greenhouse gases such as CO_2 and methane released into the air by relentless human activity everywhere.

We all know that scientists around the world have been trying for many years to convince governments (and the average human being) that human activity is the main cause of the warming of our planet (considered by many scientists, the tipping point). For governments to accept this and publish it on their websites is a giant step forward in spreading the truth. Here is a key part of the official Canadian government statement:

> Individuals, organizations, and the international community can make a difference in dealing with climate change. We must act. Measures to reduce greenhouse gas emissions are essential to slowing the rate of climate change. Raising awareness of the issues surrounding climate change can make a significant difference (climatechange.gc.ca/).

A quite detailed article was published in the international section of The Economist (May 9-15, 2015) entitled "Is it global warming or just the weather?" It provides an interesting perspective and valuable example of how scientists think, stating:

> Scientists around the world are getting more comfortable about attributing the heat waves and droughts to human influence.... Scientific attribution

does not require certainty; it deals in probabilities. Even now, doctors cannot be sure that a case of lung cancer has been caused by smoking (the patient might have got the disease anyway). Nevertheless, it is possible to say that smoking increases the risk of cancer by a certain amount and that smoking causes cancer in a general sense. In a similar way, scientists are now able to say that climate change increases the risk of a particular weather pattern by a measurable amount, and in some cases that a particular episode is almost impossible to imagine without global warming.

What can we do about climate change?

The specific and key question is: Can I, as a North American, reduce my waste or modify my daily consumption of energy so that my behaviour has an actual, positive impact on my immediate environment, the environment of my country, and even the environment beyond our borders?

The answer is: Absolutely yes! Here are sixteen practical steps that can be implemented on a personal basis while influencing the people around you through positive actions. The following are only starting points. The rest can be left to the reader's desire, imagination, creativity, and research:

1. *Recycle*: A large percentage of the North American population still does not recycle, yet this is an action that should come automatically and without even thinking about it. The more we recycle, the less garbage, less use of natural resources, and less greenhouse gas emissions. Simple!

2. *Use less hot water at home:* Wash with cold water instead of hot. According to DuPont, they have developed a soap formula that works as well or better in cold water than in hot. They claim that, if you use

cold water instead of hot water for a year, you will save enough energy to charge your cellular phone for life. It doesn't matter if this estimate of energy savings is 100 per cent accurate; there is no doubt there would be a serious positive impact on energy consumption across North America if we all washed at home with cold water.

3. *Reduce consumption and re-use*: We should all make an effort to fix things and re-use them. We do not need to maintain a high level of consumption to emulate the Joneses. There is no need to compete or prove that you have as much or more than your neighbours or friends.

4. *Use your car less and buy smart*: The average person does not really need a gas guzzler in the shape of a pick-up truck or an 8 or 6-cylinder car. For your next automobile purchase, think about going hybrid or electric. You can't do it? Okay, at least use your car less for small errands; use your bicycle instead. It is healthier as well as cleaner. European countries such as Germany and Austria are into cycling a lot more than we are in North America. We should change our attitude and use our bicycles more.

5. *Use efficient light bulbs at home*: Light bulbs were originally meant to use electricity indiscriminately and to last for quite a short time. With new energy-efficient bulbs that are ultra-low in mercury, we can all contribute to save energy. Yes, they are a little more expensive, but the return on investment is quick, and you can change all the bulbs when required. No need to change them all at once, but we all need to start. The fluorescent light (CFL) bulb is a good place to start. Then venture (if budget allows) into light-emitting diode (LED) lighting, which should be the ultimate

commercial and residential goal at this time.

6. *Cut down your meat consumption*: The more meat you eat, the larger your carbon footprint. The greater the demand for meat, the more pastures are required to feed cattle, which results in deforestation and more emissions of methane gas produced by cattle. This has proven to be a very serious and incremental problem. Time to do something about it!

7. *Turn off your lights and faucets*: It is very common to see children and even adults step out of a room without turning the lights off. The children need educating on this, and the adults need to realize what they are doing and make an effort to break the habit. It is also very common to see people washing dishes with the water running. Similarly, many men and women leave the water running when they brush their teeth or shave.

8. *Plant trees, bushes, and flowers*: Aside from being beautiful and natural to own, they contribute to the reduction of CO_2 in the atmosphere. They are our best allies in providing oxygen on land. As well, their lack of care or continued destruction is threatening our children's healthy future.

9. *Avoid planting grass in residential areas*: More grass means more water and energy consumption.

10. *Purchase energy-efficient appliances*: Make an effort to purchase energy-efficient products. Their return on investment is quick, and many products come with a government or company rebate.

11. *Inform yourselves about green government candidates*: Those in favour of our environment are the candidates we should vote for, but only if they have a legitimate

track record as green candidates.

12. *Reduce personal and business traveling*: Instead, use web conferencing, phone calls, conference calls, and online communication apps such as Skype, on-stream meetings, Yammer, chatting, Facebook, hangouts, Team on the Run, and so on.

13. *Turn off your TV and box when not watching*: Programme your monitors and all computer equipment to save-mode. We need to develop this habit regardless of whether our TV is LED or not.

14. *Purchase local fruits in season*: Avoid buying produce out of season and from other countries. Buy local to avoid higher costs and gas emissions from transportation and freight, while supporting your local agriculture.

15. *Reduce your weekly garbage*: If everybody were to produce one less bag of garbage a week, which would be quite easy, we would each prevent about half a kilo of garbage per week from going to the dump. Including only residential waste (no commercial, government, or industrial waste), we would save our landfills approximately 914,320 metric tons of garbage per year (based on 35.16 million people as of 2015 in Canada alone). If the same were done in the United States (population about 350 million), it would save the landfills from dealing with about 9.1 million metric tons of garbage per year. For Mexico, the amount would be about 2.4 million metric tons (for about 124 million people with an average lower income integrated into the calculation).

16. *Reduce home heating and air conditioning*: These have a considerable impact on our environment. As the

David Suzuki Foundation has often pointed out, the energy we consume in Canada in the form of electricity comes from either hydroelectric dams, burning of fossil fuels, or from nuclear power plants. All of these sources have negative consequences on overall global warming, global waste, ocean and air pollution, and on the loss of flora and fauna. We should seriously start considering wind and solar energy and wind turbine energy as alternatives but, above all, reduce our consumption of energy in heating and air conditioning. We can start by insulating our homes efficiently to save heating and the use of air conditioning. Both will have a major positive impact on our environment.

Optimism of Pope Francis on climate change

Already since May 18 of 2015, the Vatican published Pope Francis' "encyclical on the environment and climate change." He was very specific in warning humans that we need to take immediate action to stop drastic climate changes. From the Vatican's point of view, we humans are causing an unprecedented destruction of our environment and our ecosystem, and we need to stop now.

The Pope also expressed concern regarding our exponential and uncontrolled population growth. He also stated that we are creating consumer societies that are seriously harming the planet's natural balance in relation to its delicate ecosystem. We are destroying our water reservoirs, dumping the oceans with all sorts of garbage, plastic, and toxic waste, and altering earth's CO_2 cycle, all of which are having an immediate and strong impact on the warming of our planet.

Pope Francis invited everyone not to focus on religion nor on the Catholic Church, but rather on what is really happening on our planet. He spoke about poverty, inequality, lack of spirituality, biodiversity, economic trends, and future water and consumption needs, particularly in the rich countries. He encouraged everybody to think about the integrity of daily human life, not just the integrity of the ecosystem alone. Planet Earth is begging for humility in people, imploring them to leave behind the attitude of "mastery over everything."

In my mind, among the most important aspects of the Pope's encyclical were the following:

- Finally, somebody of significant influence who many people around the world listen to has brought to public attention how we humans are contributing heavily to the slow but relentless destruction of this planet. The Pope is afraid the speed of this destruction will increase with overpopulation and the greed of powerful companies to "satisfy the needs of the masses" while, as an excuse, squeezing the planet for more natural resources. He says that capitalism is threatening the mere survival of the human race. Again, President Mujíca from Uruguay already brought this to our attention a few years ago, but nobody really listened. I trust people will listen now, because the Pope and the Vatican have nothing to benefit from this message, and they are revered all over the world. Just imagine, when Pope Francis visited the Philippines in January 2015, more than six million people gathered to celebrate his arrival and have a chance to see him. Now imagine the Pope's influence all over the world!

- The warming of the planet, which is causing a rise in sea levels and an increase in extreme weather events, has been pushed over the limit by human activities such as increased consumption and indiscriminate and endless production of goods and services.

- The Pope is concerned about the excess use of water around the world and how the quality of this precious natural resource is constantly diminishing. He insists that drinkable water is an undeniable right of every living human, as is clean air to breathe. These two natural resources have been tampered with and seriously compromised in many cities around the world. He adds that the world has a social debt towards poor people who have been denied the right to live with dignity, while others live in excess and lavishly misuse and waste fresh water and other natural resources.

- Pope Francis is extremely concerned about the fact that thousands of plant and animal species are disappearing from the face of the Earth. He insists that the majority of them go extinct for reasons directly related to human activity. On this point, I agree with him completely. There is a strong example of what is happening in the country of Madagascar, where three very important animals are going to go extinct soon if something is not done. These are the Madagascar Lemurs, Madagascar Radiated Turtle, and Big-Head Turtle. The lemurs are being hunted by locals for food and also being displaced from their natural habitat due to deforestation. Only about 10 per cent of their habitat remains. Will deforestation stop before they go extinct? Regarding the two types of turtles, these are being hunted for their meat, medicinal uses, and for export mainly to Asian countries that want them as pets or to use their beautiful shells as ornaments. Local authorities and researchers in Madagascar are carving the shells of living turtles so they do not look appealing for the export market, which is the biggest threat due to unscrupulous exporters and local poachers.

- The Pope also mentions how major urban cities have grown numb and desensitized towards the environment and the overall nature that surrounds them. Many large cities have no connection with the reality that embraces them and which they absolutely neglect. The population in large urban conglomerates seems to completely disregard the fact that the cities they live in depend for survival on the natural resources that surround them. Instead, they are destroying them due to excessive consumption, waist, and overall lack of care, taking them for granted. These cities are also surrounded by those in poverty who do not necessarily have access to those same natural resources in the form of products and or services like the most privileged do.

- The Vatican and the Pope confirmed that the scientists are right about global warming and that their research is geared towards the protection of the future of the human race. Also, somewhere in his speech the Pope said, "We seem to think that we can substitute an irreplaceable and irretrievable beauty with something which we have created ourselves."

I consider this encyclical to be a deep, accurate, and valuable analysis. Many people do believe that humans can create something more beautiful than nature itself, but this thought alone is utterly misguided and narcissistic. There is nothing more beautiful than what nature has created in so many shapes and forms throughout the world. The Pope also said: "We cannot claim to have a sound ethics, culture, and spirituality genuinely capable of setting limits and teaching clear minded self-restraint." Unfortunately, he could not be more accurate, and I hope more people start realizing the depth of meaning in his words. Why? Because if the average person listens and acts accordingly, this will have a positive impact on the future development of the human race.

According to the Pope, God failed to say that people couldn't do whatever they want to planet Earth. Once again, putting the concept of God and religion aside, he is accurate in his thoughts that men should not do whatever they please on this planet. David Suzuki, co-founder of the David Suzuki

Foundation, posted on June 24, 2015 in the Canadian Press an interesting article entitled "Pope Francis offers hopeful perspective on global crises." Suzuki pointed out that the Pope said that humans have existed on this planet for 4.5 million years but that the population has exploded from 2 billion to 7 billion in less than 80 of those years.

Is the message from Pope Francis falling on deaf ears?

I truly hope all people and every government heed this "wake-up call" by Pope Francis. Even though many will take his message as a positive warning and guidance (again, putting religion completely aside), some will criticize him and his message, because it is what some do. The great majority of people love criticizing but fall short in providing solutions.

Karen Bartko and Emily Mertz from Global News wrote an article in March 2015 entitled "Premier's comments spark witty #Prentice blames Albertans jabs." This article summarizes what happened to Alberta's then-premier, Jim Prentice, when he was being interviewed by a radio station and said that "All Albertans are responsible for getting the province into a financial mess, and everyone has to clean it up." He also said: "In terms of who is responsible, we all need only look in the mirror." It definitely took some guts and some degree of honesty to say what he said, but he was criticized by the opposition through social media. They took things the wrong, incomplete, and irresponsible way and did not pay attention to the overall message and to another important statement of his, which was: "Collectively, we got into this as Albertans and collectively we're going to get out of it, and everybody is going to have to shoulder some share of responsibility."

I totally understand and agree that many Albertans were uncomfortable and felt blamed for something that was apparently caused, to a great extent, by the government of Alberta at the time. It seems that Premier Jim Prentice's government also pushed Albertans into an economic predicament by making wrong calls such as providing tax reductions to large corporations and wealthy Albertans. Allegedly, it also failed profoundly to diversify the province's economy or slow the expansion of the oil sands that bring economic benefits to very few, with environmental disaster to all Albertans and beyond their borders. The subject of the oil sands will be dealt with later in this book, because it is a very important matter for North America.

Albertans or not, everybody in North America should stop making a storm out of a glass of water and, yes, see ourselves in the mirror and ask ourselves how we can help reduce our consumerism, protect our environment, and produce less garbage. The great majority in North America consume more than they need just to keep up with the Joneses or to respond to their children's demands, or they simply succumb to their own weaknesses and caprices while trying to feel good about themselves. None of these are a valid reason to act irresponsibly. We should stop feeling offended and blowing things out of proportion. Time to take the bull by the horns! If we do not believe in our governments, the scientists' predictions, or in God (through the Pope's thoughts), who can we believe? Shouldn't we believe in scientists, and do our own research to evaluate the accuracy and validity of their findings? Isn't that a rational and responsible thing to do?

Canada as garbage Mecca of the world

Since 2009, a report from the Organization for Economic Co-operation and Development (OECD) stated that Canada was the greatest contributor of garbage per capita in the world, to the disbelief of most Canadians. Each of us, though in various proportions, is accountable for this embarrassing and irresponsible world title. Indeed, the OECD placed Canada in the worst spot as the leader of polluters in the world due to our mega-garbage problem. The study concluded that, in 2009, Canadians produced per capita a total of 777 kilograms of garbage a year, while Japan (which produced the least garbage per capita) generated only 377 kilograms per person a year.

At first, I could not believe these figures and have been wondering what level we had reached by now. After researching various sources, I found out that we are still (as of Sept of 2017) among the ten top garbage producers in the world. Apparently, we are in the eighth position now instead of in first place. Big improvement? I do not think so; other countries have just surpassed the amount and speed with which Canadians still produce garbage. Among 193 countries worldwide, it is still embarrassing that, as a "developed country," we are not paying proper attention to a problem of this magnitude. If we do not do something about it, we are only going to get worse instead of solving or minimizing our impact on climate change. We are literally competing with the worst polluters in the world, and we are pushing the warming of the planet instead of slowing it.

According to Mr. Len Coad, Research Director, Public Policy, for the Conference Board of Canada, Canadians are in a difficult position. He said: "Our large land mass, cold climate, and resource-intensive economy make us less likely to rank highly on some indicators of environmental sustainability, but many of our poor results are based on our inefficient use of our resources." A very good example, regardless of what the oil industry says, are the oil sands in Alberta, one of the most irresponsible projects we are inflicting on our planet, which again, we will discuss in more depth later in this book.

On January 17, 2013, CBC News reported in an article entitled "Canadians Produce More Garbage Than Anyone Else," that the Conference Board of Canada had (in relation to environmental matters) called Canada an "Environmental

Laggard." This influential think-tank is a policy and research institute. They are well acknowledged and are immersed in social policy, political strategy, economics, military affairs, technology, and cultural subjects. They confirm that "Canadians use far too much energy and water, and they produce more waste per capita than any other country on earth." This statement was also published by the CBC News on Jan 17, 2013 (cbc.ca/news/business/canadians-produce-more-garbage-than-anyone-else-1.1394020).

Since Sept of 2017, I have been dubious about this claim, so I kept researching but only found sources confirming the above statements. I will limit myself here to citing two of these. The first is an article published by the World Bank (worldbank.org in the section on "Urban Development") called "What a Waste: A Global Review of Solid Waste Management," which states:

> As the world hurtles toward its urban future, the amount of municipal solid waste (MSW), one of the most important by-products of an urban lifestyle, is growing even faster than the rate of urbanization. Ten years ago, there were 2.9 billion urban residents who generated about 0.64 kg of MSW per person per day (0.68 billion tons per year). Today these amounts have increased to about 3 billion residents generating 1.2 kg per person per day (1.3 billion tonnes globally per year). By 2025 this will likely increase to 4.3 billion urban residents generating about 1.42 kg/capita/day of municipal solid waste (2.2 billion tons per year).

The second article I want to cite is one published by a small company called Haul a Day – Junk Removal. On their website, they published this strong statement:

> And the biggest offenders? High-income countries just like Canada. In fact, OECD countries (The

Organization for Economic Co-operation and Development) produce almost half of the world's waste. It makes sense if you think about it. The higher the disposable income, the more 'stuff' people buy – and throw away. And as living standards rise and urban populations grow, the problem is only going to get worse.   (hauladay.com/top-10-garbage-producing-countries/).

The Haul a Day – Junk Removal list of the ten OECD countries with the worst garbage problems, in average kilograms of garbage per capita per day, are the following:

1. New Zealand with 3.6 kg
2. Ireland with 3.58 kg
3. Norway with 2.8 kg
4. Switzerland with 2.61 kg
5. United States with 2.58 kg
6. Austria with 2.4 kg
7. Denmark with 2.34 kg
8. Canada with 2.33 kg
9. Italy with 2.23 kg
10. Australia with 2.23 kg.

Although the United States is by far the world's largest producer of garbage as a country, New Zealand is now the biggest producer of garbage per capita.

Regarding electronic waste specifically, Niall McCarthy wrote an article in Forbes entitled "Which country is on top of the world's electronic waste mountain" (April 20, 2015), in which he reported that "the world's worst offenders in electronic equipment waste are European countries such as Norway, Switzerland, Ireland, Denmark, United Kingdom, and Netherlands. Specifically, Norway is on top of the world's electronic waste mountain, generating 62.4 lbs per inhabitant.

Switzerland is in second position with 58 lbs, while Iceland rounds off the top three with 57.3 lbs. The United Kingdom comes in fifth with e-waste per capita amounting to 51.8 lbs, while the United States is in ninth position with 48.6 lbs." What is important here is to reduce the amount of garbage per capita at all cost. The ecosystem's future is at stake!

Dumping garbage in other countries

The reader can do as much research as desired, but there is no doubt that we are among the principal leaders in the irresponsible dumping of garbage in other countries. For example, Canadian garbage in the Philippines has caused serious international protests. The Catholic priest Robert Reyes, in mid-March of 2015, went to the Canadian Embassy in the Philippines to protest and urge Prime Minister Steven Harper to immediately take back 200 containers full of garbage (which some say is toxic) that had been deteriorating in the port of Manila. According to the Canadian government, this was not our problem, because those containers had arrived in Manila as a result of a commercial agreement between two private companies, one Canadian and the other Filipino. Lee Ann of Canadian Press reported on March 20, 2015, ("Canadian Garbage in Philippines Spurs Environmental Protests) that:

> Chronic Inc., a plastic exporter based in Whitby, Ontario, shipped the containers – supposedly filled with recyclable Vancouver plastics – to the Philippines in the spring and summer of 2013. But upon inspection, the country's bureau of customs found the containers were filled with stinking household garbage, including used adult diapers and kitchen waste.

When PM Trudeau visited the Philippines in Nov of 2017, President Duterte complained but nothing was resolved.

Canadians cannot and should not export waste. This was ratified at the Basel Convention and applies to Canada and every developed country. The Philippines is right to insist that Canada has violated the convention and must take the garbage back and allow no more dumping. But guess what? On May 22, 2015, new containers dumped by Canadians were found, as confirmed by local Filipino authorities. Here is what the Basel Action Network reports:

> Following a new discovery in the Port of Manila of yet another 48 containers of rotting household garbage illegally exported from Canada, environmental justice groups BAN Toxic (BT), Seattle-based Basel Action Network (BAN), and Greenpeace Philippines strongly condemned the Canadian government for "callous disregard of international law."

Many developed countries have historically been dumping toxic waste in developing countries, and some just keep doing it. According to the United Nations, "e-waste" is an especially serious problem and is getting worse. E-waste is the waste from millions of discarded computers, modems, laptops, tablets, cellular/mobile phones, digital cameras, and other electronics that end up being thrown away. The typical North American simply exchanges older versions of electronic devices and equipment for newer versions. We all believe the older versions end up being recycled, but do they really?

The term "Transfrontier Shipment of Waste" is used among industrialized countries (IC) and less developed countries (LDC) to indicate how the LDCs import waste from the IC in the form of paper products, used electronics, plastics, metals, and other materials. Most of this waste is traded among the Organization for Economic Co-operation and Development (OECD) countries, for the benefit of the LDCs, who sort and re-use it. However, illegal dumping of waste, especially toxic waste, is prohibited internationally. The real problem since the beginning of the 19th century has always been ocean dumping, usually of seriously toxic waste such as lead, arsenic, various kinds of other chemical products, metals, plastics, and even radioactive materials. A very well-known example that the reader can confirm in Google and Yahoo (google.ca/?gws_rd=ssl#q=Ocean+Dumping) was reported as follows:

> Hundreds of tons of toxic waste were dumped into the ocean from a ship, the Probo Koala. An international oil trader in the Netherlands chartered the ship. The incident was responsible for killing at least 16 people and forced thousands to flee from their homes. The waste caused damage to the health of almost 100,000 people in the nearby areas [of Cote D'Ivoire]. The oil trader, Trafigura, paid 200 million dollars to help with cleanup. The owner of the local company that was responsible for disposing the chemicals in various places was given a 20-year jail term.

However, there are other places that are even more polluted and contaminated. Here are a few examples.

The most contaminated places in the world

Lake Karachay in Russia: According to many sources, this is the most polluted place on planet Earth. It is a dumping site for radioactive materials from nuclear plants in Russia. According to an article by Jess Zimmerman published by Grist magazine (grist.org) on Oct 03, 2012 entitled "Meet the lake so polluted that spending an hour there would kill you"

> The lake is located within the Mayak Production Association, one of the largest – and leakiest – nuclear facilities in Russia. The Russian government kept

Mayak entirely secret until 1990, and it spent that period of invisibility mainly having nuclear meltdowns and dumping waste into the river. By the time Mayak's existence was officially acknowledged, there had been a 21 percent increase in cancer incidence, a 25 percent increase in birth defects, and a 41 percent increase in leukemia in the surrounding region of Chelyabinsk. The Techa River, which provided water to nearby villages, was so contaminated that up to 65 percent of locals fell ill with radiation sickness – which the doctors termed "special disease," because as long as the facility was secret, they weren't allowed to mention radiation in their diagnoses.

Chernobyl in Ukraine: On April 26, 1986, there was a big explosion and fire that released radioactive materials from the Chernobyl nuclear power plant in Ukraine. This also contaminated various areas in Europe. Locals are starting to come back to their original homes, but many suffered irreparable health issues and even death.

Dhaka in Bangladesh: This city has serious water, air, and noise pollution that is affecting their economic growth and delicate ecosystem. It suffers some of the worst environmental water and soil pollution due to old manufacturing technologies. Some of the main industrial culprits are the old tanneries that dump more than 20,000 cubic litres of serious toxic waste on a daily basis. According to Brian Walsh in Time Magazine ("Urban Wastelands: The World's 10 Most Polluted Places." November 2013), tannery workers from the city of Hazaribagh (Bangladesh) also burn old leather, aggravating their air pollution. The most common results are skin diseases, rashes, and acid burns, among many other illnesses.

Kabwe in Zambia: This is considered Africa's most contaminated and toxic city, according to the Blacksmith

Institute (which researches and evaluates polluted places in developing countries) and Green Cross Switzerland (which specializes in repairing damage caused by military and industrial disasters worldwide).

The city has been slowly but steadily polluted by local lead and coal mining activities. Smelting operations release different heavy metals into the soil and overall environment on a daily basis, causing serious health issues for local residents, many of whom work for survival wages.

Ahvaz in Iran: According to Brian Merchant (senior editor of Motherboard-Vice magazine in an article entitled "Inside the Iranian city where the air is three times worse than Beijing's," published Mar 6, 2013), the World Health Organization (WHO) ranks this Iranian city of 1.2 million residents as home to the highest levels of air pollution anywhere. Merchant explains:

> One of the crucial measures of dangerous air pollution is the number of parts per million of particles smaller than 10 micrometers (PM10) wafting through the air. Beijing's residents breathe in air with an average PM10 of 121, but millions of people have it worse. The rankings, cobbled together using air monitoring data from a variety of sources between 2003 and 2010, suggest that the world's worst air pollution floats over Ahvaz, a city in southwestern Iran where the average PM10 level hovers around 372. By comparison, the average level of particulate pollution – which causes respiratory illnesses, asthma, even cancer – is just 71 worldwide. The air quality in Ahwaz, Iran, in other words, is over five times as bad as the air the typical person breathes.

Norilsk in Russia: According to various reliable sources, the city of Norilsk is the biggest heavy metal smelting complex of the early 2000s. Smelting releases tons of carbon into the air along with sulphur and nickel dioxide, seriously affecting the area and beyond. Since the early 1930s, the area has heavily exploited its metallurgical potential. This initially started by forcing prisoners sent to the Norillag prison camp to work in the mines and related industries; thousands died due to the very poor working conditions.

New biodegradable plastics

Does the average person wonder what happens when we place our plastics in a recyclable bin or when others just throw anything made of plastic into the garbage bin? In 2015, less than 5 per cent of all plastics have been biodegradable. This has changed very little since. With the invention of plastic, human life was completely transformed for the better, but at what cost?

Plastics, derived from fossil fuel, are obtained from either natural gas or petroleum. These types of plastics are not biodegradable. They are here to stay for centuries. Thanks to new technologies, plastics can be recycled into other products such as composite railroad ties, new carpets, new flooring for all-weather purposes, decking materials, etc. However, the recycling processes still cause added damage to our environment through the emission of methane and other gases. Therefore, the invention of biodegradable plastics known as bioplastics is not just important, but a highly responsible action in favour of our environment. These plastics are made out of renewable biomass: cornstarch, vegetable fats and oils, sugar cane, biopolymers, and other materials such as cellulose-based plastics.

Not all bioplastics are biodegradable, however. That is, not all can break down in aerobic or anaerobic environments. Thus, not all bioplastics can be treated the same. Bioplastics also have an impact on our environment, but at a lower rate than the fossil fuel plastics. The problem of some bioplastics is that if they do degrade, they do so very slowly. There is a very good website (en.european-bioplastics.org) that explains in detail and with great clarity what bioplastics are and their benefits. They make a comparison between bioplastics and traditional plastics and state:

> Bioplastics are driving the evolution of plastics. There are two major advantages of bio based plastic products compared to their conventional versions: they save fossil resources by using biomass, which regenerates annually and provide the unique potential of carbon neutrality. Furthermore, biodegradability is an add-on property of certain types of bioplastics. It offers additional means of recovery at the end of a product's life.

One of the biggest and most serious problems we have in our globe is the amount of plastic content in almost every river, lake, and ocean. It is so bad that we now have what have been called "plastic islands" (or plastic gyres). The word "gyre" refers to the rotation of ocean currents. There are five major gyres: two in the Pacific Ocean (north and south gyres), two in the Atlantic Ocean (north and south gyres), and one in the Indian Ocean. However, the oceans are now infested with plastics indiscriminately dumped by humans, and the ocean currents (or ocean vortexes) collect all the floating plastics and swirl them into a plastic "island."

According to the National Oceanic and Atmospheric Administration (NOAA), there is a huge garbage patch or island known as the North Pacific Gyre or the Pacific Trash Vortex. It is not visible to the naked eye from the deck of a ship because it is formed by very small plastic particles in a suspended and floating state just underneath the ocean's surface. According to NOAA, however, the vortex is visible by satellite and seems to be expanding. It is currently about the size of the state of Texas, which is 696,241 square kilometres, and still growing. Luckily, more and more organizations are out there trying to clean the oceans from plastic products and other types of debris.

We need to let people know about this delicate and serious problem that affects our ecosystem and directly infects our own food consumption. Why? Because fish, turtles, dolphins, whales, and all other ocean creatures are eating the plastic particles (also referred to as plastic microbeads), which are toxic to sea life. These are also passed on to humans by seafood consumption.

These small plastic particles are usually made out of polypropylene and or polyethylene, which are very toxic for any living creature in the planet. Even worse is the use of bisphenol A, which is known as BPA. It is a chemical product used by various industries to make plastics and resins. Even though the Food and Drug Administration has always maintained that it is safe at low levels, the reality is different. BPA is a serious toxic substance and is found in plastic water and juice bottles, food containers, and many other consumer products. With time, residues of BPA are leached or seeped into our foods, and experts in the industry say that exposure to BPA can seriously affect the human brain, as well as fetuses during their development. Discover Magazine published an article by Rebecca Coffey, entitled "20 things you did not know about plastics," in their November 2012 issue. Coffey based the article on a book by Susan Freinkel entitled A Toxic Love Story. This is a must-read book to understand the world of plastics and our fascination for plastics as human beings.

Among the twenty trends that Rebecca Coffey discusses in this article, I want to mention only five that are especially alarming and that should remind everybody of the need to reduce our plastic consumption in the future:

1. "In 2012, the world made and consumed about 600 billion pounds of plastic yearly, and the market is still growing about 5 per cent a year." By the end of 2105 a consumption of over 700 billion pounds of plastic were consumed.

2. "The most common plastic – polyethylene – is used in plastic bags and bottles. Since 2009, Americans alone used 102 billion of them. Strung together, they will circle the earth 776 times." This type of waste has continuously increased since in an alarming rate.

3. "Bacteria and fungi are no match for most plastic molecules, which microbes cannot digest."

4. This is why "the 31 million tons of plastic waste loaded into American landfills each year retain their Barbie doll and pink flamingo shapes pretty much forever."

5. "Some plastics photodegrade: Sunlight can break up the molecule bonds in the polymers, turning the material brittle and causing it to break into small, often microscopic pieces. Plastic litter is swept through storm drains and out to sea."

As average human beings, our responsibility is to be conscious of this problem and do our best to stop it by letting others know of the seriousness of the issue, by increasing education, by researching and providing ideas for solutions, by trying to coordinate the efforts of active groups in the banning of toxic plastics, and by advocating for the cleaning and restoration of our oceans.

We must also do our best to avoid dumping more garbage into rivers, lakes, and oceans so that we have a fair possibility of actually restoring our water sources as much as possible. It is simple: either do or die. Nature does not and will not haggle. Let us please remember that.

Bullfighting (animal abuse) in Spain and other countries

There is an international consensus that bullfighting should be banned in every country, but is this economically feasible? It has been proven throughout human history that the bottom line (economic benefit) is more important for many people than matters such as animal abuse, fairness, equality, justice, the global warming crisis, and the continued expansion of environmental pollution, among many others. It is part of human nature and part of who we are. However, there are still decent, rational, and properly educated people, and I hope and trust that, with time, these people will help to straighten up our human priorities.

Throughout my life, I have read articles about the bullfighting dilemma, but I received not too long ago an email message that I hope circulated around the world by going viral. This message (and the crude reality it describes) was the tipping point that motivated me to include this irresponsible action in my book. The message is worth quoting in full due to its barbarism and cruelty overall, so I translated it from Spanish to English as follows:

> Is it a *fiesta* or an art? It is neither, because it is a science. It is the science of torture. It is all about pain and suffering. The matador thinks he is brave, but I sincerely have my doubts. During the 24 hours prior to the *corrida* (the bullfight), the bull has been kept in a confined place in absolute darkness, so that when he is exposed to the arena with hundreds of screaming people and the burning sunlight hits his delicate eyes, he tries to escape and runs like crazy within the arena hitting the fence and threatening anything in his path.

He does this not because he is aggressive (though foolish people love to believe he is), but because he is frightened and wants to escape. To protect the matador, they hang heavy sacks of sand on the bull's shoulders for hours. They punch his kidneys and testicles to weaken him. They put a nasty ointment in his eyes to minimize his vision and add a special substance on his hooves to promote a burning feeling so he never stands still and looks even more aggressive. But the bull is simply in pain, suffering, and afraid of everything around him.

The horses chosen for the *corrida* are old and without real commercial value. They cover them with so-called protective blankets, which in reality only hide the horse's wounds. These blankets do very little to protect the horses from the brutal and desperate impact of the bull's horns. Usually, the bull ends up breaking the horse's ribs, traumatizes and damages internal organs, and on many occasions, perforates the horse's body with brutal force. The horses usually die three to four days later.

If the matador notices that the bull is charging with force and putting him at higher risk, he tells the picador riding the horse with the "protective blankets" to do his job by jabbing and piercing the muscles on the back of the bull's neck. This hurts the bull deeply, which further reduces his stamina and strength so that the matador can then go ahead with his performance and the torture of the innocent bull.

The picador helps to bring the bull's head lower and make him easier to handle for the show. The picador destroys the muscles of the neck, seriously damages the bull's spine, and cuts all the veins and arteries it passes through. All this is to maximize the "artistic spectacle" that this event is supposed to be created for. Then come the *banderilleros*, whose responsibility is to weaken the bull's stamina and strength even more with continued stabbing of the bull's back and neck using *banderillas*, barbed darts with an 8 cm (3.2 inches) harpoon and sharp, hooked blade at the end. The *banderilleros* punish and literally torture the bull relentlessly by thrusting the barbed darts into his spine and neck. The *banderillas* get stuck in the bull's back, and the considerable weight of the *banderillas* and constant moving of the bull keep cutting the inside of the animal's back and neck. They only stop when the bull can barely pick up his head. By then, the bull has bled profoundly, his neck and spine have been sliced deeply in various sections, and he has just enough strength to move slowly and exhaustedly in the arena of torture. It is usually then that the matador decides to finish him off.

The matador then enters the arena with a show of pride and arrogance and murders the exhausted and injured bull. The matador walks with his chest sticking out and swaggers his way into the arena with a kind of "artistic" flair. In the meantime, people stand up screaming and applauding the *Fiesta Taurina* (the Bullfight Festival). People react just as in the times of the Roman gladiators. Again, we humans seem not to change throughout the years of our "evolution."

While the bull is tired, confused, afraid, and desperate, the matador gets close with his 80 cm (32 inches) double-bladed sword and charges the bull with full force, stabbing him in the neck or back. If the bull is lucky, the matador pierces his heart, so he dies fast. But usually, the heart is missed, and the sword simply goes through the spine, lungs, and various arteries, causing the bull to experience a slow death. He usually bleeds to death or chokes in his own blood. But if that is not enough, if the bull is still alive, they approach the animal and with a 10 cm (4 inches) dagger, they stab and slice the bull's neck and spinal cord to ultimately finish his life. This action in Spanish is called *descabello* (neck stabbing).

There is a very interesting article published in the April 4-10, 2015, issue of The Economist entitled "Matador on the march," which provides an interesting perspective on what people in some Latin-American countries think about the bullfights. Summarized, these are the main ideas:

- In February of 2015, Colombia's constitutional court reaffirmed its earlier ruling that bullfighting is acknowledged as an "artistic expression" and should be reinstated in Bogota immediately. Trainee matadors in Colombia were on a hunger strike, with a banner that read, "We don't want food. We are hungry for bull!"

- A referendum in Quito (Ecuador) led to a ban on the killing of the bull in 2011.

- In 2012, Panama banned bullfighting.

- The Mexican State of Sonora also banned bullfighting. The number of bullfights has fallen by half in Mexico generally.

- From 2007 to 2014, bullfighting dropped by over 50 per cent in Spain itself.

The same article reports that "in 2013, over 590,000 people in Spain signed a pro-bullfighting petition, which pushed the Spanish government to recognize it as part of its country's cultural heritage, overturning the previous Catalonian ban.

Mexican campaigners have stalled a 2012 petition calling for a national ban on bullfighting. In Peru, pro-bullfighters are mobilizing to keep and protect the "sport." The department of Puno (in Lake Titicaca) has over 100 bullfights every year. In a letter to the editor of The Economist published on May 11-22, 2015, entitled "In support of bullfighting," Olaf Clayton wrote this from Madrid:

> To say that fans of bullfighting have 'little to cheer about' is somewhat at odds with the Iberian reality ("Matador on the march", April 4th). In Spain, 17,000 bullfighting festivals are celebrated each year, each with its own fighting calendar. Some 130,000 bulls are bred for this by 1,200 breeders. Spain has hundreds of permanent bullrings, and 3,000 temporary structures are set up in smaller villages up and down the country for local festivals. These provide gainful employment for many locals on top of the 2,000 full-time professional matadors and 3,000 younger n*ovilleros,* each with supporting *picadors* and *banderilleros* in what is a billion-dollar industry."

Sadly, throughout 2017 it is still happening in many Latin-American countries. It is a moneymaking "sport" like many other activities, and owners as well as employees cover their eyes about bullfighting's cruelty for the sake of the continued income and not necessarily for the "artistic expression" or the "sport" itself. Some matadors are paid between $50,000 and $75,000 per fight. Juan Antonio Ruiz (known as Espartaco) is the highest paid in the industry. There are billions of dollars at stake in the bullfighting industry, from the bullfighters all the way down to the breeders of the bulls, from TV advertising to all the infrastructure built for the "sport" through many years.

Over 60 per cent of Spaniards are against the sport, yet 57 per cent oppose a national ban. One of the biggest problems is that Spain, Portugal, Colombia, and other bullfighting countries still allow children to see the gory spectacle, but at least the majority are seriously starting to oppose the sport and do something about it by fighting back instead of just remaining outside the bullring. There are now strong movements against the bullfighting industry, one of the better-known being *"La Tortura No Es Cultura"* (Torture Isn't Culture). Please visit their website at latorturanoescultura.org, where they report that:

> The bullfighting lobby has submitted to the Spanish Congress of Deputies a Popular Legislative Initiative full of irregularities seeking to shield bullfighting in Spain by declaring it a National Cultural Heritage. This would not only include the shielding of regular bullfighting in bullrings, but also the celebration of acts as cruel as the Toro de la Vega in Tordesillas, where a bull is killed with spears by people on horseback and foot, or the Toro de Júbilo, where for pure fun a bull's horns are set on fire and it is subsequently executed.

By the end of 2016, bullfighting in Spain was still receiving the equivalent of over 600 million USD in public subsidies. Should this law be passed, it would receive still more, something totally unjustified, if we consider that, according to the latest poll by Ipsos MORI (a research company in the UK) in April 2013, only 13 per cent of Spaniards strongly support bullfighting, not to mention that Spanish people have many other priorities they prefer to direct their taxes to.

In my opinion, this so-called sport should be banned in every country. According to the Ontario Society for the Prevention of Cruelty to Animals (known as Ontario SPCA and Humane Society) the definition for animal cruelty "falls into two categories: neglect, or intentional cruelty. Neglect is the failure to provide adequate water, food, shelter, or necessary care. Intentional cruelty involves deliberate physical harm or injury inflicted on an animal." Therefore, bullfighting is simple animal abuse, where humans inflict pain, harm, and suffering on the bull. The same can be said of dogfights, cock fights, or any other type of animal fight against its own species or even other species (e.g. tiger vs. bear), and of illegal slaughterhouses.

Anything inflicting unnecessary harm and suffering on an animal should be banned worldwide, and the perpetrators should be penalized to the full extent of the law. These are barbaric acts against defenceless animals whose instincts in life are only to survive peacefully among their own species. We do not live in the time of the gladiators. We live in an age in which we should respect animal life and take full responsibility for our actions. The torture of animals in the name of "artistic expression" should be absolutely extinguished worldwide.

Expansion of marine protected areas

Marine protected areas (known as MPAs) are coastal and deep sea areas around the world that are being sheltered and carefully protected. These marine areas are safeguarded for preservation purposes. This is being practiced on lakes and oceans throughout the world and, fortunately, has been increasing at a steady pace for the past 20 years. There is an abstract I want to quote as follows:

> Because of the complexity of processes within marine ecosystems, ecological changes associated with the declaration of MPAs vary greatly from one region to another and are difficult to predict accurately. Important factors that affect the way plants and animals respond to MPAs include distribution of habitat types, level of connectivity to nearby fished habitats, wave exposure, depth distribution, prior level of resource extraction, regulations, and level of compliance to regulations. The

value of MPAs primarily relates to biodiversity conservation, fisheries, and as research and management tools, but they can also generate recreational, aesthetic, and educational benefits (Edgar, Graham J., Russ, Garry R., and Babcock, Russ C. 2007. *Marine protected areas.* In: Connell, Sean D., and Gillanders, Bronwyn M., eds. Marine Ecology. Oxford University Press, South Melbourne, VIC, Australia, pp. 533-555).

In an article in the July-August, 2015 issue of Canadian Geographic entitled "Under Pressure," Alanna Mitchell writes about the commitment of the Canadian government to protect 10 per cent of its waters by the year 2020 and brings to our attention the efforts of a professor of marine ecology, Isabelle Côte, at Simon Fraser University in British Columbia. Dr. Côte is an expert in marine protected areas and has confirmed that Canadian waters are among the richest in the world for marine life and diversity. She calls them an underwater rainforest. As of 2015, Canada's underwater marine protection areas are less than one tenth of one per cent of our total marine area, according to Ms. Côte. As a nation rich in ocean shores, we lag behind many other countries in protecting our oceans. By the end of 2017 things have not changed much. Australia is among the leaders in marine protection, with particularly strict attention given to its coral reefs, Côte says.

According to Ms. Côte, in Canada we have three groups trying to make decisions on the marine areas that need protection: the federal government, the provincial governments, and the First Nations and Inuit. These groups have different jurisdictions, powers, and interests, making it difficult to reach proper decisions in a timely manner. This makes creating marine protected areas a slow and complex process.

The main goal of a successful marine reserve is the protection of marine species and their diversity. Its objectives also include the protection and expansion of commercial fishing by seeding unprotected neighbouring areas while functioning as marine nurseries along a coastal region. A particular objective of protected areas is to monitor and reduce commercial overfishing while promoting and nurturing the overall marine ecosystem.

There is a very comprehensive 2005 study about marine conservation areas from Baja California to the Bering Sea (Mexico to Alaska) published by the Commission of Environmental Cooperation of North America and the Marine Conservation Biology Institute (authors: Lance Morgan, Sara Maxwell, Fan Taso, Tara A.C. Wilkinson and Peter Etnoyer). It is a tremendous effort in putting together a full description of the priority conservation areas by marine ecoregion on the west coast of North America. In the executive summary, there is a paragraph worth quoting in full:

> From the Gulf of California, with its deep canyons, nutrient-rich upwellings, and high levels of endemism, to the 20,000 kilometres of bays, inlets, and inland drainage systems of the Pacific Northwest and the high productivity of the Bering Sea, the west coast of North America is home to unique and important shared marine environments. It is also home to a great number of shared marine species – such as Pacific gray and blue whales, leatherback sea turtles, Bluefin tuna, black Brant geese, and Heermann's gulls – that migrate thousands of kilometres, moving across national borders without hesitation. Hence, be it through shared species or ecosystems, the marine environments of Mexico, the United States, and Canada are intimately linked. Accordingly, action or inaction on one side of a border will have consequences for the shared living organisms occupying ecosystems with no definite boundaries.

According to the BBC's Travel Show and an article published on their website on April 1, 2015, Mexico's Cabo Pulmo is the most successful marine reserve in the world and the most effective in rescuing its marine ecosystem, with more than 200 species of fish and over 70,000 hectares of marine protected area within a beautiful bay at the south-east tip of Baja California Sur facing the "Mar de Cortez" (Sea of Cortez). Please feel free to visit: (*bbc.com/travel/story/20150401-the-most-successful-marine-reserve-in-the-world*),

Cabo Pulmo is a very old coral reef (over 20,000 years old) near the small town in Cabo Pulmo where the Castro family has lived for at least three generations. Almost all the locals of Cabo Pulmo and the surrounding areas used to live from fishing-related activities. During the 1980s and the 1990s, however, the area and beyond was overfished. This impacted the local coral reefs, and the people from Cabo Pulmo realized that they had to do something to save the coral reefs before it was too late. Willing to sacrifice their fishing style of life, the Castro family joined forces with other local families and approached their local government for support in the protection of the Cabo Pulmo coral reef and the surrounding areas from fishing and development-related activities.

In 1995, the government of Baja California Sur created Cabo Pulmo National Park covering an area of over 71 square kilometres. Only 35 per cent of the park was restricted as a no-fishing area, however, and this was not good enough for the Castro family's movement. They then pressured for the park to be declared a 100 per cent no-fishing area, which was ultimately agreed by the government.

Due to their efforts, all the ecosystems of the area have improved dramatically. The coral reef has recovered, and the fish population has increased. The village of Cabo Pulmo has transformed from a fishing settlement to a tourist attraction in which almost all the families depend on the new tourist industry, while taking care of their ocean waters and expanding marine life.

Some species that had disappeared from the area are returning, including humpback whales, a variety of sharks, sea turtles, manta rays, swordfish, and many more. Some of these species rely on these waters for their reproductive cycle, but other species not native to Cabo Pulmo have made the park their home due to the protected habitat. The efforts of the locals have paid handsomely in the creation of a new industry for tourism. They let go of their old fishing activities and forged themselves a new professional life for themselves and their families. By the end of 2017, Cabo Pulmo was still flourishing.

The United Nations Educational, Scientific, and Cultural Organization (UNESCO), an agency of the United Nations, declared the Australian Great Barrier Reef a World Heritage Site in 1981. This reef is located in the State of Queensland 80 kilometres into the Coral Sea between Lady Elliot Island and the northern tip of the Queensland peninsula. It stretches over 2,300 kilometres and its marine diversity is so rich that it is a habitat for hundreds of different types of corals, rich fish varieties, and exotic marine life. However, half of the reef's corals have disappeared over the past 25 to 30 years. The situation is so bad that the World Heritage Organization plans to declare it an endangered site.

The reef is shrinking due to acidification and the warming of the ocean waters, which have been pushed over the tipping point. More and more farms have washed pesticides and fertilizers into the ocean, which benefit the eating habits of a local starfish that is reproducing exponentially and destroying the coral reef at an alarming rate.

The coral reef brings in billions of dollars through tourism every year, the main reason the Queensland state government and various local industries are working very hard to dissuade the World Heritage Organization declaring the reef endangered. Strict government regulations and bans have been imposed to at least reduce and hopefully stop dumping of toxic waste into the reef's waters.

The coal industry in the area is also to blame for some of the damage to the coral reefs, especially between the Abbot Point and Townsville areas. There is real hope of rescuing the reefs, if the new laws and regulations can keep the waters of the Great Barrier Reef clean.

Keeping wild animals as pets or in captivity

Before I get mauled by wild pet animal lovers and others, let me emphasize that my general position in life, which has guided me for over 50 years, is the expression "To each his own," which holds hands with what I was also taught since I was very little: "Respect to others means peace and harmony." Yes, to each his own!

- *"To each his own,"* as long as we respect the delicate balance of the laws of nature.

- *"To each his own,"* as long as we do not inflict any harm on another human.

- *"To each his own,"* as long as we do not inflict any harm of any kind on any other species in this world of ours.

- *"To each his own,"* as long as we respect the different human skin colours, facial features, and body types.

- *"To each his own,"* as long as we respect and protect our environment.

- *"To each his own,"* as long as we take care of our ecosystem and its delicate, fragile, and impressively beautiful structures.

- *"To each his own,"* as long as we respect all creeds, traditions, and beliefs.

- *"To each his own,"* as long as we respect women and treat them equally.

- *"To each his own,"* as long as we acknowledge and accept that we are all different.

- *"To each his own"*, as long as we respect each other's efforts, work ethics, and achievements.

- *"To each his own,"* as long as we make an effort to live in peace with our neighbours and ourselves.

- *"To each his own,"* as long as we respect and accommodate liberty of expression without hatred, disrespect, or insults.

There are various legal and ethical issues all across North America and all over the world relevant to keeping wild animals as pets. Wild animals are exotic and very interesting to watch, but to keep them at home as pets is a totally different matter. To the great majority, exotic animals belong in the wild, not in cages limiting their freedom and affecting their sanity.

Exotic animal trade is the fifth largest illegal worldwide trade, only surpassed by human trafficking, the gun trade, the illegal oil trade, and the drug trade. Whoever wants a wild animal must do very deep research about its legality and overall ethical aspects, not to mention proper and safe housing, proper food, and medical access, if required. Some lizards or iguanas are safe and relatively easy to keep, but other animals, such as snakes, wild cats, chimpanzees, raccoons, and many others, are difficult to keep and need adequate and above all, secure, confined areas. All wild animals need space and liberty to move around as they please. There is no real difference between keeping a wild animal confined to a restricted space and keeping a jailed inmate in a cell of 8 by 12 feet (2.5 by 3.6 metres). Imagine if that inmate is kept there day and night for life. There is no doubt that person will end up going mad.

Do you really think this would not happen also to a caged animal? Just because they do not talk to express their feelings does not mean they are not suffering or going insane. These things happen to animals too.

After the initial enthusiasm of having a wild animal under captivity and absolute control for an extended period of time, the owner's enthusiasm and interest fades with time and some people decide to give them away or simply release them back into the wild. Some wild pets can be dangerous and very destructive, posing a real challenge to keep, another reason why some are released back in the wild, though not necessarily in their original or adequate environments. A good example is the Burmese python released in Everglades National Park. A different release into the wild happened with the cane toad in Australia, which was brought from Hawaii to control the native grey-backed cane beetle (which was affecting the sugar industry) but got completely out of control. Without predators in the new environment, the toad's numbers increased to dangerous levels. They now represent a threat to native species, which are being pushed to extremely low levels or even to extinction. I will discuss these two invasive species in more detail later in this book.

Whether or not it is safe to keep a wild animal in captivity, we should always ask ourselves if it is an ethical thing to do. The wild animal trade has always existed and, even though it is prohibited in many countries, the demand for wild animals is still strong. That is not just sad but very wrong, and it should be stopped, using new strict laws and regulations.

Is it safe to keep wild animals in captivity?

Many wild animals are natural killers. All carnivores have a strong instinct to kill and eat to survive. It is simply their nature. Carnivores in captivity can be docile for a while, but the chances of them eventually attacking a human being are very high. In most cases, it is just a matter of time. Yes, there are exceptions, but they are few and far apart. The wild side is ingrained deeply in these animals' nature; it is part of their DNA and their natural instincts. It is not a matter of if they are going to attack, but when this will happen. Anybody can Google "animal attacks in captivity" and find literally thousands of registered cases of very nasty animal attacks. But these are only the tip of the iceberg, because the great majority of attacks go unreported. Good examples of catastrophes waiting to happen are when pythons or boa constrictors are kept in captivity and handled by the owners at leisure. Hundreds of people have been squeezed or strangled to death by their "innocent and loving" pet snakes. Here are two specific examples:

1.   In New Brunswick, two boys aged five and seven were suffocated to death during their sleep when an African rock python weighing over 45 kilograms and almost five metres long escaped from the animal pet store on the first floor. This happened August 5, 2013. The python slithered its way up to the boys' second-floor apartment through the building air ducts all the way up to the room where the children were sleeping.

2. In Florida, a two-year-old girl was strangled to death by the family's eight-foot albino pet python, which "was trying to eat the girl because it had not been fed for a month and was severely underweight" (Steven Hudack). For more information, see Steven Hudack's report in the Orlando Sentinel of August 24, 2011 entitled "Reptile-loving couple sentenced to 132 years in killer python case" (articles.orlandosentinel.com).

The April 2014 issue of National Geographic contained an excellent article entitled "Wild obsession: the perilous attraction of owning exotic pets," in which Lauren Slater reported that:

> All across the nation, in Americans' backyards, in garages and living rooms, in their beds and basements and bathrooms, wild animals kept as pets live side by side with their human owners. It is believed that more exotic animals live in American homes than are cared for in American zoos. The exotic pet business is a lucrative industry, one that has drawn criticism from animal welfare advocates and wildlife conservationists alike. These people say it is not only dangerous to bring captive-bred wildlife into the suburbs, but it's cruel and it ought to be criminal too. Yet the issue is far from black and white.

In my personal opinion, the main reasons for owning a normal pet (cats, dogs, horses, etc.) are companionship, socializing, comfort, stress relief, guidance for the blind, protection, and affection through physical contact. But owning a wild animal as a pet is a combination not just of the above but also of obsession, fixation, compulsion, status, fetish, infatuation, and fashion. People who want wild animal pets are usually powerless to resist the desire and need understanding, guidance, and discipline to take care of the wild animal, but above all, to take care of their families, friends, and themselves when that wild animal suddenly goes truly wild, that is, instinctively becomes aggressive and predatory.

Slater includes a picture in her article taken by Vincent J. Musi of over 50 exotic animals (mainly bears, tigers, and lions) shot dead in Zanesville, Ohio, by police officers. Why? Because the owner, Terry Thompson, in 2011 released 50 of his exotic pets from their cages into the local community and then killed himself. The state of Ohio imposed strict laws for the owners of wild animal pets immediately thereafter. The same article has another picture, this one of five Bengal tigers confined in a very small cage. The owner of the tigers, Mike Stapleton, admitted that he never got into the cage with them. In his own words: "You never know when that instinct they have is going to kick in."

The article shows a picture of Albert Killian, who shares his home with over 60 snakes of all colors, sizes, and inherent natural defence mechanisms. He is shown sitting on his bed embracing and being "embraced" by his pet Burmese python. According to him, he has been bitten so many times that he has stopped counting the bites. But wait, I thought pets are not supposed to bite. They are supposed to love you back, right? I can only imagine what will happen if those snakes are intentionally or accidentally released into the local community. How many people would become victims of these so-called pets? Slater's article also contains these very interesting statistics:

- Animal Ownership: private 66 per cent, zoos 28 per cent, circuses 6 per cent.
- Species in captivity: reptiles 32 per cent, big cats 19 per cent, primates 16 per cent.
- Types of incident: animal escape 42 per cent, human injury 24 per cent, death 14 per cent.

The article, which I encourage everyone to read, shows other owners with their favourite wild pets such as a deer, a giant rodent, kangaroos, lemurs, and chimpanzees. We need to face reality; we are trying to turn these wild animals into something they are not meant to be. Their deeply ingrained wild instincts can flourish suddenly with lighting speed and no remedy, although I acknowledge the position of Zuzane Kukol, a co-founder of Responsible Exotic Animal Ownership (REXANO), who said: "I'd rather die by a lion than by some stupid drunk driver." Interesting, isn't it?

Orcas in captivity

Orcas in captivity have been a worldwide concern for many, many years. There are numerous animal advocacy groups and similar organizations trying to liberate or protect many animals currently in captivity, specifically orcas and dolphins. In many places around the world, there are companies that still keep orcas in captivity confined to pools that are too small for the orca's size and natural free spirit. The orcas are trained and used in shows for tourists in order to enrich the profits of these companies.

Orcas, along with dolphins, are one of the most beautiful and gracious animals on earth. They are smart, they communicate amongst each other with impressive accuracy and understanding, they are expert group hunters, they socialize and protect each other in the vast oceans, and they are athletic marine mammals that are happy swimming an average of over a hundred kilometres a day at speeds that can reach 50 kilometres per hour or more. They thrive in the polar regions, where they flourish due to the abundance of fish, seals, penguins, and other prey. They are born in the wild, and they "perform" best in the wild, not in captivity.

In March 2014, the board of editors of Scientific American published their Science Agenda with the following title: "Free

Willy – And All His Pals (Orcas and elephants are smart, social, and way too large for captivity)." There is one paragraph that is especially worth quoting:

> Chimps, killer whales, and elephants are just as dependent on companionship as we are. A killer mother whale stays with most of her descendants throughout life, sometimes shepherding as many as four generations. Related matrilines, each of which has its own dialect, unite in pods, which merge into clans, which intermingle in large communities – akin to tribes and nations.

With the above in mind, imagine confining an orca to an Olympic-size style pool day and night for the rest of its natural life. The owners only want to make money by training the orcas to perform in shows for tourists who cannot see beyond the show itself. Orcas' life span in males reaches an average of 50 to 60 years and 60 to 70 years for females. In captivity, the average lifespan is said to be nine to 15 years. Not only is their lifespan shortened, they suffer throughout their short lives, often developing a collapsed dorsal fin as a sign of frustration, anxiety, suffering, and pain. Such was the case of Freya, an orca female that recently passed away after being kept in captivity in Marine Land in Antibes in the south of France.

A well-known case of an orca in serious distress and pain is that of Tilikum from SeaWorld in Orlando. Its collapsed fin was a strong indicator of the orca's suffering and distress, according to many scientists around the world. There is a very sad, but interesting and realistic website called "Sea World of Hurt, where happiness tanks" (seaworldofhurt.com). I urge the reader to visit this site to fully grasp the gravity of the matter. Here, for example, is the site's account of Tilikum's experience in captivity:

Over the course of 21 years at SeaWorld, where he is confined to a tank containing 0.0001 percent of the quantity of water that he would traverse in a single day in nature, Tilikum has been involved in multiple incidents of aggression. The stress of captivity drives Tilikum to exhibit abnormal repetitive behaviour, including chewing on metal gates and the concrete sides of his tank – so much so that the most of his teeth are completely worn down. The stress of captivity also causes Tilikum to exhibit aggression toward humans, which has cost two more lives – those of Daniel P. Dukes in 1999 and Dawn Brancheau in 2010. Tilikum scalped and dismembered Dawn as well as breaking bones throughout her body before drowning her.

To read more, visit: seaworldofhurt.com/features/30-years-three-deaths-tilikums-tragic-story/#ixzz3o13sQXy8

Fortunately, USA Today reported in an article by Nathan Bomey (March 17, 2016) entitled "SeaWorld to phase out killer whale shows, captivity" that "SeaWorld Entertainment said Thursday that the killer whales [i.e. orcas] currently living at its facilities will be its last, as it will stop breeding them immediately and phase out theatrical orca shows." Apparently, SeaWorld will now focus on educational programmes while trying to inspire our younger generation to respect natural encounters with this magnificent species.

This is good news, but throughout the world many other facilities still have orcas in captivity. This reminds me of the bullfighting arena, though without the grotesque savagery. It is more of a physiological and mental torture of this wonderful marine mammal, perpetrated in silence and without obvious physical harm tourists can see. Tourists are there to indulge their senses without paying attention to the silent animal's stress, frustration, and suffering inside those jail-style pools.

Dolphins in captivity

Dolphins are beautiful, intelligent, docile, and playful creatures of our vast oceans. They have amazing communication skills and love living within the pods they were born in for the rest of their lives. However, many marine parks have had dolphins captured to be trained and perform for tourists.

Tim Zimmermann wrote an article for National Geographic's June 2015 issue (pp 60-77) entitled "Born In The Wild." It is about aquatic animals in captivity, especially dolphins and orcas, and shows a picture of a dolphin called Chunsam who was released in the wild after many years in captivity in South Korea. Chunsam returned to his native pod after his release, which, according to the article, will increase his chances of survival and adaptation. The article notes that, when dolphins are in captivity, they are mainly fed dead fish by their trainers and forget how to eat, much less hunt for, live fish in the wild if released. Before they are released, they need to be trained again to be self-sufficient by triggering their natural hunting instincts. Such was the case for two bottlenose dolphins named Tom and Misha, who were kept in substandard conditions in a small pool in Turkey.

The world-renowned Born Free Foundation (bornfree.org.uk) wrote a 44-page report on the efforts undertaken to release Tom and Misha back into the wild. The report, "Back to the Blue," explains the two dolphins were trained to hunt for themselves, spend more time under water, and brought back to tip-top physical condition. Jeff Foster, a marine mammal expert from Seattle, helped retrain the dolphins. For many years, he was involved in capturing aquatic marine animals for SeaWorld's marine parks and for Don Goldsberry, who according to Zimmermann, has been the biggest collector of marine mammals in the world.

Foster realized that he was destroying marine mammals' families by separating them and semi-domesticating them while breaking their natural and wild spirit in the process. Regretting the damage he had unfortunately caused, he decided to do something to compensate for his actions, so he joined with the Born Free Foundation to rehabilitate Tom and Misha. Foster said:

> In captivity, we train the animals not to think on their own, to shut down their brains, and do what we ask them to do. What we are trying to do when we release them into the wild is get them off autopilot and thinking again. If they can make it alive through a six-month period, then we know they have been successfully reintroduced. Within six hours of release, they were eating wild fish and swimming with another dolphin. It was fabulous.

Read more at: care2.com/causes/watch-two-wild-caught-dolphins-return-home.html#ixzz3on7tf6fm

According to Zimmermann's article, by June 2015 there were 2,913 dolphins and 56 orcas in captivity in over 300 marine parks worldwide. Many of them were born in captivity, which greatly reduces their chances of survival if released in the wild. Among the main captors are the United States (18.16 per cent), Mexico (11 per cent), China (10.1 per cent), Japan (18.65 per cent), and some European countries (10.19 per cent). The rest of the world accounts for 31.9 per cent of cases.

A sad example of the above is Xel-Há and Xcaret in Cancun, Mexico, where they still enslave dolphins in captivity. They have them in painfully confined areas. Sometimes as small as a 30 by 20 metre rectangular pool. Keep in mind that a bottlenose dolphin swims at an average speed of 8 kilometres per hour, but on a busy day, they can reach speeds of 38 kilometres per hour. A bottlenose dolphin can dive up to a depth of 300 metres and these pools are usually no more than 10 to 15 metres deep. Now, kindly ask yourself, how fast can they swim in such a small size pool confined for the rest of their lives? Do you really think that a dolphin that is born and meant to be in the wild with a swim-free spirit as part of their DNA and innate nature, will keep its sanity if retained in such confined spaces for the rest of its life? Do you really think this is not torturing an animal? Dolphins in captivity will do anything for food from their trainers, but isn't their soul and spirit crushed and turned into a living, swimming ghost? In my mind, that is a very good example of animal abuse and exploitation for the sake of money; motivated by economic profit. To all those tourists that want to swim with dolphins, I only have one comment …. Please, let us not be selfish and instead, join the silent dolphin's plea for freedom. Why not join an active pro-animal rights group to protect these beautiful and innocent animals? For more information about the above example in Cancun, Mexico, please visit:

en.xcaretexperiencias.com/activities/dolphin-ride-xcaret.php

Chimpanzees in captivity

Chimpanzees are very closely related to humans; they share 98.8 per cent of their DNA with us. We are extremely similar yet still very different. Chimpanzees have been used throughout history in medical laboratories, and some have been kept in quite inhumane conditions. Scientists admit that these primates are closely related to us in their actions, reactions, sensitivity, instincts, thoughts, and even in their internal organs. Then why keep them in inhumane conditions for laboratory tests, when you can feel and see the reflection of all our feelings and overall similarities in their eyes and facial expressions? Yes, make no mistake, humans and chimpanzees appear different from each other, yet we are very close. Scientists have compared their bands and chromosomes to those of humans and found astonishing similarities. Some genes are slightly different, so chimpanzees are not affected by some human diseases, such as malaria, against which the chimpanzees blood cells are resistant. But they do get infected and are also carriers of the AIDS virus and hepatitis.

Using chimpanzees as substitutes for humans in laboratory tests may have made sense initially, but we have learned that primates have feelings too. Laboratories need to rethink their methods of researching cures for us humans, especially nowadays when we have sequenced our human genome (the complete nucleic acid sequence for humans). In the world of medicine, there is a legitimate belief that the proper understanding and use of our DNA sequencing will assist scientists to advance in all sorts of diagnoses and disease treatments and achieve successful medical treatments that will enable human evolution beyond frontiers we have never even imagined.

On the Nature of Things, David Suzuki has a fabulous video, "Safe Haven For Chimps." His video was broadcasted on CBC-TV at 3 pm EST on October 17, 2015. It is also available in a 45-minute video at: cbc.ca/natureofthings/episodes /safe-haven-for-chimps. He notes that the United States is one of the few countries that still use chimps in laboratories. I sincerely hope not for long. As Suzuki points out, "biomedical research on chimps has persisted, despite everything we've learned…. But now that's changing, signalling an evolution in our thinking."

Hundreds if not thousands of chimps have been rescued all over the world from medical laboratories. In his video, Suzuki talks about an amazing group of people who work at a place called Safe Haven for Chimps (referred to commonly as Chimp Haven) where many retired chimpanzees rescued from laboratories and other forms of captivity are living in harmony in family-style groups. They cannot be released to the wild because they are no longer capable of surviving there and because some of them were injected in medical labs with different viruses and are now carrier of those diseases. Kathleen Taylor, the director of animal services at Chimp Haven, says:

> These are feeling, caring, loving beings. And they put their life on the line for us unwillingly for so many years that it's only right that we give back. It's only right that we provide an environment where they can live out the rest of their lives.

Again, wild animals belong in the wild, not as pets. A very famous case of a pet chimpanzee gone wild was that of "Travis," who used to appear in commercial and television shows in the US. One day (February 16, 2009), he suddenly began acting aggressively and attacked a friend of Sandra Herold, his owner, leaving her blind and severing her nose, ears, and both hands. When the police arrived, Travis was still very aggressive and launched an attack on a police officer, who shot him dead on the spot. It is not a matter of whether or not a wild pet will go wild and become aggressive, it is just a matter of time. Their natural instincts will sooner or later kick in and the result may be a devastating attack on whoever gets in its way. We are all better off having a dog (*man's best friend*) or cat as a pet.

World Wide Fund for Nature (WWF)

Fortunately, there are several organizations and international agreements that work to promote animal protection and reduce the human footprint on our ecosystem. The most important are the World-Wide Fund for Nature (WWF) and the Convention on International Trade in Endangered Species of Wild Fauna and Flora (CITES). Refer to the section

"Protection of fauna vs. flora" earlier in this chapter for more information about CITES.

As for the WWF, this is a non-governmental organization that promotes biodiversity conservation and the overall reduction of our human footprint on the environment. It was established in April 1961 and is well respected and supported worldwide. I encourage everyone who reads this to support the WWF, because it is the world that surrounds you that you will be supporting.

David Miller, President and CEO of WWF-Canada, included in the 2014 WWF-Canada Annual report an alarming message regarding the world's natural diversity and its environment, which we all need to read, understand, and act on. He said:

> Together, we're facing the biggest environmental issues of our generation: WWF's recent Living Planet Report pointed out the devastating news that the population of mammals, birds, reptiles, amphibians and fish around the globe has declined by 52 per cent over the past 40 years. The health and security of critical habitat in oceans, rivers, on land, in the Arctic, and across the country remain under threat from unsustainable development and from the everyday decisions we all make.

The WWF is the world's largest biodiversity conservation organization and focuses on six main issues: endangered species, our forests, our fresh water, our oceans, our ocean coasts, and climate change. Although the WWF has offices around the world, its major influence and strength is in the United States and Canada, where it places very strong emphasis on the sustainability of our natural resources, the protection of biological diversity, the reduction of waste and pollution, and the promotion of recycling.

UNESCO has acknowledged the WWF as a non-government consulting organization. The research, analysis, and conclusions of the WWF are accepted and used as a reliable source of information for decision-making by many countries in relation to their policies on biodiversity protection and conservation and the reduction of the human footprint on our overall ecosystem (all microorganisms, fauna, flora and their immediate environment) and environment (the physical aspect of our immediate surroundings). The environment is simply limited to what surrounds us in the world we live in, while the ecosystem relates to the interactions of all living species.

The WWF has also focused on trying to reduce the illegal and unethical trade in wildlife, which they consider a major, direct threat to all species. The main threat, however, is overpopulation and the resulting human invasion into animal habitats, which are being reduced every day all around the world. Habitat destruction and the wildlife trade need serious worldwide attention and strict government controls, which the WWF is working hard to promote.

The wildlife trade (according to the WWF) is worth close to 160 billion dollars a year and involves a long list of species. In one of their sites (wwf.panda.org), the WWF writes:

> The trade involves hundreds of millions of wild plants and animals from tens of thousands of species. To provide a glimpse of the scale of wildlife trafficking, there are records of over 100 million tonnes of fish, 1.5 million live birds, and 440,000 tonnes of medicinal plants in trade in just one year.

Stopping illegal hunting and species extinction

Doris Lin has been an animal rights activist for over 30 years and has written many articles on animal rights, endangered species, hunting, poaching, and wildlife management, among other topics. She is an animal rights attorney, a member of the steering committee of the League of Humane Voters of New Jersey, and Director of Legal Affairs for the Animal Protection League of New Jersey. On her various articles published (animalrights.about.com/od/wildlife/g/What-Is-Poaching.htm), Doris Lin provides a very good definition of what poaching really means:

> Poaching is the illegal taking of wildlife, in violation of local, state, federal, or international law. Activities that are considered poaching include killing an animal out of season, without a license, with a prohibited weapon, or in a prohibited manner, such as jacklighting. Killing a protected species, exceeding one's bag limit, or killing an animal while trespassing are also considered to be poaching.

There have always been big debates regarding the ethical aspects of hunting. Hunting and killing (not catch and release) wild animals is usually practiced for food, trophies, or recreation. Without getting into the nitty-gritty of the ethical aspects of hunting, I want to express my own personal belief, which is that, since every species on earth feels hungry, thirsty, tired, stressed, sleepy, cold, warm, pain, happiness, sadness etc., every species should have its own privileges, benefits, liberty, prerogatives, advantages, and its own unique rights, all of which should be respected.

The desire to hunt an animal for recreation or trophies, in my mind, should be banned and harshly sanctioned by law. Yes, there are many macho men and macho women out there who would challenge me on this, but the day a hunter steps out of a jeep in the middle of the African savannah, with nothing but a Rambo style knife and a knapsack with a survival kit for a week, and goes hunting for hyenas, water buffaloes, cheetahs, antelopes, lions, and so on, that will be the day I will take my hat off and respect him or her as a hunter.

In my personal point of view, trophy and recreation hunters are a bunch of cowards who use powerful rifles, high-tech crossbows, or very advanced and sophisticated bows and arrows to put all the advantages in their favour and mostly hunt from a comfortable, secure position using advantageous strategies of deceit and ambush. Again, from my personal point of view and without prejudice, such is the case for all those recreational and trophy hunters who kill animals for fun and not for need. For example, we have a BC woman whose main reason to kill animals (according to her) is to connect to "the wild." Her name is Cassandra Oosterhof. She is "undeterred by death threats" and is one of five British Columbian contenders for the reality-TV title of "Extreme Huntress," according to The Province newspaper front page on May 24, 2016. Gordon McIntyre, who wrote the article, reports that Oosterhof loves nature and animals and hunts in order to conserve the wild because she says that we humans belong to "the wild." But if that is true, why go to "the wild" with very powerful and extremely high-tech rifles?

If that were not enough, she uses amazing telescopic sights to ambush and kill innocent animals who stand no chance of survival against such a powerful weapon in "the wild". In my opinion, these so-called recreational and trophy hunters are wimps who lack backbone. To my mind, they all seem uneducated people thirsty for blood, who suffer an uncontrollable urge to assassinate a wild animal that has the same right to survive as we all do, but stands no chance against tricky hunting strategies and powerful weapons.

It appears to me that these types of people like nature, or what they call "the wild," because they have a need to kill. They do not need the animal's meat to survive, but they need to feel physiologically powerful and need to collect or hang on their walls another head of an animal as a trophy. They say they love animals, but how can you kill for trophy an animal you love? When they go to Africa, they go for recreation and trophy killing of more exotic animals. They do not go for the meat, because they get rid of it with the excuse that "we give the meat to locals, camp workers, and guides to divvy up." Our ancestors hunted for food, hunters in general claim. But we need not do so anymore.

Yes, I insist, almost anybody can go out there with a powerful automatic rifle such as an AK-47, a high-tech crossbow, or even grenades, and bring an animal down (or mortally injure it). Literally anybody with a wee bit of training, a peewee brain, and some basic general knowledge can do it. But try using knives, machetes, and spears like our ancestors did. That is true heritage, contrary to what Oosterhof states, which is that "Hunting is not just about killing, it is about reconnecting with our heritage." If it is not about killing, why not use her skills and hunt with a high-tech camera to connect with "the wild"?

Imagine your dog's, your cat's, or your horse's head as a trophy on my living room wall. What is the difference from the perspective of animal rights? Just because one is wild and the other domesticated? Animal rights should cover all species. But heck, that is just me. Hunting for food is, to my mind, a natural survival instinct of every species that is carnivorous. If I had to hunt to feed my family, I would most likely do it, though against my will, desire, and spirit. I would then pay my respect to that dead animal before bringing him to the table. But if I could avoid it by putting fruits, vegetables, grains, bread, and other products on the same table, that would be the route I would take. That is just me and unfortunately, that seems to be a minority view.

There are two types of acknowledged hunting categories: legal hunting and illegal hunting. They involve killing or capturing wild animals with or without a legal permit and with or without having rights on the land where the hunting is taking place. The *animals'* rights are not considered, yet animals have rights in their native geographical area, and violating those rights should be considered a crime. Nevertheless, in this chapter, we are only interested in how to stop or minimize illegal hunting, i.e. poaching, which is penalized by law and considered a serious crime throughout our planet. Poaching contradicts all national and international laws. This activity should (and usually has) serious penalties, but people still risk their lives every day to practice it.

Elephants' relentless "donation" of ivory to the world

In January 2014, Scientific American published a brief article by Kate Wong (p.18) in which she describes how the US Fish and Wildlife Service ended up destroying a 25-year huge "stash" of African ivory. That stash was worth about 12 million dollars on the black market. All the tusks seemed to have been carved in beautiful artistic shapes. Yes, all beautiful pieces of art, but why not carve in wood, stone or marble? Ms. Wong goes on to say that the real problem is poaching, which has become a huge international business worth over 19 billion dollars. International criminal syndicates that are very well organized are perpetrating this trade within and beyond the borders of various African nations and all the way to several Asian countries, China being the most lucrative market. Already since October of 2012, National Geographic had their front page titled "Blood Ivory; 25,000 Elephants Were Killed Last Year (2011)." In this issue, there is an article by Bryan Christy entitled "Ivory Worship." Christy starts the article by reporting how, in January 2012:

> A hundred raiders on horseback charged out of Chad into Cameroons' Bouba Ndjidah National Park, slaughtering hundreds of elephants – entire families – in one of the worst concentrated killings since a global ivory trade ban was adopted in 1989. Carrying AK-47s and rocket-propelled grenades, they dispatched the elephants with military precision reminiscent of the 2006 butchering outside Chad's Zakouma National

Park. And then some stopped to pray to Allah. Seen from the ground, each of the bloated elephant carcasses is a monument to human greed.

This article revolves around the main uses of the ivory and where it is smuggled from and sold to. According to Christy, the main demand for ivory is for artistic work that ends up as religious figures and amulets around the world, but mainly in Asia and south east Asia: "Although the world has found substitutes for every one of ivory's uses – billiard balls, piano keys, brush handles – its religious use is frozen in amber, and its role as a political symbol persists." Christy says that Kenya's President Daniel arap Moi is the father of the ivory ban but once gave the Pope John Paul II an elephant tusk. This was followed by a noble initiative when he ordered the burning of 13 tons of confiscated ivory headed to the black market from Kenya.

Elephants roam freely over much of the African continent. Regrettably, poaching takes place all over Africa as well. Western Africa is known to have the strongest elephant ranger teams taking care of this beautiful animal, but poachers seem to be outsmarting the rangers' efforts to protect the elephants. In fact, the poachers themselves have killed many rangers.

The poachers have even been killing elephants in parks, reserves, and other wildlife sanctuaries, regardless of the potential repercussions if they get caught. Why? Because an artistically carved tusk can go on the black market or in fancy stores in China for over $250,000 USD. The poachers can easily get between ten and twenty thousand dollars for different size tusks (equivalent to several years of salary in those countries). According to Christy's article, the countries that demand ivory the most are (in this order): China, Thailand, Hong Kong, Taiwan, Vietnam, Philippines, Japan, Malaysia, Singapore, and India.

The majority of the ivory is artistically worked for religious purposes. The priests receive beautiful artistic and religious ivory figures in exchange for the amulets that they themselves make and bless. Some pieces or figures are even baptized. The better the gifts they receive, the better the amulets they give, which have a higher value as well. That is how many priests live and pay their everyday expenses. Amulets and religious figures are considered to protect their wearers from bad spirits, to bring them good luck, good health, a long happy life, and even money. This is why they are willing to give a priest an expensive, artistic, and religious ivory piece in exchange for an amulet. According to Christy, some people even use ivory to protect them from black magic.

The clergy's values and traditions in ivory matters

In many places all over the world, the clergy accepts valuable artistic pieces of carved ivory, and they have done so for hundreds of years, while accumulating riches and power. It is hard for me to understand how they can accept artistic carved tusks as gifts knowing that most come from animals sacrificed by poachers. Most of the ivory comes from the black market, which is fed by criminal poachers and traders, while threatening the existence of some animal species. Isn't this a very insensitive role for the clergy, one that goes against the value of preserving and respecting life in all its forms that they preach everywhere? Imagine if accepting this type of blood-ivory were banned? The demand for ivory would hopefully be reduced considerably and the elephant would be protected from extinction, contrary to its likely current fate.

Why are some clergy supposedly "so close to God" and so far from reality and from respecting life on earth? Why are they so close to goodness but so far from justice? Why so understanding of the poor but living in such opulence themselves? Why do some promote chastity while sexually abusing innocent children? Why? Sorry, but I do not have another answer aside from greed, corruption, and hypocrisy. I strongly recommend Bryan Christy's article for more information, as well as another article published by him in the September 2015 issue of National Geographic (pictures by Brent Striton) entitled "Tracking Ivory; Fake tusks carrying hidden GPS devices expose the trail of Africa's elephant poachers." In the second article, he writes:

> A booming Chinese middle class with insatiable taste for ivory, crippling poverty in Africa, weak and corrupt law enforcement, and more ways than ever to kill an elephant have created a perfect storm. The result: 30,000 African elephants are slaughtered every year, more than 100,000 between 2009 and 2012, and the pace of killing is not slowing down. Most illegal ivory goes to China, where a pair of ivory chopsticks can bring more than a thousand dollars and carved tusks sell for hundreds of thousands of dollars.

In this article, Christy allows us to understand how African terrorism is being financed to a great extent by dead elephants' ivory and how many African families are being terrorized on a daily basis by the same terrorists and traders. The Lord's Resistance Army is well financed by the ivory trade, says Christy. Africa is the perfect soil for the "seeds of terrorism", illegal hunting, and illegal trade to expand and develop. Its history has been continuously marked by the indiscriminate exploitation of its natural resources (animals, plants, minerals and more) and by abusive foreign countries throughout their history.

Almost every European and Asian country has had self-proclaimed rights to natural resources in various parts of Africa, and they still do, in sophisticated arrangements with corrupt governments. Along with the political corruption of many African countries, their natural resources and their animal kingdom are still placed at great risk beyond imagination. Christy says that the smuggler's trail was finally uncovered thanks to the creation of artificial tusks that had GPS devices imbedded inside them. National Geographic commissioned this GPS project. The artificial tusks were somehow infiltrated into Africa's smuggling chain. This helped uncover the whereabouts, sequences, mechanisms, and specific trails the tusks go through before reaching the international market. For more information about rhino and elephant poaching and the complex illegal trade system, please refer to Appendix 1, especially points five and six.

Invasive species

Let us start by defining what exactly an "invasive" species is. It is simply a plant or animal that is not native to a specific location and has the propensity to expand and spread beyond control, while affecting the native environment for the worse. The damage to the native environment is not limited to the ecosystem; it ultimately affects and endangers human health, the local society, and the local economic, commercial, and overall financial environment.

Some of the invasive species arrive by accident due to commercial activity or through human negligence, irresponsibility, or lack of care. To my mind, however, any normal person with a reasonable level of intelligence should understand that we cannot freely bring foreign flora or fauna to a new place without risking the balance and harmony of the environment, especially if we set the species free in our ecosystem without caring about the repercussions. Let's now look at a few examples of serious cases of invasive species such as:

The cane toad in Australia

Sometimes the invasive species is introduced into a new geographical area as a means of pest control. This is what happened in Australia with the cane toad. The Bureau of Sugar Experiment Stations, today known as Sugar Research of Australia, brought the toad (originally native to South and Central America) from Hawaii in hopes of controlling the Grey-backed beetle and the French beetle, which had been damaging their important sugar cane industry. Unfortunately, the cane toad did not help control the beetles as initially expected based on experience in Hawaii and other countries. Instead, the toads multiplied by the millions and now represent a serious threat to the Australian ecosystem.

Cane toads do not have serious predators because, in their backs and heads, they have glands that produce poison when triggered. Only a few species have adapted to become cane toad predators. For example, some birds and other animals attack the toad by its belly or eat the newborn tadpoles before they grow and develop their deadly poison, but not enough to control or get rid of the infestation. Many Australian species have been affected by the cane toad, which eats almost anything it can digest.

Environmental scientists cite the cane toad as an example of a very difficult invasive species that has brought many problems to Australia, though it has also promoted certain aspects of the tourism industry. Many souvenirs are made from the cane toad, such as purses, cricket balls, dissected toads, etc. Two environmental documentaries have been made about the species, "An Unnatural History" and "The Conquest."

The Australian culinary industry is even incorporating more and more toad dishes such as toad leg canapés, toad cake, fresh toad meat, fried toad meat, fried leg snacks, etc. However, the proper skinning of the toads is of utmost importance to turn "toad pest into toad pesto" as Australians say. Bon appétit, mes amis!

The Burmese python in Everglades National Park

This snake is originally from Southeast Asia. Animal traders brought them to North America, where people have bought them for pets, not knowing the challenges of owning a Burmese python. Many python owners realize they cannot handle them as pets (due to the amount of work involved or the potential danger), so they end up releasing them into their local environment, where the python does not belong. What started as a rumour is now a reality and a serious problem in places such as Everglades National Park in Florida. The python has become an invasive species there and is seriously affecting the local ecosystem, because it feeds on various local mammals and birds. It competes with local predators, of course, but with its faster rate of reproduction, it is leading the survival game in the Everglades.

Burmese pythons grow 12 to 22 feet long (3.6 to 6.7 meters) and have extremely powerful constricting abilities, to the extent of being able to suffocate an alligator. They are threatening already endangered species like the Florida native wood rat (also known as the Key Largo wood rat) and are also invading wildlife sanctuaries to hunt and feed on otters, flamingos, parrots, and other species. The natural order of life of many native species is now at risk. The National Park Services have been working along with other government and private agencies to try to control the expansion of this new species, which is still very foreign to the Everglades.

The Japanese Kudzu vine

This vine is known in North America as the "mile-a-minute vine." It was brought to North America from Japan because it was known to be a very fast-growing and resistant plant that would help control soil erosion, or so it was hoped. It is also native to eastern Russia and all the way down south to India and New Guinea. Initially, the US imported the plant because it was known to provide quick shade and to assist in stabilizing soil.

There are three competing versions of when and where it was first introduced into North America: Portland, Oregon, in the early 1980s, Philadelphia at the Centennial Exposition in 1876, and Beltsville, Maryland, in 1937. Whatever the history, scientists agree that the kudzu also accelerates climate change, because it seems to accelerate the release of carbon accumulated and stored in the soil and in the native plants. The kudzu is a very fast-growing plant and, by overrunning the local plants, affects the soil and the proper storage of carbon dioxide, which the local environment needs. According to a paper by Mioko Tamura and Nishanth Tharayil entitled "Plant litter chemistry and microbial priming regulate the accrual, composition and stability of soil carbon in invaded ecosystems" (US National Library of Medicine, National Institute of Health, April 11, 2014), "changes in leaf litter associated with kudzu infestation result in changes to decomposition processes and a 28 per cent reduction in stocks of soil carbon, with potential implications for processes involved in climate change."

The kudzu is a self-pollinating plant that, if helped by regular pollination (done by the birds spraying the seeds), reproduces at the rapid pace of at least a foot per day. It also has good anti-inflammatory and anti-microbial attributes, but the speed with which it covers terrain threatens the existence of native plants and even animals. It competes for light while covering other local plants, which then end up dying due to lack of sunlight. Indeed, the kudzu covers everything in its path, regardless of whether this is a natural setting or a city concrete-style jungle.

Scientists still have not found a way to get rid of it or to stop its fast pace of expansion without harming the native environment. The only way to stop kudzu is the traditional method of pulling it up with its roots.

The Zebra mussel

These mussels are native to the Black Sea and, specifically, to the Eurasian region connecting Ukraine, Russia, Georgia, Turkey, Bulgaria, Romania, and Moldova. The mussels were brought to North America in the ballast water used to provide stability and improve manoeuvrability of ships. Ballast water is pumped in and out of ballast tanks in a process (called ballasting) that is fundamental for safe control of ships on the high seas, but, according to Transport Canada and other government sources in North America, these waters often carry various kinds of species, from microbes to different aquatic plants or fish. When the ships later discharge (for safety reasons) the ballast water, the foreign species are discharged as well, which can bring serious ecological problems affecting the environment, the economy, and even the health of humans.

Due to ballasting, Zebra mussels, along with Quagga mussels, another invasive species, have been found in different areas of the Great Lakes and in rivers such as the St. Lawrence and the Mississippi, among other places. They damage their new environment by affecting the production of plankton when the mussels filter their water, which allows more sunlight to go through, therefore increasing the underwater vegetation that affects the marine stability of the area.

Their microscopic larvae swim freely everywhere and cling to rocks, ships, anchors, pipes, chains, and almost anything they come in contact with. This also constitutes a serious technical and economic problem for water treatment plants around the world. The mussels even represent a constant danger to people's feet and hands, which can easily be cut by accidental contact with the sharp, hard shells.

The Asian carp

By Asian carp, the world of science refers to various species of fish originating from Asia. They were brought to North America to promote the aquaculture industry, but while they were being farmed, some were accidentally released or escaped into the wild, causing infestations in various rivers and lakes. The most invasive species of Asian carp are the Grass carp, Silver carp, Black carp and the Bighead carp. They have overwhelmed river systems such as the Illinois and Mississippi. These carp are ferocious eaters and have the same diet as native species, so they end up competing for survival in an already stressed environment. Various microscopic microorganisms and general algae (plankton) are the carp's main dietary meal, which robs the food chain supporting local fish and is now affecting the food balance of rivers and lakes.

The carp congregate in large schools, displacing and pushing the local fish out of their native habitats. The carp is also economically less beneficial for fishermen than native species, which are more lucrative per pound. Silver carp are very sensitive to noise and, when startled by an engine, they literally jump from four to eight feet out of the water, constituting a serious threat of injury when colliding with people on boats passing by.

The Asian carp poses a real threat of getting into the Great Lakes and causing irreparable damage to the aquatic food chain of the lakes. As voracious eaters of plankton, the carp cause a serious imbalance in the food chain when challenging other native fish for food. Some of the rivers affected by the Asian carp have electric meshes to contain and keep the carp from spreading into the Great Lakes, which would seriously affect ecological, economic, and even recreational environments in this part of the United States and Canada.

Invasive species real threat

Invasive species can come in the form of either terrestrial or aquatic animals and plants. When a foreign species enters a new environment, the biggest threat is that of altering the food chain and food-web mosaic of the new environment. This deeply affects or even exterminates some native species that have lived in the area for tens of thousands of years peacefully and in perfect balance.

An article by Carl Zimmer in Scientific American (October, 2012, pp 60-65) entitled "Ecosystems On The Brink" discusses the need to keep jellyfish, fungi, and other creatures from overpowering healthy environments. He notes how scientists are continuously researching and exploring the various food webs and tipping points of different environments around our globe. Using the example of aquatic animals, he includes a very interesting diagram in which he explains that the food chain is not necessarily controlled from the bottom up, as many scientists have believed for years. He confirms that, according to other scientists and his own research, top predators can also control the food chain. His diagram explains how big sharks (such as the Hammerhead, Tiger, Bull, Short Fin, Great White and Dusky) are the top predators of smaller sharks and various types of stingrays, which, in turn, prey on smaller species such as scallops, clams, and oysters, which depend on plankton.

Plankton are known as "floaters in the ocean." They are microscopic organisms that drift freely with the ocean currents throughout our globe, mainly in the form of protozoans, phytoplankton, jellyfish, small crustaceans, diatoms, and others. One important source of food for them are the larvae and eggs from bigger animals of the aquatic kingdom, also drifting in the ocean currents.

Zimmer says that when the wolves were removed from Yellowstone National Park, the elk population increased. The elk feeds on tree leaves such as aspen. While feeding, the elk started killing young aspen trees, which consequently affected the local ecosystem. According to Zimmer's article, Stephen Carpenter from the University of Wisconsin at Madison, is "developing an early-warning system that can reveal when a food web is about to flip and [can then] offer guidance about how to pull it back from the brink." This would be of great value when foreign species suddenly show up in a new environment, or when species are removed from their native environment.

Proactive organizations against invasive species

There are organizations that are very proactive in trying to educate our world about controlling and avoiding the spread or introduction of invasive species. One of the most important is the Invasive Species Council of British Columbia (ISC). They have a very interesting website that I encourage the reader to visit (bcinvasives.ca).

The ISC invites everybody to "spot and report any invasive species in your area" and to cooperate in the efforts of the local community to keep the native environment protected and pristine. In Ontario, the Invading Species Awareness Program (ISAP) website (invadingspecies.com) has at least 25 very important links to similar and related organizations in North America, which I encourage the reader to visit in order to get a deeper understanding of the dangers that invasive species represent and the amount of effort out there by volunteers, non-profit organizations, and others to fight invasive species.

Another organization that is very important to mention is the International Union for Conservation of Nature (IUCN), which gives special attention to the conservation of our natural resources and overall environment, as well as the sustainability side of our natural resources to maintain our balance with nature that is under constant threat of overpopulation. The IUCN is assisting our society in the selection of sustainable businesses appropriate for growth and expansion with the best interest of our environment in mind. The IUCN has a well-known "Red List of Threatened Species." They work in conjunction or parallel with nations around the world, who produce the "Regional Red List" assessing the balance, threat, or actual extinction of species within their boundaries every year. Shouldn't we all be motivated to research and take serious action in protecting our rich and diverse biological world in relation to any specie (animals or plant)? I encourage the reader to visit the following links to learn more about IUCN and about how we can all work together to help it achieve its goals, which are of extreme importance to every human:

iucnredlist.org
britannica.com/topic/International-Union-for-Conservation-of-Nature

Swaziland teenagers' innovation and tree-free paper

For the last of the responsible actions to be highlighted in this chapter, I decided to include two that I deeply acknowledge and feel fond of. Both are responsible actions that can bring a lot of benefit to humans in almost any corner of the world.

Swaziland teenagers' innovation

They say that "if there is a will, there is a way," and that is exactly what two 14-year-old teenagers in Swaziland proved. They joined the second annual Google Science Fair and won the Scientific American-sponsored Science in Action Award (2012). The winners were Sakhiwe Shongwe from the town of Siteki and Bonkhe Mahlalela from the sugar mill town of Simunye. Both towns are located in eastern Swaziland. The two teenagers decided to tackle head on the problem of low food productivity in their country. Swaziland has long received food aid from other countries. Their goal was to engineer a solution to food shortages in their country and reduce the cost of food due to high distribution and transportation expenses. Their goal was to assist farmers to achieve a sustainable growth in their harvests of grains, fruits, and vegetables without the need for more land.

Their method relied on increasing farmers' yields with a simplified (but effective) hydroponic system based on recycling resources in order to make farming more self-sustaining and cost-effective and eliminate the need to import food and the high distribution and transportation costs. The hydroponic system eliminates the need for soil, reduces the farmer's need for water, and makes farmers more self-reliant. It also helps farmers to recycle materials that previously were considered garbage and that ended up in local landfills. Their contribution was targeted initially at their local communities, but it has now been studied and applied beyond their borders.

Jeff Golfman and tree-free paper

Jeff Golfman has been working diligently for many years to create public awareness of the serious worldwide deforestation problem. He realised that organized protests do not necessarily have the impact and effect on public awareness and positive thinking that he would like. Therefore, he decided to take immediate and direct action through green manufacturing processes to try and achieve a cost-efficient tree-free paper. Others have tried this before in various parts of the world, using fibre from agricultural products (such as bamboo), but there are no paper mills capable of producing cost-efficient, tree-free paper that meets the rigorous demands of the printing industry. This is one of the reasons Golfman decided to get actively involved in the search for a good quality and cost-efficient tree-free paper.

According to an article entitled "Environmental Innovation" by Jake McDonald in Canadian Geographic (April, 2014, pp.46-48): "If Jeff Golfman's … paper catches on, it could dramatically reduce deforestation in North America." Golfman's vision is to recycle the waste from wheat fields instead of tilling it back into the soil, which can be hazardous and far from environmentally friendly. The tilling of wheat straw into the soil is practiced all over North America, but the wheat straw-fibre could easily be the solution for tree-free paper, according to Golfman.

His challenge is to increase the demand for this type of tree-free paper, although the supply is not there yet to achieve his target. According to Golfman, the feasibility of manufacturing cost-efficient good quality paper from wheat straw "will be economically viable once demand is sufficient to support a 300,000 ton per-year operation." McDonald adds that Golfman's critics "say he faces a thorny logistical challenge in gathering widely scattered straw and affordably trucking it to a mill," but Golfman is convinced he will solve this problem. He currently has an amazing number of supporters who are powerful in various industries, some with a deep interest and strong financial support. They all have a keen interest in bringing Golfman's dream to fruition for what he calls an eco-friendly paper mill to help protect the forests of North America.

CHAPTER THREE: ATTITUDE

Introduction

Humans tend to be dynamic and in search for a continued state of evolution in one way or another. The way that people comport themselves is referred to as human behaviour.

Depending of the society in question, the interaction among the members of that society varies greatly. Such differences constitute a very unique and important aspect of each society and of human behaviour overall. There are many angles from which to interpret, understand, and justify the different ways in which people behave towards each other. There is a wide range of behaviours that humans practice, but they are all influenced by their geographical area, personal backgrounds, values, emotions, states of being, and specific cultures. But above all, they vary based on each individual's personal experiences and unique personalities, mental dispositions, and attitudes.

Human behaviour is very complex and difficult to understand and even sometimes to justify. The historical background of a society helps us understand typical behaviours in the society in question. This is known as social behaviour. If we dissect and study social behaviour, we can understand isolated and unique behaviours in context. Therefore, specific cultural background is of extreme importance for understanding the behaviour of individual human beings, and, above all, for understanding their inner responses and overall attitudes, which have led to hundreds of years of unique traditions.

The most important factors that help understand the behaviours of humans are their backgrounds, ethics, religions, geographical locations, and the times in which the behaviours took place (e.g.1917 vs. 2017). These factors shape the way humans conduct themselves. Their behaviour or response to these can be favourable or unfavourable to a specific place and time. Their attitudes will determine how they respond to a specific scenario. Their strength and ability (or lack thereof) to respond to a predetermined situation unsuccessfully or successfully determines, in turn, their immediate and long-term future.

In all societies, there are norms, rules, and regulations that aim to guide and control the people living in that society and direct them towards reasonable, fair, respectful, positive, and promising behaviour for the benefit of themselves and everybody around them. The sum of these individual behaviours will determine and chisel the final outcome and the quality of their social behaviour. Depending on the norms, rules, regulations, ethics, and creed of the society in question, people's behaviour can either "sculpt" a beautiful statue, such as a Minerva or a David, or an awkward and unbalanced one such as the Hunchback of Notre Dame or a heinous gargoyle.

Individual behaviour can be rational and planned. Behaviour can also be instinctive, which lacks any planning. People tend to follow rules and regulations, but they can also act by pure instinct in many of their daily activities, disregarding rules and regulations. The philosophy of every individual shapes and guides the actions of that individual and leads to behaviours that will take them along a unique path in life and equip them with a specific set of attitudes, habits of mind, prejudices, inclinations, and so on.

Strength of character

Strength of character, or lack thereof, is one of the key elements that indicate the personality of each individual and help explain their behaviour. There are two very interesting websites – livelifehappy.com and feelmylove.org – about living a happy life in harmony with your surroundings that provide two quotes worth mentioning about strength of character.

These two quotes are:

1. "Strength of character is not always about how much you can handle before you break, it's also about how much you can handle after you've broken." – Robert Tew

2. "Anyone can be a gracious winner, but being gracious after losing shows strength of character." – Donald Lynn Frost

These are some of my favourite quotes with which I could not agree more! I am a true believer that the power and strength of humans are in their character and their attitude towards different situations. A person with a strong character should have the ability to help the weak, to pull them up, and to assist and rescue them when they slip and fall. A person with the right attitude will certainly do just that.

A strong character and a positive attitude together constitute the pillars of a healthy person in any given society. Strong minds with character are the creators of new opportunities that break new boundaries to the unknown. The timid souls with weak characters and negative attitudes will remain on the dark side without ever being able to see the beauty of light. It is never too late to do your best to try and improve your strength of character and, above all, to develop a positive view and a progressive attitude. Indeed, it is never too late!

As human beings, it is in our nature to wish for, and try to live, dynamic, productive, meaningful, and happy lives. A strong character and a positive attitude will definitely augment our experiences at work and at home and help us enhance the way we see art, music, sports, nature, love, and the mirror in which we see ourselves. The more fulfilling a person's life is, the more the opportunities for new challenges and innovations will arise. Such people are very valuable to their society, which, in turn, will assist them to expand their prosperity and their horizons. This will definitely enable the community to thrive and boost its competitiveness relative to other societies.

Both strength of character and a good attitude are first taught at home. It is a sin for the weak and the lazy to remain passive and not try to strengthen their character, improve their attitude, and, above all, influence the next generation. Children are very easy to mould, guide, and teach. If they are not taught properly in their early stages of life to develop the right attitude and a strong character, whoever is raising them is actually betraying them. This sounds harsh, but let's face it; it is a concrete jungle out there, and, as we all know, it is survival of the fittest. Simple examples are how the animal kingdom survives in Africa, the Amazon, Siberia, the Arctic, the Antarctic, the oceans, rivers, and lakes, and in every forest and desert on our planet. Only the fittest physically and mentally survive. Every human should wake up with the right attitude, which will enable them to enrich and strengthen their character.

Perseverance

Perseverance and persistence are crucial ingredients in the formula to achieve the right attitude and, of course, success in whatever a person is trying to attain. Some define perseverance as "steadfastness in doing something despite difficulty or delay in achieving success." There is a very fine line between perseverance and persistence. The latter is defined as "firm or obstinate continuance in a course of action in spite of difficulty or opposition." The source of these two definitions is English Language and Usage at: stackexchange.com

There are two quotes about persistence that I particularly like. They come from Michael Pollock (michaelpollock.com):

- From Swami Vivekananda: "To succeed, you must have tremendous perseverance, tremendous will. 'I will drink the ocean,' says the persevering soul; 'at my will mountains will crumble up.' Have that sort of energy, that sort of will; work hard, and you will reach the goal."

- From Albert Einstein: "It's not that I'm so smart, it's just that I stay with problems longer."

Even though I like and agree with these quotes, I still want to emphasize that a crucial part of the definition of persistence is the quasi-hidden action of repeating something again and again until you achieve your goal. In my view, being persistent has an inherited negative connotation compared to that of perseverance, which tends to be accepted as a more positive attitude.

A well-known basketball player named Michael Jordan once said, "I can accept failure, but I can't accept not trying." My understanding is that, in his mind, this is the way he envisions perseverance, which I personally like. There is a famous poster about perseverance called the Cliffhanger that reads, "What the mind can conceive and believe, it can achieve." This quote shows a specific angle about perseverance, but it also reveals what the right attitude and mindset can do.

Both of the above quotes prove my point that perseverance is usually seen in a better light than persistence, but both contribute strongly to create and shape the right attitude. Henry Roosevelt (former assistant secretary of the United States Navy) once said, "When you come to the end of your rope, tie a knot and hang on." Muhammed Ali once said that he would rather endure pain now and live like a champion later. To my mind, these are wise words, because we all know that where there's no pain, there's no gain. At least that is how some of us were brought up. My grandfather used to say: "Where there is commitment, there is sacrifice, where there is sacrifice there is pain, and where there is pain there are endless possibilities of success, because you are forced to focus absolutely while trying to leave the pain behind."

One of my favourite sayings is by Dr. Martin Luther King, whose philosophy was: "Try your best to fly, but if you can't fly, then run, and if you can't run then walk, but if you can't walk, then crawl. But whatever you do, keep moving." Dr. King's philosophy of life was something I always agreed with and admired. He was an extremely proactive and persevering individual. His death was a tragic loss to the United States and to the world. While I was reading his biography, and after understanding his concept of perseverance, endurance, and attitude, an old Swahili parable came to mind, which is parallel to Dr. King's quote. I searched for it to confirm its origin, and I found several slightly different versions, but the message in essence is just the same.

The version I like the most is the following:

> Every morning in the African savannah, the sun rises.
> Every morning in the African savannah, a gazelle wakes up.
> The gazelle knows that it needs to outrun the fastest lion to survive.
> Every morning in the African savannah, a lion wakes up.
> The lion knows that it must outrun the slowest gazelle to survive.
> It does not matter if you are born a gazelle or a lion.
> But in the African savannah, when the sun rises, you better be running.

Perseverance and persistence are synonyms for continuous action, decision, commitment, and a decisive attitude. Steve Jobs (founder of Apple) was convinced that what separated successful and non-successful entrepreneurs was pure perseverance, not persistence. For Jobs, perseverance was equal to success! The great majority of people give up, so the road of perseverance tends to be very lonely, but it certainly pays off.

Yes, you have to be on the move every minute of every day. You need to be proactive and positive to achieve success. Unfortunately, not everybody makes an effort to achieve success. Everybody seems to want to achieve it, but is everybody making a real effort, while sacrificing a bit of pleasure for a bit more work on a conscious productive scale? That is the question everybody should ask themselves, and then provide a sincere and honest answer. Are we putting the time, effort, focus, dedication, and our heart into it?

Ability

The word "ability" refers to the particular skills, expertise, and talents an individual possesses. Ability represents the specific set of skills a person has compared to his peers. The more education a person has, the more this will assist him or her to develop higher levels of accomplishments due, in part, to the development of better skills and, therefore, abilities.

Ability can also be thought of as the power and capability to achieve goals above and beyond those of the average person. Those with better ability stand out from the crowd and tend to influence others. The more ability people possess, the better they will portray themselves due to a stronger and more focused attitude.

Joyce Mayer has a quote on brainquote.com that demonstrates the power of ability: "Patience is not only the ability to wait – it's how we behave while we're waiting." To my mind, perseverance improves the level of ability a person can achieve. Ability shows your talent and capability and your potential to accomplish things. But the initiative, inspiration, motivation and tenacity of a person sharpen their focus, determination, and achievements, which ultimately reflect their real perseverance and attitude.

This is the reason why, in many environments, attitude is acknowledged as a better trait than just knowledge, memory, or overall education. You do not necessarily reach success with more knowledge but you sure need the right attitude to be successful. That is the importance and real relevance of assisting a child to develop the right attitude during their infant years. But the question remains, whose responsibility is it to teach an infant the right attitude? The parents, the school system, or both?

Tenacity

While perseverance means to repeat something until it works, tenacity implies the use of new information, facts, data, events, or knowledge during the decision-making process, while trying to achieve our goals in the most efficient, shortest, and easiest way with the least resistance or effort.

Tenacity has a more positive meaning than perseverance, and even more than persistence. It implies a more rational and systematic pursuit of a better goal. Contrary to persistence, which is a repetitive action, tenacity is a planned and repeated action. It is a thoughtful action that provides faster and better results.

Tenacity needs more effort and focus to achieve. The great majority of people have persistence, fewer have perseverance, and even fewer have tenacity. To succeed in life, you need all three in the right proportion while, in my view, focusing more on tenacity. If you add cogency to the equation, that means you are being lucid, clear, and convincing as well. This allows people to have clear, specific goals along with a relentless and committed attitude. Cogency is a fantastic quality that, when added to persistence, tenacity, and perseverance, creates clear, logical thinking and a better outcome in whatever you are trying to achieve.

Here are a few quotes about tenacity that I particularly like:

- "There can be no success in sales without tenacity." – Chris Murray

- "Never give up; go over, go under, or go through, but never give up." – quotessays.com

- "Let me tell you the secret that has led me to my goal: my strength lies solely in my tenacity." – Louis Pasteur

- "If we have the courage and tenacity of our forebears, who stood firmly like a rock against the lash of slavery, we shall find a way to do for our day what they did for theirs." – Mary McLeod Bethune

Some of my own personal definitions and interpretations of tenacity include:

- Tenacity is the repetitive effort in a cognitive mode to achieve victory.

- Oxygen is to water as tenacity is to triumph.

- Tenacity possesses the proper state of cognition in parallel with a positive attitude, which is conducive to the oasis and gardens of success.

At this stage, we have evaluated various concepts that bring together and strengthen the overall cohesion and concept of "attitude," but we haven't talked about attitude itself yet and have not defined it fully.

Questions: Is attitude less important than knowledge, tenacity, strength, and ability? Does the average person pay attention to their daily attitude? Does the average human being try to polish and enrich their attitude to improve themselves and their behaviour towards others?

Answers: Unfortunately, the answers are all "No!" There are lots of very smart, knowledgeable people out there who have the wrong attitude and do nothing to improve it. Even worse, some do not even realize they have the wrong attitude. Most may simply have a totally different interest from their counterparts, and this is the reason why their attitude has that negative, unproductive, and even sometimes destructive flair. For example, try again justifying George W. Bush's invasion of Iraq in search of "weapons of mass destruction", whose attitude and actions are still a mystery, but in the minds of many, utterly abusive and wrong.

Attitude is everything! With the right attitude and only average knowledge, strength, ability, or tenacity, a person can succeed. Your attitude is what portrays you and places you in better positions in society. It assists you to higher plateaus within your social and economic environments. With the right attitude, a person can become aware of their strengths and weaknesses and implement strategies to improve. Without the right attitude, even with above-average knowledge, strength, ability, or tenacity, a person will not necessarily succeed at the levels they initially targeted or want to achieve.

For Steve Jobs the correct state of mind was always important, but the right attitude was everything. During his speech at Stanford University, he challenged the audience to ask themselves: "If this was the last day of my life, would I want to do what I am about to do today?" He even asked them to stand in front of the mirror and ask themselves that question every morning. Would they change their attitude if they were to sincerely answer that question? Steve Jobs was convinced that this would force people to bring their focus in line with the goals that really mattered to them, making their day much more productive and happier.

Something else to admire about Steve Jobs' philosophy was that he was averse to, even terrified of, stagnation, which for him meant total lack of growth. There was not a day that went by in which he did not make an effort to improve his attitude, his focus, and his overall end result for that day. On a daily basis, Steve Jobs assigned himself enough time for every task. He recommended to others to get used to tackling every task with a sense of urgency, because he was convinced that, if you give yourself too much time, you will be less productive. He constantly told his teams that a positive attitude would bring success, and that "success begets success." This was a very famous line of his. True commitment and positive attitude, in Job's mind, were the pillars to achieve success.

He had contact on a daily basis with a young and energetic group of technically oriented people who, at the click of a button, were used to getting whatever they desired. He was very clear in making them understand that they should not expect immediate gratification and that they should get rid of that attitude of entitlement. These two expectations, if not handled properly, would only bring them grief and frustration and would put the brakes on their healthy growth and minimize their achievements. He used to say: "Go to work in a happy mood." Happiness brought productivity, and productivity would lead to triumph, which would ultimately provide enjoyment, fulfilment, and pleasure, known by many as happiness!

One day while I was working on my computer, a little window popped up saying: "It is never too late to start over. If you were not happy with yesterday, try something different today. Do not stay stuck. Do better." At the bottom of this window, I was asked if I agreed or disagreed. I obviously ignored the message. Who knows where it would have taken me? But what would have happened afterwards if I had replied is not as important as Jobs' message. Why? Because it is often common for the great majority to do something on a daily basis without being truly interested and happy. This was something Steve Jobs was totally against. His message was to go to work happy, work hard against a due date, and not expect immediate pleasure and indulgence. Unfortunately, the younger generations nowadays expect immediate gratification in whatever they are involved in and, if they don't get it, feel frustrated.

Where are the days when you had to work smart and hard for your achievements and your money in order to be able to save? Where are those days in which you needed to increase your savings in order to accumulate enough money to purchase something in cash? Nowadays, the ease with which people purchase any item on line with a click of a button and the use of a credit card often lands them in deep financial distress, from which it is very difficult to recuperate.

There are so many people who do not care about the future repercussions as long as they get what they want in the present and as soon as possible. But we need to keep in mind that "easy comes, easy goes." The more easily a person attains something, the sooner the satisfaction of having that item disappears into thin air, and then they are looking for something else to satisfy their need for new things. They do not seem to grasp the fact that people are richer and happier the less they need and not the more they have.

It is unfortunate that the more these people have or buy, the more they need and want to continue purchasing. Some develop what is called an impulse control disorder (or shopping addiction). What induces people into these dangerous habits is the ease of use of plastic (credit cards). We do not even need to go to the store to buy something. We can do it at home through our computers and have it delivered. In the old days, you actually needed hard cash to purchase something, cash that you would have earned with hard work. To spend this hard-earned money required careful thought, not an impulsive reaction.

Attitude

For many people, attitude means the mental state of any human at any given place and time. Attitude includes, in many instances, facial expression and body language. If we try to connect the facial expression and body language, then we can easily perceive the attitude and commitment of the person we are dealing with in their unique social environment at that specific moment in time. Attitude is reflected in how a person responds to their environment and is interpreted through the path they have chosen to proceed on. The reaction of a person helps us to understand their attitude at any given time and place.

Attitude is a very powerful tool to achieve any goal. For example, only the right attitude can lead you to the top of Mount K2 or Mount Everest. You might have the right equipment, desire, and knowledge, but the real and winning determination comes from your attitude towards adversity. Our attitude, in cohesion with our knowledge, helps us reach the top in a more determined and efficient manner. An interesting website called Rogers Business Solutions (businessdictionary.com) provides a very good definition of attitude:

> A predisposition or a tendency to respond positively or negatively towards a certain idea, object, person, or situation. Attitude influences an individual's choice of action, and responds to challenges, incentives, and rewards (together called stimuli).

The four main components of attitude are:

- Affective: emotions or feelings.
- Cognitive: belief or opinions held consciously.
- Conative: inclination for action.
- Evaluative: positive or negative response to stimuli.

According to the Merriam-Webster dictionary, attitude can be understood as:

- The way you think and feel about someone or something.

- The feeling or way of thinking that affects your behaviour.

- A way of thinking and behaving that people regard as unfriendly, rude, etc.

Another definition worth mentioning was retrieved from Wikipedia:

An attitude is an expression of favour or disfavour toward a person, place, thing, or event (the attitude object). Prominent psychologist Gordon Allport once described attitudes as 'the most distinctive and indispensable concept in contemporary social psychology." Attitude can be formed from a person's past and present. Attitude is also measurable and changeable as well as influencing the person's emotion and behaviour. In lay language, attitude may refer to the distinct concept of mood or be especially synonymous with teen rebellion.

To me, attitude is a form of behaviour that can either be spontaneous, subconscious, or planned in advance. It can be accidental or intentional, but the most important and valuable aspect of attitude is that anyone can willingly modify it, for better or worse, at any given time if so required. Anyone can change his or her attitude for better or worse at any given time. It might not be easy to change our attitude, but it can be done. Unfortunately, when a stubborn, hard-headed, or, simply put, a limited person refuses to improve their attitude, then missing the target is often the end result. A positive change of attitude can avoid disasters while allowing the sun to shine brighter on a person's path, but only if that person decides to change for the better.

There are many quotes that can assist the reader to see and evaluate the depth and magnitude of the right attitude. For me, attitude is absolutely everything. Throughout my life, I have failed in many things like anybody else, but that is one of the reasons I learned to understand the importance of attitude. Usually, when failure happens and repeats itself, I end up regretting it, but when I have the strength, discipline, vision, and the required will to change and adopt the right attitude regardless of the situation, things always change for the better. No doubt about it!

There is a very good website, which I encourage the reader to visit. It is called goodreads.com and has many quotes about attitude (and many other subjects) that I like. This site will undoubtedly help the reader to grasp the power of attitude. Some of my favourite quotes from that website (and other sources) are:

> "Keep your thoughts positive, because your thoughts become your words. Keep your words positive, because your words become your behaviour. Keep your behaviour positive, because your behaviour becomes your habits. Keep your habits positive, because your habits become your values. Keep your values positive, because your values become your destiny."— Mahatma Gandhi

"Attitude is a little thing that makes a big difference."—Winston Churchill

"Life is 10 per cent what you make it and 90 per cent how you take it." — Irving Berlin

"Our life is what our thoughts make it." — Marcus Aurelius

"If you think you are beaten, you are; If you think you dare not, you don't. If you'd like to win, but think you can't, it's almost a cinch you won't. If you think you'll lose, you've lost, for out in the world we find success being with a fellow's will. It's all in the state of mind. If you think you're outclassed, you are. You've got to think high to rise. You've got to be sure of yourself before you can ever win a prize. Life's battles don't always go to the stronger or faster man. But soon or late the man who wins, is the one who thinks he can." — Walter D. Wintle

"Life is not a matter of chance...it is a matter of choice." — Ka

"Just because I face a defeat does not mean I am defeated." — Jeffrey Fry

"No guts, no story." — Chris Brady

"Attitude is everything." — Diane von Furstenberg

"Your attitude determines how you experience the world." — Sanaya Roman

"Happiness is a conscious choice, not an automatic response." — Mildred Barthel

"Your appearance, attitude, and confidence define you

as a person."— Lorii Myers

"Self-affirm – build yourself up with honest and genuine praise." — Lori Myers

Stop blaming. Take responsibility for your thoughts and your actions." — Dee Dee Artner

"Our perceptions are influenced by our surroundings."— Asa Don Brown

Now, I would like to add my own personal thoughts about attitude, which are:

The reflection of your own persona is the result of the shadow or the light emanating from your attitude.

You need a strong attitude to succeed, to never give up, to trust yourself, and to realise that sometimes "it is what it is," so buckle up and learn the lesson.

We are very lucky that we live in a dynamic world, but sometimes it spins too fast. Things change; circumstances change. Learn to adapt and to keep yourself in a constant adaptive mode. Channel your efforts to what is important to you, so you can respond accordingly. Never see change as a threat: with the right attitude, it can be an opportunity to learn, grow, evolve, and advance beyond the rest.

There is an intrinsic value and great power in people with the right attitude. In the eyes of many people, those who lack the virtue of an attitude (positive or negative) are ordinary, forgettable, and uninspiring. They go through life in the midst of indifference, lack of excitement, and in a very nonchalant, apathetic, and uncaring world of their own. In the dictionary of some, these people are called mediocre. Is that how we want to be? Certainly, not me. Mediocrity for some is not bad, but it is far from being ideal. We need to learn how to control ourselves and get our act together, in the blink of an eye if need be.

If we change our attitude, then we are chiselling and sculpting a different type of life, a different outcome, and we are ultimately changing our future, hopefully for the better. It is not easy, but it is definitely doable. Nothing good and valuable comes easily, and if, by chance, something good and valuable comes knocking at your door, embrace and treasure it! To some, it could be superficial and without real value. Therefore, that opportunity can also slip away very quickly, the same way it suddenly knocked on your door.

It has been said that "the difference between failure and success lies in the substance (or lack of substance) of your attitude. Perfection is achieved with practice, patience, pride, self-esteem, and a positive and consistent attitude. These characteristics are certainly not gifts; they are achieved with effort, sweat, and risk. I have learned over time that the impact of whatever happens to me will depend on how I perceive things and events and, above all, how I react to them, which brings attitude into play as the key element.

We are all far from perfect, and we tend to overreact to things that happen to us. But when we are under control, with a calm and peaceful attitude, our interpretations, reactions, and overall response lead us to a better path in pursuit of real satisfaction. Personally, I have to make a continuous effort to control or guide my attitude. Some people say that, with time, the right attitude comes naturally, but I have my doubts. I believe that you always need to be in control and conscious of your efforts to have the right attitude for the circumstances around you. Nothing really valuable comes naturally; you have to work for it and make it happen, at least in my world! I know that the height of my success and happiness is measured by my ability to adapt and change my attitude.

Out in the real world, they say, "We all need to learn to accept people the way they are, not the way we want them to be." I always make an effort to accept people the way they really are. Unfortunately, there are some people out there whom I will never be able to accept as they are, because they go against my values, education, principles, and overall way of thinking, especially those people with wrong or negative attitudes. But let's face it; there are certain types of people we will never understand, much less accept. I never confront them. I just keep my distance, switch them to invisible mode, and keep on with my life; it's that simple. Respect for others means peace. But it is a two-way street, they also need to respect you and your surroundings.

As I have gotten older, I have become less patient about certain things. Therefore, I try to deal only with people who have similar values, principles, and levels of education. I've noticed that, with age and the passage of time, I am less willing to spend time with people who are totally different from me. I have fewer days left on my horizon than I used to have, so why waste the precious time I have left with people I cannot relate to? They say that you learn to be more patient with age. This is true, but we also learn to be more selective in everything we do as well. Hey, nobody knows how much time we have left, so I have decided to be selective from now on, and, therefore, my family and close friends are number one.

Also, as I have gotten older, I have learned to listen. Yes, to really listen. Listen with full attention and legitimate interest, while doing my best to understand the meaning and depth of what I am being told. To listen to somebody with undivided attention and patience is an art. Even more of a challenge is to provide an intelligent comment or answer to the problem of the person I am listening to. It is always difficult to provide meaningful advice that is enlightening and helpful to the other person.

Our response has to come from carefully calculated reasoning and from the depths of our heart. Sincerity is crucial. If we cannot provide positive reinforcement, or if we are going to hurt others with our comments, we should not say anything at all. If we are going to disrespect or dishonour somebody with our comments or make wrong assumptions based on unfounded statements, we are better off keeping quiet. If we are just going to judge others, we should stop and consider that others can judge us too. We need to try to be discreet, sincere, honest, and altruistic, while using positive reinforcements. To learn how to listen properly and then formulate an intelligent and respectful answer is a skill worth developing and worth putting effort and work into. I remember my grandfather used to tell me: "If they laugh at you because you're different, stop and look straight into their eyes and just smile at them, because sadly, they're all the same. Be proud of who you are and of being different, but within the ethical parameters of the society in which you live and that you have been taught at home."

Attitude and perspective

It is very important to keep our lives in perspective. We need to discover and define what is important to us, so that we can then choose the battles that are worth fighting.

One day I received an email message from a friend of mine in which he said that we need to think outside the box and that, when we encounter a problem, we need to put things in perspective. I believe this email has circulated around our world several times. I verified its legitimacy, and I did not find anything contrary to its content, which is the reason why I will shortly be using it as an example. His message was in relation to the average problems we encounter on a daily basis in life and how we handle them to make them small or big issues.

When we have a problem, sometimes we are overwhelmed by

it. We should stop, step out of our spinning world, and look at the problem from the right perspective and proper angle. We should not exaggerate or make a problem bigger than it really is. Again, my grandfather used to say, "Do not drown in a glass of water," meaning take it easy, calmly and rationally. He also used to say, "If there is no solution, why worry? But if there is a solution, why worry?" Conclusion: "Do not worry and always keep calm," he used to insist. Within his simple approach to life, he was a genius who observed the world with calmness and friendliness, regardless of the problems around him. The proof that he was 100 per cent correct is that he lived a long, happy, and prosperous life, until he passed away at age 86, from natural causes.

Earth vs. our galaxy, the universe, and beyond

Planet Earth is huge and full of surprises and wonders. All humans (over 7.5 billion of us) live on this blue planet. Earth is very small within our own solar system. Our solar system is proportionately smaller within our own galaxy, the Milky Way. Our galaxy, in turn, is almost nonexistent in that mysterious but fascinating space called the universe. Then, how big is Earth really? I will try to answer this question using two simple approaches.

First, according to astronomer Carl Sagan (world-renowned US scientist in the 1980s and 1990s), planet Earth is only one-sixth of a pixel within our own solar system. This is based on scientific information from brighthub.com and from solarsystem.nasa.gov/planets. Our solar system is only 0.032 per cent of our galaxy. If our galaxy is 100,000 light years in diameter and about 1,000 light years in thickness, can you really fathom how insignificant we are in our own Milky Way?

Second, I once received an email from a friend of mine with an attachment that helped me put things in perspective, although I first confirmed its validity and accuracy. This attachment was related to the use of astronomy to help evaluate things from a different angle and to allow us to comprehend that we are really insignificant in the universe. Some say we should try to see our problems in the same proportion, if possible. If we were to see the size of the earth compared to Jupiter, Saturn, and our sun, we would realize that our planet is extremely small. Earth would fit into the sun 1,300,000 times. Can you imagine that?

Comparatively, our sun can barely be seen at one-pixel scale, if we place it just beside the star called Antares. This star is 10,000 times brighter than our sun. It burns energy much faster than our sun, and, even though it is massively bigger, has a shorter life expectancy. Antares is the fifteenth most brilliant star in the sky, located more than 1,000 light years from earth. Now, please stop for a minute and imagine the following three scientific statements:

1. By considering the equatorial diameter of earth as equal to 1, then Mercury's equatorial diameter is 0.382, Saturn's is 9.449 and Jupiter's is 11.209. This simply means that Jupiter is 11.209 times bigger than earth.

2. The radius of the sun is about 109 times the earth's radius (695,800 kilometres compared to only 6,371 kilometres).

3. The radius of the star Antares is approximately 840 times larger than our Sun's radius (584,472,000 kilometres).

After understanding the magnificent and impressive size difference between earth, our sun, and Antares, the message of the attachment I received shows us how small and insignificant we are in the universe. Therefore, our problems are literally insignificant or practically non-existent within the universe. We need to see them with a different attitude and in real perspective. Our planet is insignificant in size compared to other planets and stars in our solar system, which is also very small within our galaxy, which is also extremely small and insignificant compared to other galaxies, and so on. That is how small and insignificant earth is, which ultimately borders on the edge of non-existence.

A delicate conclusion

This goes to show how fragile Earth is and how imperative it is to take care of this place we call home. It is the only home we have. A positive attitude in everything we do, together with correspondingly positive actions towards the environment, will have a positive impact in the preservation of our planet. We all have to cooperate if we want to keep having a sustainable life on this planet. We all have to do our part, regardless how small or big that part is. Why? Because the alternative of finding another planet where humans can live is not just very difficult, but if we ever find a planet, rest assured it will be pretty darn far away, measured in thousands of light years.

Humankind does not seem to understand (or does not care) that the balance of nature has its limits and can be destroyed irreversibly if we all do not put our hearts and efforts into taking care of our environment and ecosystem. In the name of profit and money, we have been raping earth's innocence, but earth has grown up and is about to show us its wrath. In fact, it has already started, but we refuse to see and acknowledge this. Personally, I am convinced that only an ignoramus searches for logic and common sense in the chambers of the pounding human heart driven by profit and gain. It is a recipe for disaster in the ephemeral existence of the confused and pitiful human soul. But the little angel on my right shoulder says: "Have faith, do not give up."

CHAPTER FOUR: HUMAN ATTITUDE AND OUR PLANET

We live in a world of limited resources. The more we exploit our world's resources through unlimited human activities, the more we push it to the brink of exhaustion, that is, to the irreversible depletion of its delicate balance in the four basic elements: air, fire, water, and earth. Throughout history, greed and the need for more and more power has shadowed the ultimate human goals of proper and balanced responsibility, integrity, honesty, and loyalty. This affects humanity's performance and attitude towards its environment and its ecosystem, which are being mistreated, taken for granted, disrespected, and figuratively raped every day by individuals, corporations, and corrupted, blinded governments around the world. These are the reasons I want to focus the rest of this book around the following main subjects:

- Earth's four basic elements for survival.
- Population explosion: overpopulation vs. invasive
- species.
- Energy and oil.
- Global warming and the future of "blue gold."

Anthropocentric vs. biocentric attitudes

We all need to rethink seriously our relationship with nature. There are no two ways about it. If, to date, we have not realised or cared about the real importance of nature, then we should carefully, thoughtfully, and immediately act and make an effort to get involved not just for our own benefit but for the benefit of all those we love and care about. Anthropocentric individuals only care for nature if they can get material or economic benefits from it. Otherwise, they tend to feel apathetic towards it. They do not really seem to care for nature and end up acting towards it with absolute disregard.

Biocentrism is a disposition of respect for nature and a strong interest in our ecosystem. Biocentric individuals tend to protect nature at all times. It is therefore of utmost importance to be less anthropocentric and more biocentric. That is, we need to realize that not everything revolves around us humans, that there is a lot more than just us on this planet, and that we cannot survive on our own in the long run.

All those anthropocentric people are committing the same mistake our ancestors made before Galileo proved that we were not the centre of the universe and that it was earth that orbited the sun, not the other way around. Respectful and careful coexistence with nature (animals and plants regardless of geography) is crucial for our own survival. We need to educate our children on how to avoid anthropocentrism and how to focus on the value of our environment, our ecosystem, and all the living species in it, regardless of what we might perceive, feel, or experience subjectively. It is simply a fact that we need to educate the younger generation to respect our world and its environment, as much as they are taught to respect their national anthem, their flag, their home, their grandparents, their parents, their teachers, and themselves.

The older generation should lead the younger generation by example, not just through words of wisdom and advice. They need to walk the talk. Children learn by example more than by words. They copy, mimic, and emulate what they see and even try to exceed those mirrored actions. We most certainly also need to teach them how to obey the law and live in harmony, not just with their brothers and sisters, but with every other human being and every other species on earth.

Earth's four basic elements

The adults and the elderly have the utmost responsibility to teach their youth the value of the basic elements of life, which are air, fire, water, and earth (soil). The adults and the elderly need to inculcate with crystal clarity in children at a very early stage in life (from one to 12 years old) an absolute respect for the four most basic elements on earth. Teenagers all think they know better than anybody else, and so it can be a real challenge to teach children new philosophies of life after the age of 12 or so. The great majority simply disrespect, abuse, mistreat, or take for granted some of these elements that are absolutely crucial for our survival as human beings.

Young people who manage to connect early in life with these four basic elements will mature more happily, more positively, and with less stress. According to David Suzuki, we need to add to the four basic elements three more basic components as well, which are love, spirituality, and biodiversity. Yes, I agree with these extra elements. They are very important for a productive life, but I think we should even add two more, which are crucial for a good balance in life: respect for others and respect for oneself. Without these two components, our life will always be limited, and above all, at very high risk. In the rest of this chapter, we will briefly focus on each of the four main elements in turn.

Importance of air

Clean air is almost a synonym for a healthy life. Without clean air, we will simply get sick, slowly but surely, as is happening in many cities around the world that are suffering from air pollution. According to the government of British Columbia, in western Canada air quality is extremely important to support and maintain the proper and delicate balance of life on our planet. On their website (gov.bc.ca), they publish the following statement:

> Clean air is essential to maintaining the delicate balance of life on this planet – not just for humans, but wildlife, vegetation, water, and soil. Poor air quality is a

result of a number of factors, including emissions from various sources, both natural and human-caused. Poor air quality occurs when pollutants reach high enough concentrations to endanger human health and/or the environment. Our everyday choices, such as driving cars and burning wood, have a significant impact on air quality.

Air quality is measured in terms of both indoor and outdoor air quality. Indoor air quality, although important, is less critical than air pollution outdoors, which affects all types of life. Bad air quality indoors will only affect those living inside those quarters, though it can cause serious health problems and severe allergies if the problems are not addressed adequately. It is important that we have companies dedicated to provide good indoor air quality using better and more efficient building codes, heating systems, air purifiers, and other equipment.

We all react differently to air pollution, but one thing is certain: we all end up reacting negatively and being affected by lung, heart, skin, or multiple other diseases. The energy we use at home and at work in the way of electricity still contributes strongly to air pollution. Also, the fuels used to run our cars, trucks, and factories contribute the most to air contamination, which are mainly operated using fossil fuels along with natural gas. The use of coal in many countries is a big detriment to our air quality, because the pollution travels around the world through the planet's natural air currents and winds. Factories and motor vehicles create serious pollutants such as sulphur dioxide, lead, nitrogen dioxide, carbon monoxide, and other particulate matter, which are very harmful to our health. Ozone, which is a form of gas, is also a contributor to bad air quality. All the chemicals and harmful biological materials released by humans into the air put at risk our lives and those of our children.

The Environmental Protection Agency (EPA) collects air pollution statistics and confirms that poor air quality, present in all medium and large cities, causes serious health issues mainly in the form of brain damage, heart disease, lung cancer, kidney and liver damage, and respiratory disease. The average person cannot understand or even believe that we all breathe each other's breath. In fact, what a person exhales in a distant country such as Australia, we end up breathing the same air here in North America. This reminds me of what David Suzuki once wrote about the sacred and untouchable balance of nature in his book "The Sacred Balance: Rediscovering our Place in Nature." Suzuki wrote:

> Every breath is a sacrament, an affirmation of our connection with all other living things, a renewal of our link with our ancestors and a contribution to generations yet to come. Our breath is a part of life's breath, the ocean of air that envelopes the earth.

Importance of fire

There is no doubt that the environment has influenced humankind's development throughout history, but humankind has likewise influenced the environment and the ecosystem in which we all live. When Homo erectus set foot on earth, he was influenced and totally controlled by the environment, which he depended on and adapted to. But when the first humans discovered how to manipulate and later create fire, they started having some impact or control over the environment in turn.

The concept of fire has been instrumental for human development and growth, but it has also been detrimental. Controlled fire provides warmth, protection, the ability to cook food, to see at night, better ambience, and many other benefits. Fire also produces destruction, pain, and economic loss. Above all, it affects the delicate balance of our air quality and, therefore, our health, which has a fundamental and important impact on our societies.

Our forests every year (as has been the case for centuries) are at risk of natural wildfires, mainly caused by lightning. Recently, however, the worst fires in North America, and some in Australia, have been caused by human negligence and even mischief. Nobody in their right mind would cause fires like the one called Cedar Wild Fire in California in October 2003, which burned over 273,200 acres, or the Rim Wildfire in August 2013, which burned over 257,300 acres. Both were caused by human negligence. We all still remember the wildfire of 2017 in Fort McMurray (BC, Canada), where over 2,400 buildings were destroyed. In 2017, catastrophic wildfires in California destroyed over 1,381,000 acres, followed by killer mudslide in Jan of 2018.

Wildfires can also be good for the environment. They sometimes create desirable changes in the soil that ultimately benefit many life forms within the forest. Wildfires contribute to early plant successional stages that positively impact the wildlife in the area. Control of prescribed fires in the forests can be an effective fuel management tool. They assist in reducing fuel accumulation that collects with time, increasing biodiversity, improving wildlife habitats, promoting new growth, and controlling undesired forests encroachments.

Fires literally clean the forest floors from various types of debris, allowing the sunlight to get through while nourishing the soil. With less competition for soil nutrients, both new and established trees absorb more nutrients from the soil and grow faster, stronger, and bigger. The more efficient nutrient absorption, together with the extra space, allows for healthier future forests and consequential benefits for their wildlife.

Unfortunately, there are serious downsides to wildfires, which put both human and animal lives at risk. For example, 10 per cent of the world's species live in the Amazon rainforest. According to the November, 2015 issue of National Geographic, the Amazon has 16,000 known species of trees and over 2,500 known species of fish. Just between 1999 and 2013, some 1,661new species of vertebrates and plants were discovered. Brazil and Peru own the largest portion (about 70 per cent) of the Amazon rainforest (along with seven other countries), which absorbs at least 25 per cent of the carbon dioxide being emitted and produces a substantial proportion of the world's oxygen. However, the November, 2015 issue of National Geographic published an alarming supplement regarding how human impact (human encroachment) is affecting and actually destroying the Amazon rainforest, all in the name of progress and economics:

> Amazonia is a huge carbon sink. Its soil and vegetation hold roughly a fourth of all the world's carbon that's stored on land. But scientists say a tree die-off in the past decade is shrinking the region's capacity to absorb the planet's carbon.

If this is true, which absolutely makes scientific sense, then the Brazilian and Peruvian people have in the palms of their hands the future of 25 per cent of the air quality of the world. Should only Brazilians and Peruvians have such influence and control of the air we breathe? Shouldn't there be an international institution that actually controls and implements monitoring techniques, strict international methods, procedures, and policing to ensure the efficient management of forests like that of the Amazon?

Brazilians are mainly responsible for changing the landscape of the southeast section of the rainforest forever, and they are getting deeper into the jungle at an alarming pace. According to National Geographic, NASA found that 3 per cent of the rainforest had been destroyed by slow-burning blazes between 1999 and 2010. The rainforest is being cleared mainly to make space for more human habitat and for cattle ranching, because the export of beef is a multibillion dollar part of the Brazilian economy and a considerable contributor to Brazil's GNP. The demand for beef is growing throughout the world, pushed by fast food companies like McDonald's, Burger King, and others. But they are just responding to the demand for beef worldwide. Deforestation in Brazil has been rampant by the desire to harvest more and more soybeans, a cash crop exported to many countries. Commercial agriculture is one of the strongest drivers of deforestation in Brazil and in many other Latin American countries. There is an interesting article written by Stephanie Nolen, published in the Globe and Mail, January 28th, 2018. She states that "Brazil is home to 15% of all species on Earth, it recycles 20% of the world's rainfall, and it stores over 150 million tons of CO_2." Sadly, illegal deforestation, farming, mining, and sawmills are destroying the Amazon rainforest. Shouldn't this require the attention by the UN, regardless of national sovereignty?

There is a website worth citing that I also used as reference for the worldwide deforestation information I am about to present in summary form. I encourage the reader to visit their site called *allianz.com* because of the valuable content they have collected throughout the years. There are many other forests around the world being affected for the same reasons and at similar speeds. The six most relevant are the following:

1. The Amazon Rainforest, with over 5.5 million square kilometres (2.1 million square miles). Located in a section known as the Atlantic Forest (Gran Chaco) with an amazing diversity of life, this massive rich rainforest is occupied by Argentina, Brazil, and Paraguay. El Gran Chaco, as it is known, has suffered severe deforestation due mainly to overpopulation in that area. The clearing of forest for cropland and pasture has been growing exponentially in the past 20 years, and unfortunately, it is still happening in 2018.

2. There is another area in South America known as Choco-Darien, which is located on the northwest Pacific coast. Mainly in the Colombian, Panamanian, and Ecuadorian areas, the forests are being threatened and damaged due to oil exploration, mining activities, and the creation of new highways and roads for industrial, commercial, and residential development in the area.

3. Canadian natural forests, which cover 4.2 million square kilometres, over 45 per cent of Canadian territory, the second largest country in the world. The biggest threats to the forests are the expansion of hydroelectric plants, mining, and, above all, logging. Twenty-five per cent of the world's paper consumption comes from Canadian exports.

4. East Siberia's coniferous forests, with over 3.8 million square kilometres. Russia is the biggest country in the world, with the largest forest area.

5. The United States has about three million square kilometres of forest that, although more or less managed, is being slowly fragmented and degraded as human population expands.

6. The Scandinavian taiga, with about 2.1 million square kilometres, is also extremely important, along with the Russian taiga, for the amount of carbon dioxide absorbed.

Other countries with considerable forests and impact on wildlife and on humans include the tropical basin of the forests of Congo in Africa (containing 20 per cent of the world's tropical forests and the highest biological diversity in Africa), the tropical forests of the Republic of Mexico, the forests of

Malaysia, Indonesia, and Brunei (known as the Borneo territory), the New Guinea rainforest, and the forests of Rumania and Bulgaria. Together, all these forests cover an area larger than 2.7 million square kilometres. They are also in danger of being depleted by human activity in the form of industrial and residential developments, clearing land for plantations of various types, such as coffee and palm oil, illegal logging, wildlife exploitation, and urbanisation, among many others. There are also other forests around the world, not mentioned previously, that are quietly and slowly suffering serious deforestation. This is happening mainly because local farmers are clearing land for survival purposes in a slow but relentless manner, affecting their surroundings, while destroying their forests. Such is the case in East Africa where farmers carry out illegal logging to open up space for livestock and cash crops. They also overharvest to meet their needs for timber and fuel wood. This is happening in various eastern African countries, being the worst Somalia, Kenya, Tanzania, and Malawi.

One of the places on earth with the highest risk and strongest threat of deforestation is the island of Madagascar, where mainly Chinese corporations are now focusing their attention on Madagascar's natural resources and are committed to huge investments with the local government to exploit them. Some of the fauna and flora found in Madagascar is unique to the island, for example, many subspecies of lemurs, bats, and rodents that exist only on this African island. Madagascar's biodiversity is extensive, beautiful, and impressive but, sadly, at high risk of continued exploitation and imminent extermination.

Importance of water

Water is vital for human survival. Everyone in this world knows that. So why does the average person take water for granted and waste it as if there were unlimited supplies, when it is the most valuable natural resource of all, and above all, has limited supplies in most countries? Canadians have easy and inexpensive access to water in general, but that does not grant us the right to waste water when other countries have serious drought problems. In fact, even in Canada, we have water shortages in different areas during specific times of the year.

Water (H_2O) is two parts hydrogen and one part oxygen. It makes up more than two thirds of human weight. Without H_2O, we would die in just a few days. Many people do not realize that, if they feel tired or have a headache, it is most likely because they are dehydrated and just need a glass of water. We should not just drink when thirsty, but on a regular basis to keep the body hydrated. Yes, hydrate your body several times a day, though without falling into the exaggerated mode of some by walking around with a water bottle and sipping it all day long.

The human brain is 90 per cent water, and water constitutes about 80 per cent of your blood and about 65 to 70 per cent of our lean muscles. Water is essential for the absorption of nutrients, for the proper chemical reactions in our bodies, and, above all, for proper digestion. Water aids us as a lubricant as well and helps regulate our body temperature. All minerals, proteins, and carbohydrates are metabolized within our body and then transported through our bloodstream to our extremities thanks largely to water, in this way providing the required energy for our daily activities. Water is also our strong ally in getting rid of unwanted toxins for a healthier body.

Questions: Why does the average person waste water and take it for granted? If they do not consider water important and crucial to their survival, what do these people consider important? Should we assume that a careless attitude and overall ignorance are the answers?

This also reminds me of something David Suzuki once wrote and with which I agree totally: "If we humans are good at anything, it's thinking we've got a terrific idea and going for it without acknowledging the potential consequences or our own ignorance." The average person lacks information about the real value and scarcity of fresh water and its relationship with the delicate balance in this world. Not all the water available to us is as easily accessible as ground water or the water in lakes and rivers. In many countries, they need to drill thousands of metres to find reliable sources of water.

Wasting water is a serious problem in North America, where the average person uses water indiscriminately during their daily lives and where industrial, commercial, and farming activities use even more. From brushing our teeth while leaving the water running to manufacturing that glass of wine we enjoy so much (120 litres of water are required to produce one glass of wine). Seventy per cent of our water is used for industrial and commercial purposes, about 23 per cent is used in farming, and the remaining 8 per cent is residential use. The proportion – and the waste – is similar in many other countries around the world.

Contrary to what many believe, according to experts around the world, water is going to be the biggest and most expensive commodity in the future of mankind. So why do we waste this natural and limited resource, already known to many as "blue gold?"

There are some very interesting water facts and figures published by the International Fund for Agricultural Development (IFAD), which was established in 1977 as a specialized financial institution and agency of the United Nations to assist in funding specific projects for agricultural development, mainly in developing countries. They have always targeted food production projects for areas or countries in need. For full details and more water facts and figures, please visit their site at ifad.org/english/water/key.htm

Here are some of their figures:

1. Water pollution, environmental degradation and disasters:

   - Every day, two million tons of human waste are disposed of in water courses.
   - In developing countries, 70 percent of industrial wastes are dumped into water, where they even pollute the usable water supply.
   - Since 1900, we've lost half of the world's wetlands.
   - Between 1991 and 2000, over 665,000 people died in 2,557 natural disasters. 90 percent were water-related.

2. Water footprints:

   - 13 litres of water for a tomato.
   - 25 litres of water for a potato.
   - 35 litres of water for a cup of tea.
   - 70 litres of water for an apple.
   - 75 litres of water for a glass of beer.
   - 120 litres of water for a glass of wine.
   - 140 litres of water for a cup of coffee.
   - 170 litres of water for a glass of orange juice.
   - 184 litres of water for a bag of potato crisps.
   - 200 litres of water for a glass of milk.
   - 2,400 litres of water for a hamburger.
   - 16,000 litres of water for one kilogram of beef.

3. Drinking water and sanitation:

   - The UN suggests that we need 20-50 litres of safe fresh water a day for drinking, cooking, and cleaning.
   - Two in six people worldwide (894 million) don't have access to 20-50 litres of safe fresh water a day.

- The daily drinking water requirement per person is 1-2 litres, but it takes 2,000 to 5,000 litres of water to produce one person's daily food needs.
- 2.5 billion people, including almost one billion children, live without basic sanitation.
- Every 20 seconds, a child dies as a result of poor sanitation – 1.5 million preventable child deaths each year.
- Globally, diarrhea is the leading cause of illness and death, and 88 per cent of diarrheal deaths are due to lack of access to sanitation facilities, together with unsafe drinking water and inadequate availability of water for proper hygiene.

Importance of earth (soil)

Soil, also commonly referred to as dirt, is generally disregarded by the great majority of humans, who don't fully grasp that it is a finite resource as well and that it is as important to earth as the human stomach is to a person's life. Why? Because the soil actually recycles almost everything that goes into it due to the thousands of microscopic organisms living there. Soil consumes, digests, and recycles all nutrients and every microbial organism in it. Good, healthy soil contains minerals, gases, and liquids that help support life. While some people refer to dirt as "displaced soil" (i.e. not on the ground), we will use both terms as synonyms to make overall understanding easier and to avoid technicalities. According to the Soil Science Society of America, one gram of soil can contain one billion bacteria.

The majority of those bacteria are aerobic, meaning they need oxygen to survive and reproduce (contrary to anaerobic bacteria that can grow in the absence of oxygen) but excel under 10 per cent of carbon dioxide. Some sources refer to soil as anything located underfoot in the way of dirt, clay, rocks, or any other kind of ground material. Soil supports life as much as water, but from a different perspective. Without proper, nutritional soil, we would not have good, healthy forests, jungles, wetlands, savannahs, grasslands, and other areas.

Good quality soil is fundamental for proper water recycling, which enables animals and plants to grow and reproduce healthily anywhere on the planet. The quality of soil is an important part of the shaping of the geography in which it is located and ultimately forms part of. It shapes mountains, rivers, lakes, canyons, steppes, meadows, deserts, and other landforms.

Soil is an integral part of our daily lives in almost every aspect of human expansion and growth. We use it to plant, to build houses and dikes, and for innumerable medical and religious purposes. Soil has an enormous array of uses, but, unfortunately, most people do not know that good soil is very scarce on our planet. Some civilizations completely disappeared due mainly to their failure to protect the natural nutrients of their soil through their farming practices and techniques. One example is the Mayan civilization of Mexico and Central America.

Organics

Many people around the world are consuming more and more organic produce in search of tastier and more nutritious foods, but above all, healthier foods. The less pesticide we use, the better off people are when trying to achieve a better quality of life for themselves and for their children. Organic food on the family's table is of utmost importance for their future well-being.

There is a local magazine in Kelowna, BC, called All One Era, published by Stephen Cipes. In their October Moon 2015 issue, they celebrated the event called Okanagan Water

Forum held by the Okanagan Nation Alliance on October 14, 2015. David Suzuki participated in the event and, among his most important comments, was this:

> There is a suite of problems with young people – attention disorder, bullying, hyperactivity – that all comprise what is known as "nature deficit disorder." Take these kids out into nature, and all these issues disappear. We all need to get out and make contact with nature.

There is a website called - helpguide.org – that, in a down-to-earth manner, clearly describes the concept and benefits of organic products with six different and brief examples, which are:

- Organic products contain fewer or no pesticides.
- Organic food is often fresher and healthier.
- Organic farming has been proven to be better for the environment and even the local economy.
- Organically raised animals do not receive any type of antibiotics or growth hormones and are never fed animal by-products.
- Organic meat and milk are richer in several different nutrients.
- Organic products are free from any kind of GMO.

Personally, I would add a very important factor to the above list, and that is that organic products taste much better than non-organic ones. They are nurtured by Mother Nature, which provides more care and love to her products than anything created by humans.

Message from the Hopi Tribe

Nature consists of air, fire, water, soil, and every living creature (animal or plant), including humans, but excluding human creations. Nature is breathtaking 24/7. Nothing is as perfect and exquisitely balanced, but nature is fragile and needs taking care of on a daily and continuous basis. Indigenous people across North America used to admire, protect, and revere nature. Among the most celebrated indigenous civilizations was the Hopi of northeastern Arizona, with their unique Uto-Aztecan language. When the Spaniards arrived on the American continent, they referred to the Hopi as the "Pueblo People." They were good farmers and lived in peace, believing that "Earth needs man's respect to survive in harmony and be plentiful."

Their ancient stories, teachings, art, and music were geared to connect with and embrace their environment in harmony with their own lifestyle. They understood that a strong and stable environment promoted respect, self-esteem, peace, and cooperation among the people of their tribe, as well as with other tribes. There is website that shares part of the Hopi Tribe's philosophy (quoteinvestigator.com/2011/10/20/last-tree-cut/), which shares a thought worth quoting:

> Present needs and present gains were the rule of action. It seems to be a sort of transmitted "quality" which we in our now enlightened time have not wholly outgrown, for even now a few men can be found who seem willing to destroy the last tree, the last fish and the last game bird and animal, and leave nothing for posterity, if thereby some money can be made.

The Hopi (Pueblo People) are known for a short but powerful prophecy that says:

> When all the trees have been cut down,
> When all the animals have been hunted,
> When all the waters are polluted,
> When all the air is unsafe to breath,

Only then will you know….
You cannot eat money.

Greenpeace's version of a similar Cree prophecy is as follows: "Greenpeace believes that after the last tree is cut, the last river poisoned and the last fish dead, you will find you can't eat your money. In that interest, we strive to bring public and legal pressure against those who pollute the environment, deplete our resources and threaten rare species for private profit."

The Hopi prophecy made me remember a wise sentence that David Suzuki once wrote in his book entitled "From Naked Ape To Super-Species: Humanity and the Global Eco-Crisis." He said: "A balance between sustainable ecology and sustainable human life, on the one hand, and the unfettered drive for profit, on the other, is just an oxymoron."

World population: A frightening forecast

I have always been a firm believer that technology will outpace the Malthusian theory of geometrical population growth vs arithmetical food production growth. With each technological advance in agriculture, humans have been proving Malthus wrong. But for how long? Some people believe that, regardless of how much the population grows, humans will always be able to produce enough food, water, and energy through the discovery and implementation of new technologies.

The January, 2011 issue of National Geographic published an article by Robert Kunzig (who works for Discover Magazine and often contributes articles to National Geographic as a senior editor on the environment) entitled "Population – Seven Billion." He includes an alarming graphic (p. 35) that shows that, according to the US Population Reference Bureau, the world's population had reached 7 billion people by 2011 and was forecast to reach 9 billion by 2045 (a 28.6 per cent increase in 34 years). If we do a simple calculation by applying the rule of three, we can extrapolate the corresponding percentage growth for the year 2100. Using year 2011 as a baseline, this would mean that, within the next 89 years, the population will increase by 74.8 per cent, and the total global population will reach a staggering 12.24 billion people.

Kunzig questions whether the planet can "take the strain" of supporting nine billion people by 2045. Birth rates have been falling in developed countries, while continuing to grow in most developing countries that are trying to propel themselves out of poverty. But will the globe's natural resources support that growth and beyond? Kunzig says that the population is growing by about 80 million people per year, while "water tables are falling, soil is eroding, glaciers are melting, and fish stocks are vanishing."

One important factor that is boosting human population growth is modern medicine. According to Kunzig, "the development of medical science was the straw that broke the camel's back." In industrialized countries, life expectancy jumped from 35 to 77 years and, even factoring in declines in child mortality, the aging population is living longer. This is putting a serious strain on the economy and is the main reason immigrants play such an important role in modern industrialized societies all around the world.

Kunzig quotes Paul Ehrlich (Noble Prize in Science winner in 1980) as follows:

> I have understood the population explosion intellectually for a long time. I came to understand it emotionally one stinking hot night in Delhi a couple of years ago…The temperature was well over 100, and the air was a haze of dust and smoke. The streets

seemed alive with people. People eating, people washing, people sleeping, people visiting, arguing, and screaming. People thrusting their hands through the taxi window, begging. People defecating and urinating. People clinging to buses. People herding animals. People, people, people, people.

George Pydias Mitchell once said, "If we can't solve the problem for seven billion people, how will we do so for nine billion people?" Mitchell was born in Galveston, Texas, of Greek immigrant parents. He was an expert geologist who was fascinated with the idea of freeing and trapping natural gas from shale. Even though he was not the first in the fracking industry, he was the strongest pioneer and considered by many the father of modern hydraulic commercial fracking. Though environmentally controversial now, it was a highly-regarded innovation of his time. He was a visionary who understood the laws of physics and geology and the limitations of our natural resources. One of his main concerns was how the world could actually support the accelerating human demographic explosion.

Producing enough food for the growing population is definitely possible with new farming technologies, but doing this without depleting natural resources such as soil and water is going to be an enormous hurdle for humanity to overcome. Regardless of how sophisticated some technological advances are, if we consider all the fresh water on the planet, plus all the limited good soil essential for proper agriculture, plus all the food production, plus all the energy consumption, the day will come when it will not be sufficient to support all human life on this planet, at least if we keep reproducing at current rates and continue doing so until the year 2100 or beyond. Also, important to consider is the amount of CO_2 that will be generated by a growing population along with the waste that will end up in landfills all over the world.

The constant struggle by humans for more energy and new sources of energy is also a vital aspect of the survival of our species. With sufficient energy, we can cope with population growth a lot more easily, meet our fresh water needs, rejuvenate our soil, and achieve adequate food production levels.

The Economist published an article on demographics entitled "Baby Love" in their July 25-31, 2015, edition. They confirm that some developing countries such as Nigeria, Indonesia, Bangladesh, and Uganda have excessively high birth rates, while other countries have the opposite. The common denominator seems to be women's level of education. There is a direct correlation between the education level of women and their desire to have fewer children. The more educated women are, the fewer children they want to have, and the less prone they are to early marriage.

South Korea, Italy, Hong Kong, Japan, Germany, Switzerland, Belgium, and so on are good examples of countries that demonstrate these direct correlations. Their fertility rates are between 1.2 and 1.4, which means that with each generation their population will fall by roughly half incrementally, unless replaced by immigration. Countries that are predominantly Muslim (and a few that are predominantly Catholic) are the most fertile and are the sources of most immigrants to European countries and many other parts of the world, including North America.

The key element to increase the rate of fertility in developed countries is for governments to offer better social housing programmes, tax benefits for families with children, and cheaper day-care facilities so that parents can leave their children while at work without draining their bank accounts. These countries need a younger population base to increase productivity and sustain their retirement pension plans.

To some critics, it is a contradiction for developed countries to try to increase their birth rates while supporting women's education and professional advancement. However, women have the same right to education as men, the same right to choose where and when to work, whether to marry or not, whom to marry, and, ultimately, an absolute right to choose whether they want to have children or not. The latter includes their absolute right to have an abortion. It is their body, nobody else's! Women should have the absolute right to do whatever they want whenever with their own bodies. A large majority of the population believes it is nobody else's business, and especially not the business of religious or fanatic anti-abortion groups.

In developing countries, the overprotection of women, along with efforts by men to keep their women at home, ignorant and completely outside any professional circles in their society, is keeping the fertility rate high. It is an axiom that the overprotection of women works to their detriment by keeping them uneducated and, even worse, keeps them benighted, without being able to learn and develop themselves to their full capacity.

Meanwhile, governments in developed countries are very worried about the dropping birth rate. The Economist article referred to above (entitled "Baby Love") states that many environmentalists are against population growth rates over 2.4, which seems to be the magic number to keep the population of a country stable. They insist that fewer people are definitely better for the planet and its limited natural resources. The opposition agrees to some degree, but they also insist that people matter too and that we all have the right to procreate as we please, to my mind a very obtuse and limited perspective. They also argue that a sudden population crunch would have negative and painful repercussions, such as happened in Greece (according to The Economist article), where the fertility rate has fallen to under 1.3, and the resulting "shortage" of younger people has had a detrimental impact on pension funds for retirees.

The most dangerous invasive species of all time

There is a very interesting article published by Scientific American in their August, 2015 issue, entitled "The Most Invasive Species of All." Author Curtis W. Marean describes how several human species coexisted on our planet without colonizing other species until one decided to do it, and then colonized the entire world. How did they do this, and why were they so successful? Marean outlines the following steps:

- Homo sapiens originated in Africa about 200,000 years ago.

- About 160,000 years ago, Homo sapiens learned how to take advantage of all the rich coastal resources, after which they intensified their territorial confrontations. They then went to what Marean calls "selection for a hyper-pro-social behaviour," and, finally, they started creating intergroups (different groups interacting with each other) and intragroups (a group with various members and specific cooperative behaviours).

- Around 71,000 years ago, Homo sapiens started to move beyond the African continent, invading Europe (45,000 years ago), the Middle East and Asia (about 55,000 years ago), and North and South America via the Bering Straits (about 14,000 and 13,500 years ago respectively). According to Marean, "Homo sapiens did not merely follow in the footsteps of its predecessors. It blazed trails into entirely new lands – and transformed the ecosystems wherever they went."

The main reasons (according to Marean) that Homo sapiens decided to cross continents, venture into new lands, and conquer their rivals were:

- A desire to expand partly for the sake of survival and partly just to expand their territory and explore further lands beyond their initial reach. "Wherever Homo sapiens established itself, they left behind burned ecosystems, exterminated species, and environments reshaped to our predecessor's purpose," Marean observes.

- They became, with time, "team players," which gave them strength in numbers and within groups properly organized with common goals. They developed unrivalled collaborations and became fearless opponents of other tribes.

- They developed a magnificent "weapon of war" for the time. They promoted the ability and skill to group together totally unrelated individuals but with similar goals and under a rudimentary organizational structure that actually worked. Together they developed what Marean calls "projectile weaponry," which gave them a clear competitive advantage over other species and tribes. With every tribe they conquered, they got new ideas and developed spears, arrows, and darts with very finely sharpened stones that would bleed their enemies more and faster than the sharpened wooden branch tips they had used previously. According to Marean, "they used tiny stone blades, or microliths, attached to wood shafts to form an arrow or dart," which were definitely more lethal than plain sharpened wooden spears, arrows, or darts.

The last element that gave the invaders the advantage was what Marean calls "the force of nature." To best explain this, I want to quote a very descriptive, well-written paragraph in the article by Marean as follows:

> With the joining of projectile weapons to hyper social behaviour, a spectacular new kind of creature was born in Africa about 71,000 years ago. One whose members formed teams that each operated as a single, indomitable predator. No prey – or human foe – was safe. Availed of this potent combination of traits, six men speaking six languages can put back to oar and pull in unison, riding 10 metre swells so that the harpooner can rise to the prow at the headsman's order and fling lethal iron into the heaving body of a leviathan, an animal that should see humans as nothing more than minnows. In the same way, a tribe of 500 people dispersed in 20 network bands can field a small army to exact retribution on a neighbouring tribe for a territorial incursion.

That is how the new invaders – the first modern humans – invaded and drove the Neanderthals to extinction. The Neanderthals did not stand a chance against the newcomers' organizational skills and weaponry. The newcomers killed all the Neanderthal men and children but kept the women for procreation. Humans have been savages since we first started walking and thinking. The previous illustration briefly indicates that, throughout human history, it has been humankind's nature to invade every corner of our planet and leave destruction and desolation in our path. Nowadays we are more civilised, or should I say more "diplomatic" or more "politically correct," but our inner instinct and nature are to acquire more and to invade other countries in the name of protection, peace, and progress. In reality, we have not changed. By far the worst invasive species is the human being! It is in our nature, imbedded in our spirit and soul.

That is who we are, whether we like it or not. We may do things in a more sophisticated way nowadays, but, ultimately, we still tend to destroy everything in our path, regardless of the methods and techniques at our disposal. I do not mean that we create total alienation and destruction, only that we use technology to manipulate nature to our advantage through GMOs, oil, plastics, and so much more.

We humans also have the strongest instinct for survival, and we have proven this throughout history. It is the reason why, in the twenty-first century, we are even looking for life beyond our stars while venturing more and more into space in the hope of one day colonizing other planets that can sustain human life. I am personally convinced that there is still a thread of hope, because we all seem to want to survive in peace. But to succeed, we ought to adapt our technological advances in favour of healthy, equitable and controlled survival in parallel with our need for water, energy, good soil, food, and any other natural resource available. How are we going to do that?

Protection of natural resources

Some natural resources are limited and, therefore, not renewable. Even renewables represent a real challenge to maintain healthy levels, and some are sliding through our fingers' grasp. And if this is happening today, imagine 50 or 100 years from now. Many species have already been extinguished by human greed and barbarism. Others are on the brink of extinction, and many more will follow, because we humans fail to synchronize our worldwide efforts to reduce waste and stop the indiscriminate use of our natural resources. Everything, absolutely everything, has its limits, and everything comes to an end sooner or later. Let me provide you with one small example of what happened in India not too long ago.

According to an article by Michael Webber in Scientific American (February, 2015), India's regional electric grids failed in July 2012. Webber (director of the Energy Institute at the University of Texas in Austin) reported that more than 620 million people were without electric power. This was due to a major drought at the time in India, which had forced farmers to draw more electricity for their electric pumps in order to get more water from deeper aquifers. The hydroelectric dams also had lower levels of water, which contributed to the overall power failure and left the equivalent of nine per cent of the world's population in absolute darkness. It is not surprising that, with the world population we currently have and its continually increasing demands, our systems often fail to provide the essentials when pushed to their limits.

For how long can our natural resources and technological advances support us? California and many places in Australia and Africa have exactly the same problems: droughts, population growth, and depleted natural resources. With all its desalination plants, even the Red Sea is being depleted by the surrounding countries that desperately need water for agriculture. All around the world, countries are trying to supply more energy, food, and water to growing populations, but they are doing it independently, states Webber. They are not coordinating their goals and strategies, as they should be.

Webber does raise a note of hope:

> Reducing waste food can conserve energy and water. Indoor farms can use city water to grow crops and power the buildings in which they are housed. Algae production next to power plants can turn wastewater and carbon emissions into food or biofuel. Wind turbines in the desert can convert brackish water into fresh water. A smart grid for water delivery can save water energy. Energy, water, and food planners and policy makers have to stop working in isolation and

devise integrated policies and infrastructure solutions.

However, he then adds:

> We do not live in a world of unlimited resources, of course. We live in a world of constraints. The likelihood that these constraints will lead to cascading failures grows as pressure rises from population growth, longer lifespans, and increasing consumption.

Webber also gives an example that almost everybody in North America already is aware of – the problems that Lake Mead outside Las Vegas is suffering due to the continued depletion of their water reservoirs from the Colorado River. It is so bad that, according to Webber, some scientists at the Scripps Institution of Oceanography in La Jolla, California, predict that Lake Mead will simply run dry by 2021.

Webber observes that The World Bank and The World Business Council for Sustainable Development agree that, in our world's complex system, we need policies that are linked together to solve our problems in coordination and harmony with our systems as a whole. Webber provides several ideas that, if synchronized around the globe, will greatly assist in the maintenance and management of our delicate environment and its limited resources. Here are seven ideas humans should implement to slow down, and in some cases, stop the depletion of our natural resources include:

1. Boosting food production with less use of soil and water. "Vertical farming" is being practiced around the globe by a select group of people. Vertical farming, also known by some as urban agriculture, is being implemented in greenhouses, skyscrapers, or any other indoor facility where clean, efficient agriculture can be practiced. Good vertical farming can grow produce in half the time, with less water, no soil, and no direct sunlight. It uses very little

fertilizer and no herbicides or pesticides. Vertical farming is capital-intensive, high-tech, and typically produces only for the local market. These farms grow crops in stacks using artificial light, hydroponic cases, and a temperature-controlled climate. This type of agriculture has another competitive edge over regular agriculture; it is not subject to seasons. It is an indoor activity, so weather conditions do not affect production. With all this in mind, we can now see how positive and important this new form of agriculture is for the conservation of our environment and the enhancement of food production.

2. Webber also proposes better management of wastewater. He gives the example of New York City, which produces a billion gallons per day of wastewater. Instead of cleaning the wastewater before it is dumped into the Hudson River or re-used for other purposes, why not utilize part of it to irrigate the vertical farms, he asks. Cleaning wastewater will save money and energy, which will definitely have a positive impact on the city's finances. Solids recovered from liquid waste are usually just burned but, Webber asks, why not use the process to produce more electricity?

   The first example mentioned above could also help reduce farmers' demand for water outside the city, while the second example would assist the city in getting more electricity at a cheaper cost and simultaneously reducing its overall energy demand. This will also help reduce the costs of transporting produce into the Big Apple. We would not only save energy but also reduce carbon dioxide emissions, a win-win scenario for all concerned.

3. Nowadays a big trend in many countries around the world is the farming of algae (known as Algaculture). Algae have amazing nutritional attributes as well as commercial and industrial uses as a source of energy in the form of biofuel. According to Webber, many companies, during their start-

up stage, are now using wastewater and CO_2 directly from power plants to grow algae: "The algae eat the gas and water, and workers harvest the plants for animal feed and biofuel, all the while improving the environment by removing compounds from water and CO_2 from the atmosphere." As food, algae is an excellent source of omega-3 fatty acids. Commercially, it has many uses in pharmaceutical products, fertilizers, feedstock and colorants. One of the most important uses of algae from the industrial point of view is the production of bioplastics, which have a very positive impact on our environment due to their biodegradable capabilities compared to plastics originating from fossil fuel (petroleum).

4. A very important contribution in Webber's article is the idea of "smart conservation." As he points out, we humans use more water through our electrical outlets and light switches than from our garden hoses, faucets, and showers. Why? He states that billions of gallons are used to cool down power plants on a daily basis all around the world. We also use more energy to start, heat, and run the pumps and other equipment that many cities use for lighting.

Webber's final and very valuable message about smart conservation is this: "Turning off the lights and appliances saves vast amounts of water, and turning off the water saves large amounts of energy." This is very down-to-earth advice that everybody can implement at home, at work, and at school, and thereby contribute to a cleaner environment. How difficult it is to train ourselves and our children to always turn off the lights behind us?

To complement the above, it is worth listing "humanity's top ten problems for the next 50 years" according to Nobel Laureate Richard E. Smalley of the Institute for Nanoscale Science and Technology. In order of importance these are: energy, water, food, environment, poverty, terrorism and war, disease, education, democracy and population growth. For more information on how Smalley came up with this list, please refer to the following link: cnst.rice.edu/content.aspx?id=246

5. Webber mentions the potential of brackish water, wind power, and solar energy for many human requirements in residential, commercial, and industrial contexts. Brackish water, a mix of fresh and salt water, is not as salty as seawater, so it is more energy-efficient to use in many instances. It is plentiful around the world and is commonly found in mangrove swamps, estuaries (where rivers meet the ocean), and even in the Black and Red Seas. It is better to use brackish water for desalination plants than ocean water. Wind power and solar energy are wonderful sources of renewal energy.

6. Large energy companies are using hydraulic fracturing (fracking) in the gas and oil industries. Unfortunately, there is a big problem with fracking, since it releases methane gas, which rises to the surface and from there to our atmosphere. It also contaminates nearby water sources, causing lots of health problems for locals. A lot of this methane gas coming out of the man-made wells is burned instead of being capitalised on for its potential uses. According to Webber, "smart operators can use methane to power distillers or other heat-based machines to clean the water, making it re-usable on site, which spares fresh water while avoiding the wasted energy and emission of a flare."

Webber here presents a very strong point, because fracking is an extremely lucrative part of the oil industry. All oil companies should build up the proper infrastructure to trap and pipe methane gas, which they can later sell as another source of immediate energy.

7. The last two suggestions from Webber's article are related to high-tech, efficient sensors that can be installed in gas and water meters (currently done in some developed countries) and on food packages to determine the expiry date before the food goes bad and starts decomposing.

Conclusion

Without a doubt, population growth will continue. But since growth is uneven among countries, it is important for developed countries with lower birth rates to increase their immigration using reliable and efficient, custom-made, selective immigration strategies. Our planet is still capable of sustaining and supporting a larger human population, but how much more and for how much longer? We are pushing it to the brink, which is the reason why countries need to harmonise their development strategies and work together so that technological advances are applied efficiently to their industries. Government policies need to go hand-in-hand with technological advances in every commercial or industrial application, residential included. New policies and regulations for control of new technological breakthroughs are required. Without these measures, population growth will overpower the capacity of governments to provide for their people.

CHAPTER FIVE: CLIMATE CHANGE AND GLOBAL WARMING

Global warming is a hotly debated subject nowadays throughout the world. There is no doubt that it is indeed taking place; the question is whether we humans are causing it to go over the tipping point, that is, beyond the point of no return. Most scientists are convinced that global warming is happening mainly due to human activities that are negatively impacting our atmospheric composition above and beyond the natural balance of our planet, but there are always sceptics who argue otherwise and blindly deny that humans are the ultimate cause. Some even go to the extreme of denying global warming altogether, considering it as part of earth's natural cycle and normal behaviour. Assuming this last statement is true, isn't it our responsibility as humans to try to stop the accelerated process of global warming anyway?

There is scientific evidence that the ice sheet in the Arctic Ocean is disappearing much faster than expected and that ice fields that were once attached to land in the Antarctic regions are detaching and floating into the Antarctic Ocean. Originally, it was thought by scientists that by keeping our planet's warming process under two degrees Celsius would prevent serious ocean level rises, strong droughts, massive wild fires, and much more. Before the Industrial Revolution, there were roughly 280 parts per million (ppm) of carbon dioxide in our atmosphere. According to many scientists, carbon dioxide needs to be kept under 450 ppm to avoid apocalyptic levels of climate change. As of October, 2014, we were pushing 395.95 ppm. In the same month of 2015, we reached 398.29 ppm. Scientific America then confirmed that in April of 2017 we surpassed 410 ppm. This showed a rapid growth of 1.3 per cent over a twelve-month period, that is, 11.7 ppm more in two years. If we project the same growth rate for the next 22 years, we will reach the tipping point of 450 ppm by 2037.

Permafrost, methane gas, and CO_2

Evidence has proved that the permafrost belt around the world is releasing large amounts of methane gas into the air along with more CO_2. Global warming is not just melting the polar regions (and beyond) but accelerating the methane gas release process in areas such as Siberia and the Antarctic and Arctic hemispheres. Permafrost is a zone on earth with thick layers of ice that do not melt year-round and that have been frozen for millennia. Permafrost currently accounts for 20 per cent of land in the northern region and for 22 per cent of fresh water supplies worldwide. The permafrost's upper layer (known as active permafrost) thaws in summer and freezes in winter. Unfortunately, the permafrost's original natural balance has been seriously challenged in recent decades by the continued increase of carbon dioxide in our atmosphere, now mainly emitted by human activity.

It has been scientifically proven that global warming is causing the active permafrost layer to melt sooner and for longer periods of time, releasing even more quantities of methane gas. Soil, rocks, water, and sediments (organic material) make up the permafrost. When the average annual global temperature is less than the freezing point of water, permafrost thrives. But if the temperature rises, it allows the organic materials to thaw, grow, die, and decompose, which immediately releases methane gas into the atmosphere. Methane gas is a member of the alkane series of hydrocarbons and is among the most harmful greenhouse gases that can be released into the atmosphere.

Added to the above issues, more and more extreme weather phenomena have been taking place in the last decade. The hotter the weather, the more the sea ice melts, allowing the sun to melt even more. This happens in the permafrost regions as well. These permafrost zones allow more CO_2 and methane gas to be released into the air, which accelerates the permafrost melting process. It is a vicious cycle that is hurting the earth and causing stronger and more erratic weather conditions, endangering life in many places. These conditions include floods, killer mudslides (i.e.: California – Jan 13 of 2018), hurricanes, tornadoes, volcanic activities, droughts, torrential rains, dangerous wild fires, and rising ocean levels.

John Carey wrote an article for the November 2012 issue of Scientific American in which he notes that "the feedback scientists fear most is loss of ice, uncovering darker land and seas that absorb solar heat, melting even more ice, amplifying global warming." Carey highlights research from glaciologist W. Tad Pfeffer of the University of Colorado at Boulder that concludes that the maximum conceivable ocean rise for this century is less than two metres, not five as predicted earlier by other scientists. The Business Insider (Science Section) published an article April 22, 2014, "Rising Sea Levels Could Cause Staggering Damage To These Cities," by Gus Lubin and Mike Nudelman, in which they give as an example the city of Kolkata, India, where, with just a 0.5 metre rise in sea level, more than 14 million people would be in duress and $0.2 trillion in assets put at risk. Pfeffer urges countries to take action and implement new policies to control greenhouse gas emissions, because even small changes are a serious menace to the stability of many cities around the world. He observes that we have had a "remarkably stable climate … [but] that these creeping disasters [ocean level rising] could really wipe us out."

In his article, Carey mentions that glaciologist Sarah Das of the Wood Hole Oceanographic Institution has seen impressive cracks on the ice floor that have drained and swallowed lakes of glacial melted waters. The ice floor, according to Das, is about 3,000 feet thick (900 metres). When the ice floor cracked open, the currents into which the melted waters were drained and sucked were so powerful that the ice cap was lifted from the solid bedrock and pushed at a very fast speed into the ocean. The acceleration, according to Das, was from one metre per day to as much as 18 metres per day on average. Carey also cites Pfeffer's research showing how those once-thick layers of ice are being seriously compromised due to the reinforced impacts of an ever more acute global warming process.

Ocean level rise and its cost impact

If Pfeffer is correct in his forecasts regarding the ocean level rise, can we even fathom the perilous position of cities that are currently just a foot or two above sea level? Cities like New York, Sydney, Vancouver, Fort Lauderdale, Mumbai, Tokyo, Hong Kong, Miami, and many more that are currently just a few feet above sea level, will require enormous investments to protect their assets and people.

That is the reason many cities around the world are building sophisticated and highly engineered dikes to protect them from rising sea level. There is a very interesting article by Evan Lehmann regarding this matter in Climate Wire from Scientific American (February 4, 2014) entitled "Sea Walls May Be Cheaper Than Rising Waters." Lehmann suggests that research shows it would be less of a financial burden to build dikes and walls sooner rather than later in order to protect cities in imminent danger from sea level rise. Lehmann writes:

> The encroaching seawater threatens to flood hundreds of millions of people every year by 2100 as homes that are already below flood heights, or will be, succumb to climbing oceans. If governments fail to take any action, the annual cost of damage stands to reach hundreds of billions of dollars, at best, and as high as $100 trillion under grimmer scenarios, according to the paper "Coastal flood damage and adaptation costs under twenty-first century sea-level rise" published in the

Proceedings of the National Academy of Sciences (Jochen Hinkela et. al.).

For more details about this paper, please refer to: http://www.pnas.org/content/111/9/3292.abstract

Hinkela predicts that 5 per cent of the global population will suffer yearly floods, which will impact the global economy by 10 per cent. Even though the cost of building dikes is high, they will be less costly than doing nothing. Therefore, they are a must, but poor countries are really going to need strong financial support to save their cities in this way, although building dikes will still cost less than the alternative of being under water. Lehmann predicts, using mathematical formulas and correlation analysis, that the worldwide cost of dealing with rising sea levels could reach close to $100 trillion dollars with defenceless and unguarded cities, but, with investment in dikes, can be held to about $80 billion.

The high cost of protecting coastal cities has been tested and proven with the $14 billion dollars that the US government incurred to rebuild and protect New Orleans after Hurricane Katrina in 2005, according to Lehmann. As coastlines shrink, we are going to have more and more people living on or near them. Lehmann therefore argues that we have to be realistic and expect a high financial burden on all taxpayers in order to protect the coastal cities in developed countries that can afford to do so, some of which already have plans to implement measures all the way up to year 2100. Developing countries will have to go hugely into debt, or many of their cities will end up under water.

Main sources of carbon dioxide (CO_2)

There are both human and natural sources for the CO_2 being released into our atmosphere. The main causes in each of these two categories are:

- Human: The use of fossil fuels (generally in the form of gas, oil, and coal), antiquated industrial processes, deforestation, and animal agriculture.

- Natural: The ocean's constant release of CO_2, volcanic activities, forests, weathering of carbon rocks (thermal decomposition of limestone), decomposition, respiration, and even changes in solar radiation.

There is proof that the more meat we eat, especially beef, the more damage we do to our environment. I know some people will say, "I will never stop eating my steak," but it would be hugely beneficial and intelligent for humans to at least reduce their consumption of beef. The billions of tons of grain fed to cattle worldwide are not just seen by many as detrimental to our environment but also inhumane, when every day in many countries people are dying of hunger and malnutrition.

There is a very interesting and well-made documentary called Cowspiracy (see: cowspiracy.com) produced and directed by Kip Andersen and Keegan Kuhn. A new cut from executive producer Leonardo DiCaprio is streaming exclusively on Netflix (netflix.com/ca/title/80033772). The film helps people open their eyes, minds, and understandings regarding the detrimental environmental impact of animal agriculture. The average person only sees a steak on a plate, but never stops to think about the real short-term and long-term costs of that steak that is about to be devoured and enjoyed. I am not suggesting going vegan, but we have to understand that everything in excess is detrimental not just to our health but to our society.

If we reduced our consumption of beef even by half, we would be doing a great favour to our world. We do not need to completely eliminate beef, but a partial switch from beef to vegetables and grains would have a major impact on the reduction of CO_2 in our atmosphere. Some of the main points and facts in the Cowspiracy documentary are quoted below:

- "Animal agriculture is responsible for 18 per cent of greenhouse gas emissions, more than the combined exhaust from all transportation."

- "Transportation exhaust is responsible for 13 per cent of all greenhouse gas emissions."

- "Livestock and their by-products account for at least 32,000 million tons of carbon dioxide per year, or 51 per cent of all worldwide greenhouse gas emissions."

- "Methane is 25-100 times more destructive than CO_2 on a 20-year time frame."

- "Methane has a global warming potential 86 times that of CO_2 on a 20-year time frame."

- "Livestock is responsible for 65 per cent of all human-related emissions of nitrous oxide – a greenhouse gas with 296 times the global warming potential of carbon dioxide and which stays in the atmosphere for 150 years."

- "Emissions from agriculture are projected to increase 80 per cent by 2050."

- "Energy-related emissions are expected to increase 20 per cent by 2040."

- "US methane emissions from livestock and natural gas are nearly equal."

- "Cows produce 150 billion gallons of methane per day."

- "Converting to wind and solar power will take 20+ years and [cost] roughly 43 trillion dollars."

- "Even without fossil fuels, we will exceed our 565 gigatonne CO_2 limit by 2030, all from raising animals."

- "Agriculture is responsible for 80-90 per cent of US water consumption."

- "2,500 gallons of water are needed to produce one pound of beef."

- "1,000 gallons of water are required to produce one gallon of milk."

- "Only 5 per cent of water consumed in the US is by private homes; 55 per cent of water consumed in the US is by animal agriculture."

- "Animal agriculture is responsible for 20-33 per cent of all fresh water consumption in the world today."

- "Livestock covers 45 per cent of the earth's total land."

- "Animal agriculture is the leading cause of species extinction, ocean dead zones, water pollution, and habitat destruction."

Carbon dioxide (CO_2) vs. chlorofluorocarbon (CFC)

CFC, short for chlorofluorocarbon, is an organic compound made out of chlorine, fluorine, and carbon. Its production is based on methane and ethane, which have a direct, detrimental impact on our ozone layer when released into the atmosphere.

On May 30, 2013, The Waterloo News from the University of Waterloo published an article entitled "Global warming caused by CFCs, not by carbon dioxide, study says." The article was based on a study by Qing-Bin Lu (a professor of physics and astronomy, biology and chemistry in Waterloo's Faculty of Science), which was published in the International Journal of Modern Physics. The study concluded that, since the early 1970s, CFCs have been the main culprit in planetary warming, not CO_2. CFCs have been proven to contribute to the depletion of the ozone layer of our planet and are also considered to be the key element in global climate change.

Professor Lu writes:

> Conventional thinking says that the emission of human-made non-CFC gases such as carbon dioxide has mainly contributed to global warming. But we have observed data going back to the Industrial Revolution that convincingly shows that conventional understanding is wrong. In fact, the data shows that CFCs, conspiring with cosmic rays, [have] caused both the polar ozone hole and global warming.

The main sources of CFCs are the combustion of fossil fuels (man-made), the combustion of wood (man-made), hydrogen production (man-made), the fermentation of sugar in the brewing of alcoholic beverages, and the production of aerosols and Freon gas used in refrigeration equipment all around the world.

Some scientists believe that it is also produced naturally, though in smaller amounts than man-made, through the thermal decomposition of limestone and from natural CO_2 springs. CFCs break down the ozone gases in the ozone layer and cause the depletion of the ozone, which is a thick layer in the stratosphere meant to protect earth from our sun's harmful radiation.

Professor Lu concludes:

> My calculations of CFC greenhouse effect show that there was global warming by about 0.6 °C from 1950 to 2002, but the earth has actually cooled since 2002. The cooling trend is set to continue for the next 50-70 years as the amount of CFCs in the atmosphere continues to decline. The climate in the Antarctic stratosphere has been completely controlled by CFCs and cosmic rays, with no CO_2 impact. The change in global surface temperature after the removal of the solar effect has shown zero correlation with CO_2 but a nearly perfect linear correlation with CFCs – a correlation coefficient as high as 0.97.

Ultimately, it does not matter, at least to my mind, whether it is CO_2 or CFCs that are causing the continued relentless warming of our planet. Why? Because a normal intelligent human being understands that both are detrimental to our environment and that both affect (to a greater or lesser degree) our atmosphere and contribute to global warming. This is the reason why common sense, logic, and ten grams of human wisdom, together with another ten grams of moral and ethical responsibility, clearly indicate that we have to stop being selfish and irresponsible about global warming.

We definitely need to start actively participating in global efforts to reduce the use of anything that causes the release into our atmosphere of CFCs and CO_2 for the benefit of the clean air we breathe. By doing so, we will start diminishing and hopefully slowing the speed with which the planet is warming up. But if you do not believe any scientific theory, any government's opinion, any university professor's research, or simply do not care about our environment, then the following will happen if we all adopt that passive and careless attitude of some narrow minded and presumptuous individuals:

Nisbet's own 'nightmare scenario' starts with a blip in methane emissions and a very warm summer that leads to massive fires, pouring carbon into the atmosphere. The smoke and smog blanket Central Asia and weaken the monsoons, causing widespread crop failures in China and India. Meanwhile, a large El Niño pattern of unusual warm water in the tropical Pacific brings drought to the Amazon and Indonesia. The tropical forests and peat-lands also catch fire, injecting even more CO_2 into the atmosphere and putting the climate on the fast track to rapid warming. 'It's a possible scenario,' Nizbet observes. 'We may be more fragile than we think we are.' (Source: Carey Euan Nisbet, Professor of Earth Science at the Royal Holloway, University of London, as quoted by John Carey in the previously acknowledged article).

The following is an interesting, though hard-to-believe, statistic. The Daily Courier in the city of Kelowna, BC, published an article by "BrainTrust Canada" (see: braintrustcanada.com) on December 7, 2015, entitled "Stop being stupid and wear a helmet." It stated that 87 per cent of snowboarding and skiing deaths are due to traumatic brain injury caused by recklessness in the sport. Yet BrainTrust Canada confirms that 80 per cent of those brain injuries could have been prevented simply by wearing a protective helmet. Amazing but true.

Sometimes I feel incredulous when I read statistics like that while I am trying hard to make a point in favour of our environment by writing and publishing this book. How can I expect average citizens to practice due diligence in protecting the air we all breathe and the environment where we all live if they cannot even protect their own head and brains?

A similar thing happens with those cyclists who do not wear helmets and who seem to believe they are exempt from any accident, until one day they land and kiss the floor. Some are simply ignorant, dumb, or lazy, while others do it for religious reasons, such as Sikhs who stubbornly do not want to wear custom-made helmets and are allowed to do so by a weak and deficient legal system. Ultimately, if the law allows them to ride without helmets, then let it be; it is their own heads and brains that are at risk. This reminds me of a short poem I once read, which goes as follows: "Men go abroad to wonder at the height of the mountains, at the huge waves of the sea, at the long courses of the rivers, at the vast compasses of the oceans, at the circular motion of the stars, and they pass by themselves without wondering" (Augustine of Hippo).

Government actions vs. national safety

Governments often make decisions dictated by private interests, social pressures, "political correctness," self-interest, or plain ignorance. It is only once in a while that they make decisions exclusively focused on the benefit and well-being of their people and their country. A good example is a project called - Site C Dam. In 2014, the B.C. government approved the construction of the dam with an initial budget of $8.3 billion. But as of Feb, of 2018, there is a confirmed budget of $10.7 billion. A "slight" increase of $2.4 billion in just three years. How much will it really end up costing by the time they are done (somewhere in 2024)? This project will flood about 83 kilometres of the Peace River valley. The goal is to generate enough electricity to power 450,000 homes, but with costly environmental and economic sacrifices. In my view, this decision, strongly puts the brakes on research and development for alternative renewable energy sources so badly needed for our future, such as:

- *Geothermal heat*: Earth's internal heat can be captured and turned into electric power production. It can be used to heat or cool building structures of any kind and is already in wide use in some parts of the world.

- *Solar power*: This is the most renewable of all energy sources. It comes directly from sunlight and can be used for many different applications.

- *Ocean energy*: This comes from tidal and wave energy that can be captured and converted into electricity.

- *Wind power*: Wind produces energy that is captured by wind turbines. It has been very successful in many European countries.

- *Bioenergy*: This is produced from the organic matter that comes from plants, which is then mainly used for fuel, electricity and chemicals mainly.

- *Hydrogen power*: When hydrogen is separated from other elements, it can be used to generate electricity or burned as fuel.

There is an article entitled "Site C Is a Climate-Change Disaster, Says Suzuki" published on February 23, 2016 by Mychaylo Prystupa on The Tyee (news, culture, solutions). In this article, David Suzuki is quoted as stating that by flooding valuable farmland for the creation of the Site C Dam Canada is clearly going against the climate-change reductions agreements it has signed, which are targeted at reducing carbon dioxide emissions.

This is clearly a violation of international agreements to make Canada a low-carbon economy. It also pushes our country deeper into a high-carbon food production economy. Our farmland is required to reduce dependence on food from other countries such as China and Chile (among others) from where many of our vegetables and fruits are imported.

In Prystupa's article, Suzuki makes accurate and strong

arguments against Site C Dam worth quoting:

> "It seems to me crazy to put farmland in the north underwater," [Suzuki] said. We live in a food chain now in which food grows on average 3,000 kilometres from where it's consumed. The transport of all that food is dependent on fossil fuels.

> "Food has got to be grown much closer to where it's going to be consumed. Instead of building dams and pipelines, Canada should massively encourage wind, solar and geothermal energy projects and put a stiff price on carbon emissions," he said.

The Site C Dam is located in a privileged geographical area. It is an integral part of the most important wildlife trails in the Yellowstone to Yukon corridor chain, where many species migrate every year in large numbers. It also covers very fertile agricultural lands where old boreal forests grow.

There is a very good and interesting article written by Wilderness Committee (wildernesscommittee.org/sitec) where the following strong and valuable statement is made:

> BC Hydro says it is because BC needs the energy, but we don't: Hydro's own reports say BC can meet current demands through energy conservation. Site C is not about meeting the electricity demands of British Columbians; it is about subsidizing BC's oil and gas and mining industries. It's an $8 billion taxpayer subsidy to a dirty fossil fuel industry that needs cheap energy to expand.

I strongly encourage the reader to research more about this project, and if possible, try doing something about it. If that corridor of valuable land is flooded, it is going to be gone forever; like the Three Gorges Dam in China that had a very strong negative impact on China's environment and ecosystem in a desperate quest for hydroelectric energy.

Important Report:

CBC News published (April 19, 2017) an article entitled "Site C dam project has become 'uneconomic' and should be suspended: University of British Columbia (UBC) report". Researchers Karen Bakker, Richard Hendricks, and Philip Raphals published this 168-page report on water governance; where several important elements on Site C have profoundly changed. Initially, alternative options to generate electricity have become much cheaper. Such is the case of wind and solar power, along with energy conservation systems. BC Hydro's prediction said the demand for electricity has "dropped significantly," as per the UBC researcher's report.

The electricity from Site C would not be required for at least ten years after its completion, which would force BC Hydro to export the energy at prices below cost and with a forecasted loss of $1 billion dollars, the report confirms. There is a 25 per cent cost overrun ($2.4 billion) as of 2018. Most importantly, the report states: "Under BC Hydro's forecast demand, the analysis found, cumulative losses would be nearing $2.7 billion by 2036." Shouldn't BC Hydro cut their losses and suspend or cancel the construction of the environmentally and economically damaging Site C immediately? Shouldn't Prime Minister Trudeau and his office focus on renewable energy projects instead of putting more money in a lost cause? Financially and environmentally, it would only make sense. It is worth quoting the summary of the report as follows:

> The decision to approve the Site C Project in 2014 will cost ratepayers on the order of $1.4 to $1.7 billion dollars more than had an alternative portfolio of resources been pursued at that time. Our analysis indicates that cancelling the Site C Project as of June

30, 2017 would save between $500 million and $1.65 billion, depending on future conditions. Suspending Site C Project is preferable to cancelling the Project by up to $350 million. Both cancelling and suspending are preferable to continuing with the Site C Project.

Our recommendation is: <u>Suspend the Site C Project</u>, and refer the Project to the BC Utilities Commission for a full review. Table 42 summarizes the net present value benefit (cost) of continuing with the Site C. Projected under the various scenarios. These results indicate that it was not prudent to proceed with the Site C Project, and it remains imprudent to continue with it.

Impact of the Kyoto Protocol

In 1997, the signatories to the international treaty known as the Kyoto Protocol promised to reduce their greenhouse gas emissions over two decades. Some have complied with that pledge, but others have failed, sometimes in a large and embarrassing way. According to an article entitled "World" published in the November 2015 issue of National Geographic (p. 31), only three countries have contributed more than the protocol specified to reduce greenhouse gas emissions – Costa Rica, Egypt, and Morocco. The countries that have met their targets are the United States, Mexico, Peru, Brazil, all the EU members, Kazakhstan, China, Indonesia, and India. Those lagging behind are Canada, Ukraine, Chile, Russia, South Africa, and Australia. Other countries either were not rated or never made a pledge to reduce their emissions.

It is not just alarming but also tragic that some developed countries have failed in their promise to reduce greenhouse gas emissions due mainly to the strong economic and political influence of some of their private industries. The main problem is that these governments favour distinctive sectors of their economies and protect specific industries that contribute highly to the government's tax base, external balance of trade, or gross national product (GNP). These countries are among the biggest producers and exporters of natural gas, oil, and coal, still the major sources of energy throughout the world. Their governments do not want to alienate the private enterprises that are exploiting their country's natural resources and pushing greenhouse gas emissions to ever higher levels.

This reminds me of something I read in All One Era Magazine (October Moon 2015 issue), where Cameron Esler quoted South African social rights activist and retired Anglican bishop Desmond Tutu as saying that "people of conscience need to break their ties with corporations financing the injustice of climate change." Esler's article was especially interesting in the context of the Canadian Medical Association (CMA) taking a strong position on climate change because of the negative health impact it has on their patients. Apparently, the CMA has voted to divest its holdings in fossil fuel companies. It is never too late for such things to happen, and I truly hope many others will follow suit.

According to the CMA, people in northern Canada (Yukon, Northwest Territories, and Nunavut) are more conscious of their environment, because their livelihoods are more closely related to the environmental health of their surroundings. Therefore, the relationship between the health of their environment and their own health is clearer to them than to those living in southern, urbanized regions. Esler's article also mentions that the World Health Organization has launched a worldwide campaign to make people more conscious of the relationship between their health and their environment. The campaign is called "Our Climate, Our Health."

It is funny, but all the above brings about two specific

reflections that are worth always keeping in mind:

- The more I live, the less I understand human nature.
- The more I know people, the more I love my parrot.

Why? For many reasons that I am sure the reader already knows, but let me give you two quick examples of what happens in China (as in many other countries worldwide), where many cities suffer serious air, soil, and water pollution far beyond the minimum needed to affect the health of their populations. It is so serious that many people are dying as a result. Ironically, the Chinese are also the most to blame for relentlessly hunting wild animals, due to their excessive and irrational demand for certain animal parts. Yes, they seem to be the main culprits and worst silent predators in pushing to extinction species like the rhinoceros because of the apparent valuable properties of some of its parts to cure diseases and, above all, to allegedly help men with erectile dysfunction, instead of being humble and accept with dignity their reality.

But why do you need the rhinoceros or tiger's miracle benefits when many are already dying from pollution in the cities where they live? It certainly contradicts logic and common sense. I wonder if such people will ever see clearly the relationship between a clean environment and their health, or is their need for quick sexual gratification or greed for money and power so strong that it prevents logical thinking?

International efforts to achieve change

Many countries have been getting together to implement coordinated measures to reduce greenhouse gas emissions (GGE) by 2020. The United Nations conference on climate change that took place in December, 2015 confirms that the biggest polluters (regardless of whether they have met their targets or not) need to reinforce their efforts with solid programmes to reduce their GGE. The biggest polluters (Canada, the United States, China, and the European Union) also need to protect vulnerable countries that are being exposed to the damaging effects of indiscriminate GGE.

Some countries are already making great efforts and strenuous financial sacrifices to reduce their carbon footprints. Robert Kunzig, in an article in the November, 2015 issue of National Geographic describes the impressive advances of Germany in its goal to reduce its GGE. According to Kunzig, in the last decade Germany has achieved the following:

- Near the coal-fired power plant in Gazweller (western Germany), they have been installing wind turbines for electrical power. Germany currently generates 27 per cent of the electricity requirements of their country from wind. A decade ago they only generated 9 per cent.

- Germany intends to have shut down all its nuclear power plants by 2022. As Kunzig notes, "workers have been taking apart the Soviet-era nuclear plant near Greifswald in eastern Germany since 1995, cleaning radioactive surfaces with steel grit so the metal can be recycled."

- A nuclear reactor at Kalkar (a municipality in the district of Kleve in North Rhine-Westphalia) was completed just before the 1986 explosion at Chernobyl, Ukraine. Because of that accident, the plant, though ready, was converted into an amusement park known as Wunderland Kalkar. There are beautifully decorated mountain views painted on the exterior walls of the nuclear plant. The central nuclear tower is being used as a flying-chair carousel-style ride. Please google it!

- Germany's goal, says Kunzig, is to reduce its overall

energy consumption by half and get 80 per cent of their energy from renewable sources.

- In the Baltic Sea, Germany is building 19 wind farms about 50 kilometres offshore and planning even more in its continued efforts to promote the clean energy movement and serve as an example to the rest of the world. The goal is to get one-third of Germany's energy from wind farms alone. A single wind turbine can currently cover the need for electrical power of 6,000 homes.

- Of 17 operable nuclear reactors, nine have been closed so far, and the rest are programmed to close by 2022. In the meantime, writes Kunzig, 90 per cent of Germans accept paying higher electrical costs as long as the electricity comes from clean, renewable sources. Germans are among the people of the world who respect their forests and their environment the most, the reason they are leaders in the development of cleaner, renewable energy sources.

- Germans were the first to mass-produce electric cars (by BMW). Although not the current leaders in this, they are trying hard to produce more.

- Germany has installed more photovoltaic panels to trap solar energy than any other country in the world. Good examples are the thousands of panels surrounding the Eberswalde-Finow Airport, 48 kilometres north of Berlin.

- Although Germany is moving towards renewable energy, they are still having trouble (as of December, 2015) reducing their use of the dirtiest form of coal (known as lignite). They extract over 22 million tons of lignite per year and seem unlikely to stop soon.

Kunzig's research shows that, in 2014, Germans met 18 Per cent of their energy needs from hard coal, which is mostly imported, and about 26 per cent from lignite.

The United States has also been making efforts to develop renewable, cleaner energy sources in the past decade, though not at the same speed as the Germans. In the US, there is a new solar technology that uses mirrors that centre and direct sunlight to heat liquid salt. This heat can then be used during the day as well as after sunset, according to Craig Welch in an article in National Geographic (November, 2015) entitled "A Blueprint for a Carbon-Free America." Welch notes that the US has detailed plans for solar panels all across the country, using extensive research on where the sun shines the most (and at what times of the year). Wind turbines are planned as well. According to the research, the strongest winds in the US are found in the Great Lakes region, offshore New England, and in the Great Plains. Welch explains in his article that the road map for the United States' future in relation to their needs for renewable energy is:

- 1.3 per cent geothermal.
- 0.1 per cent tidal.
- 3 per cent hydroelectric.
- 7.2 per cent photovoltaic (mainly rooftops).
- 30.7 per cent utility PV (utility-scale solar).
- 7.3 per cent concentrated solar power plant (CSP).
- 19.1 per cent offshore wind.
- 30.9 per cent onshore wind.

Welch believes that, just as mass production brought down the price of cars after Henry Ford's Model T, the same thing will happen with solar and wind power as demand increases. The cost of clean, renewable energy is still high compared to energy from fossil fuels, but there is no doubt it will come down as demand goes up. According to Welch, California has a wealth of potential renewable resources. Using information from Stanford professor Mark Jacobson, Welch writes:

> From rivers to ocean waves, the Golden State's natural riches offer many clean-energy options. California has set ambitious goals for renewables and is reducing regulations and costs for solar and wind projects. This could create jobs, reduce the state's severe air pollution, drive innovation, and jump-start a national movement. Land-use battles seem inevitable, whether over raptor deaths at wind farms or the risk that solar projects pose to endangered tortoises. California, already crowded, is still growing fast, but its progressive political bent has not resulted in a commitment that comes close to eliminating fossil fuels.

Learning to live with climate change

In November, 2015, National Geographic published a well-researched and well-documented article entitled "How To Live With It" in which Patricia Edmonds acknowledges that there are thousands of sources of information about how to live with climate change. She starts by saying:

> If it's true that we learn by doing, then the learning has begun. What we face is daunting: extreme heat and weather; threats to water, crops, and health. But with technology and ingenuity, earth's custodians are finding new ways to manage our changed reality.

There is no doubt she is on to something accurate but frightening. I personally do not believe that technology is going to defeat nature or even work at par with it. As humans, we are going to continue demanding more and more from our planet, pushing it to the limits, unless we do something to reduce the demographic explosion. We will always be patching our mistakes, while playing either catch-up with nature or applying desperate survival techniques such as building high walls and dikes in major coastal cities.

Edmonds' group of contributors (Jeremy Berlin, Eva Conant, Karen de Seve, Daniel Stone, Lawson Parker and Mathew Tuombly) summarize our strategies for survival and adaptation in five main areas:

1. Warming Water: We all know that we depend on fresh water for our survival as humans. All species on earth require fresh water on a regular basis. No exceptions. All human crops require water in large amounts. All the animals we raise, from goats to pigs, require water on a daily basis. In fact, we depend on ocean water as well, because when it heats up and absorbs more of the CO_2 that we humans produce, this actually increases the acidity of the water, modifies the chemistry and temperature of the ocean overall, and has an immediate impact on microorganisms that end up affecting the food chain. Along with shifts in sea levels, Edmonds states, warming causes new risks to all humans and strong impacts on the economies we live in. According to Edmonds, we need to apply different strategies to harvest rainwater more efficiently, and we need to re-use our consumed water and improve our water storage systems. Edmonds also mentions the urgent need to shift crop production to less thirsty fruits and vegetables. She states, "When permafrost thaws, land changes. People in the north rethink land and buildings, relocate cellars that store frozen game, and move from vulnerable areas." It is simply a game of strong human survival instincts; adapt or die. Hopefully, the human gift for reasoning will prevent us from totally destroying our planet's rivers, lakes, mountains, oceans, etc.

2. Crop Changes: Warmer weather is not necessarily bad for crops. Why? The farming season is extended due to longer warm seasons. Unfortunately, critics also say that this will cause more CO_2 to be released into the atmosphere, which

contributes yet more to the warming of the planet and to more droughts, floods, and pests. Edmonds and her team recommend that we:

- Utilize farming modernization techniques.
- Apply new methods to save water during farming processes.
- Diversify crops.
- Increase yields by 60 to 70 per cent by the year 2050 to cope with population growth.
- Promote drought-tolerant grass and seeds to help plants survive, reproduce, and increase yields.

She notes that the earlier arrival of spring can assist the pollination process, which is expected to increase. African yields will double, mainly in rice, which grows in both cold and warm weathers. There are also new water allocation plans guided by NASA's satellite technology. Others people, like the native Americans (Haudenosaunee), are adapting to warmer weather through seed banking to protect their biodiversity.

3. High Heat: As average temperatures rise; we are going to have to adapt. It is forecast that more air conditioning will be used worldwide, which will further contribute to the warming of the planet. Edmonds and her team state that all landscapes will eventually change, from urban to rural and from inland to shoreline, and suggest the following adaptation techniques to start with:

- Implement vegetation-rich roofs that help cool all buildings.
- Promote urban forestry and vegetation everywhere to lower temperatures through shade and evapotranspiration.
- Develop reflective "cool roofs" to block solar radiation.
- Make pavements more permeable and reflective.
- Focus on more heat-tolerant livestock such as pigs,

goats, and sheep as substitutes for cattle, chickens, and other livestock in order to help farmers decrease their risks while diversifying their animal stock and market supply.

- Use technological advances to focus on breeding stronger and more heat-resistant livestock.

4. Wild Weather: Edmonds and her team insist that all citizens, regardless of where they live, will need to adapt to these new natural conditions. According to Edmonds:

> In 2012, a nine-foot storm surge from Hurricane Sandy hit New York at high tide, making the water 14 feet higher than normal at the tip of Manhattan. Flooding destroyed neighbourhoods and beaches in outer boroughs. The sea level in this area is rising by more than an inch each decade – twice as fast as the global average – and is predicted to rise 11 to 21 inches by 2050. To prepare, the city is implementing coastal resilience measures. A multiuse project will create more green spaces for city residents as well as systems of floodwalls, berms, and retractable barriers for enhanced storm protection.

5. Health Risks: According to Edmonds, the weather changes will affect not only our planet's overall condition and environment but its people as well. The effects will vary, she says, by gender and geographical area. We are going to adapt by discovering and implementing new medicines and remedies in general. However, "a potential catastrophic risk to human health" could undo 50 years of global health, Edmonds writes, citing the medical journal Lancet. Climate change and extreme weather will cause serious health and economic problems. It is well known that health authorities and insurance companies are worried about the impact of heat waves in already warm countries due to the potential

expansion of diseases such as dengue fever, malaria, African Trypanosomiasis (also known as sleeping sickness), diarrhea, Onchocerciasis (an infection by a worm whose larvae moves under the skin and can penetrate the eyes), and others. All these diseases are common in the Asian-Pacific regions and Africa, but now in South America (Brazil, specifically) we have new threats through the Zika virus, which is affecting a large section of the population. The main concerns expressed by Edmonds and her team regarding what they fear will happen are:

- Respiratory problems, mainly caused by wildfire-sparked pollution, expansion of industrial activities to cope with population growth, and the decrease of our ozone layer.
- Climate refugees, who are going to move somewhere else due to rising seas and flooding. There are thousands of farmers who have run away to escape nations in civil unrest due to droughts or private and government abuses. This has pushed many societies into social violence, which then pushes people to look for new frontiers in the search for food, security, and peace.
- Mental health problems, caused by stress, anxiety, desperation, and depression.
- Power outages, that will seriously affect how our communication and transportation systems work and will disrupt healthcare provision, as our clinics and hospitals are bound to suffer power outages and their consequences, regardless of whether they have their own power plants, which will fall short in supplying all their medical equipment and more at peak demand.
- Worldwide under-nutrition, due to crop failures, lack of water for irrigation, and more carbon dioxide in our atmosphere. All this, together with higher transportation costs for vegetables and fruit, will have a severe impact

on worldwide malnutrition and hunger.

- <u>Heat-related illnesses</u>, for which children and the elderly will be at higher risk, in every major city inland and on shorelines.
- <u>Freshwater supplies</u>, which will be at risk due to higher sea levels and extreme storms and rain, which will cripple the sewer systems and the storage capacity in urban areas, while flooding urban areas.
- <u>General worldwide conflict</u>. As Edmonds explains, "soil degradation, freshwater scarcity, population pressures, and other forces related to climate change are potential causes of conflict." This is going to be a serious problem that will go beyond the borders of the affected nations, regardless of any barriers that can be implemented. It is already happening in some African countries, and it is just a matter of time and population growth before it happens more widely.

Technological advances

Throughout the world, technological advances are taking place focused on cheaper, cleaner, and more reliable energy sources, as we try to move away from fossil fuels that we all know are so detrimental to our planet. Basically, wind, solar, hydroelectric, biomass, geothermal, or nuclear will be the sources of carbon-free power in the future. Scientists are currently working to capture and store carbon being burned from traditional fossil fuel processes and convert it into a harmless gas for storage deep underground. Scientific American published an article written by David Biello on December 15, 2015 entitled "An Unusual Tech Bet Could Slow Climate Change" in which he states that ethanol, saltwater, and fermentation are all involved in the process. He writes:

That is why ADM has partnered with the US

Department of Energy to bury some of that CO_2 in a saltwater aquifer that fills porous rock 7,000 feet below the facility. If all the brewery's CO_2 could be stored in this way, the ethanol could become a biofuel to burn, one that actually reduces the amount of CO_2 in the air, and that seems to be one of the last hopes on offer to keep global warming below 2 degrees Celsius. "The world depends on removing large amounts of CO_2 from the atmosphere in order to bring concentrations well below 450 ppm in 2100," said economist Ottmar Edenhoffer, when laying out the United Nations Intergovernmental Panel on Climate Change's views on how to combat climate change in 2014. "The fact that agriculture provides options to remove CO_2 from the atmosphere means this sector has a unique role."

Bob Weber (from The Canadian Press) wrote an article entitled "Study suggests we could refreeze Arctic," published in The Okanagan on Sunday, December 30, 2012, around the time when the melting of Greenland's ice cap was making worldwide news. Weber wrote that, according to some scientists (among them David Keith, Calgarian professor of applied physics at Harvard University), the Arctic could be refrozen.

There was an interesting article by David Rotman in the MIT Technology Review, entitled "A Cheap and Easy Plan to Stop Global Warming," in which he states that David Keith and his team published a scientific paper on a theory based on injecting reflective particles into the high atmosphere to significantly reduce the amount of sunlight reaching earth's surface. This would compensate for part of the greenhouse gas emission effects. Apparently, there is technology in many areas that could reduce the impact of climate change, but the question remains: Is it morally correct and at what cost will we consider doing it?

Unfortunately, all these technological advances seem to be made at a slower pace than population growth. Some people talk about an apocalyptic process coming about. We need to emphasise, understand, and keep in mind that the air pollution in Shanghai (for example) does not just stay there. It travels silently and almost invisibly throughout the world's wind currents, changing the air we all breathe. Just because we do not see it, smell it, or feel it does not mean it doesn't exist. Denying this is like covering our eyes with our hands. Who are we trying to fool? That is another reason the United Nations Intergovernmental Panel on Climate Change got together with the brightest minds on earth to try and provide potential solutions. Obviously, this excludes all those obtuse scientists and some groups of religious people who insist that climate change is either not happening or is a natural cycle for which humans are not to blame.

There is an interesting and down-to-earth article by Steven Mufson in the business section of the Washington Post (March, 30, 2014) entitled "U.N. climate panel: Governments, businesses need to take action now against growing risks." As Mufson notes, it is important to compare the panel's conclusions with those of the Climate Change Summit that took place in Paris in November 2015. It is worth quoting what Mufson wrote in his first three paragraphs:

> The world's leading environmental scientists told policymakers and business leaders Sunday that they must invest more to cope with climate change's immediate effects and hedge against its most dire potential, even as they work to slow the emissions fueling global warming.

> The U.N. Intergovernmental Panel on Climate Change said that climate change is already hurting the poor, wreaking havoc on the infrastructure of coastal cities, lowering crop yields, endangering various plant and

animal species, and forcing many marine organisms to flee hundreds of miles to cooler waters. But the Nobel Peace Prize-winning group said that climate change's effects will grow more severe and that spending and planning are needed to guard against future costs, much as people insure themselves against possible accidents or health problems.

The report said that damage from climate change and the costs of adapting to it could cause the loss of several percentage points of gross domestic product in low-lying developing countries and island states. It added that climate change could "indirectly increase risks of violent conflicts in the form of civil war and inter-group violence' by 'amplifying' poverty and economic shocks."

It is evident that we humans need urgent adaptive and protective measures, but everything starts in our own homes, companies, industries, and cities. Re-using, recycling, and moderating our consumption are a good start, but we would still barely be in first gear. We would still have five or seven more gears to kick in, so the time to start is yesterday! There is no running away from this, regardless of what sceptics believe or feel. The writing is on the wall, in every language known to humankind. There is no excuse not to read it, digest it, and act accordingly.

NASA's OCO-2 satellite and the world's CO_2 distribution

In the November, 2015 issue of National Geographic, Peter Miller shares an amazing image taken by NASA's OCO-2 satellite that shows the world's CO_2 distribution per country as of June, 2015. It shows how the average parts per million of CO_2 is 400, with Central and North America being among the worst contributors at 405 or more parts per million. The northern part of South America, which includes countries such as Bolivia, Peru, Colombia, and Venezuela, is a big contributor. Brazil, although it is a contributor, does not show much because the rain forest absorbs millions of tons of CO_2 per year, along with the Atlantic Ocean. But if Brazil were to also decrease its emissions of CO_2, it would benefit our worldwide atmosphere.

Europe, with 405 or more parts per million, is also a big contributor, along with North African countries such as Morocco, Mauritania, Mali, Libya, Egypt, Sudan, Niger, and Chad. Asia is also a very strong contributor of CO_2 in the atmosphere. Among the worst countries are Kazakhstan, Uzbekistan, India, China, Taiwan, Thailand, the Philippines, and Indonesia, but all their smaller neighbouring countries are as bad, pushing way over 405 parts per million. The smallest contributors in the world with about 395 or less parts per million are Russia, some eastern European countries, the southern parts of Africa and South America, and the Australian continent. I truly hope National Geographic publishes – in a year or two – an updated image for a proper comparative analysis, so that we can really evaluate where the CO_2 is coming from, which countries are complying with the Kyoto Agreement and the targets of the recently concluded Climate Change Summit in Paris (November 2015), and where exactly the CO_2 is manifested the most, along with its likely future path.

Paris Agreement on climate change

We are not going to go into what for many might be a boring account of the details of the Paris Climate Change Summit. I will just summarize seven important points we all need to keep in mind as the years go by. Anyone wanting to read the 32 pages of the Paris Agreement can go to the following link: unfccc.int/resource/docs/2015/cop21/eng/l09.pdf

The Paris Agreement is the major international agreement on

climate change to date. The participating countries agreed on a common goal and accepted various degrees of commitment with the same altruistic goals in mind and in a highly synchronized worldwide programme. If implemented, the agreement will be powerful and instrumental for our survival on this planet.

However, it is one thing to promise to do something and quite another thing to actually do it. When I was a kid, my grandfather used to say: "You can promise as much as you want, but the moment in which you start delivering your promise, you then start committing and limiting your resources, so it better be a good cause and well thought-out in advance." This reminds me of what Ron Robinson, from Nelson, BC, wrote to the editor of the Kelowna Capital News last December 18, 2015. He noted that climate change information has been dully collected and analyzed and that what we now require is immediate and serious implementation. In his letter, Robinson states:

> After all the work done by individuals, organizations, and the Climate Leadership Team, for our government to suggest further consultation is needed before any action is taken is an insult to the electorate and a real indication of our government's [lack of] commitment to effective climate action.

Unfortunately, Canada (along with other countries) has failed the world in the past and seems likely to continue to do so again. I truly hope I am wrong, because it is a betrayal of the people who, with trust in hand, elected them to be our leaders and our protectors. In the minds of many politicians, economic progress and power go against environmental protection programs, especially in a semi-developed country like ours.

We do not need to discuss this further, if we stop and intelligently analyze the damage to our environment and the amount of CO_2 released into the atmosphere with the exploitation of the oil sands in Alberta. Once again, we always need to remember what Desmond Tutu very accurately and bravely once said: "People of conscience need to break their ties with corporations financing the injustice of climate change." Tutu should have continued by saying "… for the sake of money, personal ambition, and selfish greed."

The seven main points reached and agreed upon in Paris were:

1. All participating countries will make an effort to reduce global greenhouse gas emissions. They all acknowledged that climate change is a concern for all humans and that we all have to address it to protect human rights and human health, among other concerns. They put special emphasis on the protection of gender equality and the empowerment of women as well.

2. Developing countries, therefore, are mandated for the first time to commit to this comprehensive worldwide climate change agreement. Most importantly, the 55 countries and major contributors of global greenhouse gas emissions agreed to sign the agreement and abide by it.

3. The agreement emphasizes keeping the global average temperature increase below two degrees Celsius compared to the average temperature of pre-industrial times. Their goal is to do their best to limit the temperature to no more than a 1.5 degree Celsius (or less) increase. Many scientists around the world have insisted that the threshold to reduce worldwide catastrophes is below two degrees Celsius.

4. The goal is to make our world (with the participation of every country) carbon neutral sometime after the year 2050 and definitely before 2100. This will allow our oceans, soils, and forests to absorb naturally what is in the atmosphere.

5. Poor countries will be assisted in their efforts to control their own greenhouse gas emissions. Financing will be available for all poor countries that need to reduce their emissions and, most importantly, to deal with extreme weather conditions in the way of flooding, wildfires, droughts, rising sea levels, etc. All those countries that suffer weather-related disasters will be provided with urgent and immediate help. Developed countries have committed to avail $100 billion per year by 2020 to assist poor countries to cope with climate change.

6. In relation to the efforts to be done by developing countries, the agreement commits developed countries to assist them with clean and renewable sources of energy. This will help them keep their greenhouse gas emissions to acceptable levels and to have access to new technologies for renewable energy. The Canadian government alone committed to spend $2.65 billion dollars to help developing countries reduce their emissions and to finance them to achieve clean power generation instead of focusing on fossil fuels.

7. The agreement challenges all countries to reduce their carbon emissions as soon as possible and to keep detailed logs of their emissions in order to compare net reductions to those they committed themselves to achieve. These targets are going to be confirmed and revised every five years, as of 2023.

According to Fiona Harvey in an article entitled "Paris climate change agreement: the world's greatest diplomatic success" (The Guardian December 14, 2015), the Paris Agreement is a huge international compromise to put a cap on emissions and avoid breaching the two-degree Celsius threshold, which has sadly been breached by October of 2017. Harvey says:

> Paris produced an agreement hailed as "historic, durable and ambitious." Developed and developing countries alike are required to limit their emissions to

relatively safe levels of 2C, with an aspiration of 1.5C, [and] with regular reviews to ensure these commitments can be increased in line with scientific advice. Like any international compromise, it is not perfect: the caps on emissions are still too loose, likely to lead to warming of 2.7 to 3C above pre-industrial levels.

Without urgent action, it is possible the warming of the planet could reach as much as five degrees Celsius over current temperatures, according to Kumi Naidoo, Executive Director of Greenpeace International. As Naidoo warns:

> What is more, infrastructure built today – coal-fired power plants, transport networks, buildings – that entail high carbon emissions will still be operating decades into the future, giving the world a narrow window in which to change the direction of our economies.

The gift of fresh water ("blue gold")

The term "blue gold" has been used by many organizations, corporations, and individuals in their efforts to make us all understand that fresh water is the most precious and limited natural resource.

No water, no life! It is the invisible strand that entwines human lives and the lives of all species on this planet. From the coffee or tea, we drink every morning, to the brushing of our teeth, to the clothes we put on when we wake up, to the dinner we eat at the end of the day, from the lights we turn on before the sun rises to the toilets we flush throughout the day, water keeps our countries safe, our cities running, and our communities healthy. It allows our societies to survive healthily and progressively and properly pursue our industrial, commercial, and residential activities. Since water is our everything, it is time to stop treating it with absolute disrespect, arrogance, and contempt. It is time to care!

The majority of human beings in almost every American country (from Chile and Argentina to Alaska) and in many European and Asian countries take water for granted. They simply turn on the faucet and "voila," there it is! Other, less fortunate communities in Australia and Africa truly know the value of a single drop of water.

To my mind, there is no better gift than clean air and clean drinkable water. Both are now scarce in many places on earth and literally non-existent in others, where water needs to be brought from remote and faraway places. Clean air is continuously being affected by human industrial activities and damage to the air we breathe is not being reduced, much less stopped.

According to the Population Institute of Canada, more than half of the world's population is going to be living in areas of "high water stress" in the future. Since July of 2010, the Population Institute published the following alarming figures:

> The global population is expanding by 80 million people annually, increasing the demand for freshwater by about 64 billion m3 a year. In fact, water withdrawals tripled over the last 50 years due to population growth. This rapid growth rate also caused the potential global availability of water to decline from 12,900 m3 per capita per year in 1970, to 9,000 m3 in 1990, to about 7,000 m3 in 2000.

The institute is worried because their forecast is that the population affected by water scarcity in the near future will increase from 8 per cent to about 47 per cent in only three decades. That was their estimate back in 2010, but it is clear that, with global warming, water scarcity has been increasing even faster than they originally expected five years ago.

Population growth and the numbers related to it matter, and matter a great deal. Many groups, religious or not, believe God or nature will provide, so why worry? North Americans, and especially Canadians, like people in only a few other countries in the world, have been blessed by abundant natural resources. Unfortunately, Canadians have also been cursed; instead of making a bigger effort to industrialize, a great number of corporations only want to exploit the natural resources (raw materials) and fail to put more effort into researching, manufacturing, and exporting finished goods. Sadly, Canada is a country that likes to exploit resources such as fossil fuels, minerals, lumber, fish, etc. from Mother Earth, but we pay little attention to value-added industries, finished products, and the demand for them in foreign markets. With industrial value-added work, we could do much better than just exporting our raw natural products.

We are not even close to the shadow of a truly industrialized country such as Germany, Japan, South Korea, or China. We blame this on cheaper manufacturing costs or even sometimes on higher capital-intensive industries in those countries, but in reality, we lack the entrepreneurialism to manufacture and compete at the same level. We seem to lack industrial vision, diversification techniques, government assistance programs and tax incentives, entrepreneurial initiative, and guts. But what we lack most is a very valuable factor and the mother of all creation – real need and hunger.

Our resources are so plentiful that we have become lazy as an "industrialized country". But if the prices of particular commodities suddenly drop in the international market, as the price of oil did throughout 2015 to 2017, our economy nosedives. Our dollar devalues, and our imports of finished goods get a lot more expensive, while we have to increase our exports of raw materials. We allow the world to exploit our natural resources, which we are forced to export in larger quantities at lower prices. Wow, that is surely good business sense and benefits our international balance of trade. (Yes, I am being sarcastic).

Let's go back to the main natural commodity we Canadians have plenty of, which is liquid and frozen water. Every city requires development and growth. Both need good planning and always with an environmentally sustainable population growth strategy in mind. We have plenty of water, but we are not taking proper care of it, mainly due to excessive use, contamination, and lack of strategic planning. There are a lot of naïve and ignorant people around the world (and always will be) who believe that water is plentiful and that we will always have access to it. That every drop of water we use will simply come back to us because it cannot just disappear into thin air forever. People do not want to understand the complexities of reusing, cleaning, and accessing clear drinking water, with the added pressure of the extreme weather patterns currently being suffered by many countries and that will become even worse in the future.

Let me provide the reader with two interesting examples for those people who believe that nothing is really going to happen, or for those who cannot see beyond their noses to the cruel realities of unstoppable and relentless human consumption and waste.

Example No. 1
Nobody saw this first example coming, and when people finally realized it was happening, it was already over the tipping point and too late to reverse. I am talking about what happened to the Aral Sea that for thousands of years was a magnificent jewel of nature and reigned as one of the planet's largest inland bodies of water. Mark Synnott (National Geographic June, 2015) clearly describes how the Aral Sea, located between Kazakhstan and Uzebekistan, was fed by two important rivers called the Amu Darya and the Syr Darya. According to Synnott, the sea maintained itself for millennia

through these rivers and natural evaporation processes. According to Synnott, locals say the Russian government at the time built a dam while knowing very well the future disaster that was bound to happen. They say that the famous climatologist Alexandr Voeikov (1842-1916) used to refer to the Aral Sea as a "mistake of nature and a useless evaporator." The Russian government was convinced that crops were more valuable than fish.

According to Synnott, in the 1920s, Stalin decided to expand the Uzebekistan cotton plantations, but this type of agriculture is very thirsty, so it was decided to dig by hand "thousands of miles of irrigation canals." The goal was to use the water from the Syr Darya and the Amu Darya for cotton plantations in the surrounding deserts. Apparently, the rivers managed to sustain expansion in the cotton fields, but, as we humans do, it was decided to expand the irrigation canals again during the 1960s. As Synnott observes:

> That was the straw that broke the camel's back. Suddenly the system was no longer sustainable. They knew what they were doing, but what they did not realize was the full range of the ecological consequences – and the rapidity with which the sea would vanish.

So, the Russian government knew very well from day one that the region would be doomed if they were to build more irrigation channels. Unfortunately, their political arrogance and determination to profit from agricultural methods that went against nature were too strong. This negligence caused irreversible damage to the area in total disregard for the welfare of the local people. Some insist the strain that was put on the natural aquifers could not have been foreseen, but in any case, beginning around 1977 the Aral Sea started drying up at an accelerated pace, and today over 90 per cent is just sand dunes with rusted, abandoned ships lying on what used to be the bottom of a beautiful sea that supported the region's agricultural and fishing needs and tourism.

The point of the story is that the overuse of any natural resource will detrimentally affect its sustainability. If we do not take care of our water, if we keep misusing it and taking it for granted, we are heading for an unpleasant surprise, especially when other countries are going to be suffering serious droughts and water scarcities. Again, nothing, absolutely nothing, lasts forever, much less with a constantly growing, thirsty, and reckless population.

Example No. 2
This example is about how really rich Canada is compared to the rest of the world, and how this might put us at a high risk internationally, if other countries want access to our fresh water. Again, we all know, even children at elementary school, that without water we cannot survive. In fact, let us jump to high school level, where also everybody knows that there are places on earth with enough water and others with very scarce amounts of this invaluable commodity. If we then jump to university level, everybody there knows that countries with scarce access to fresh water are prone to serious economic development constraints, stress and damage to their environment, and, above all, serious impacts on their agricultural land and, ultimately, on their access to food for their population and farm animals. Their mere survival will be at risk, whether they like it or not. Now, if we hop up to the master's level, we know that water, aside from being limited, is the most precious commodity in human history, always will be, and needs urgent protection. And if we jump to doctorate level, we know that we need to research the implementation of policies, strategies, and methodologies to protect our watersheds from industrial activities and from foreign threats. If we do not get serious about this, we have much more to lose than meets the eye. Our peaceful and secure existence will be at risk and our souls will live in pain. If countries can

invade others for oil, imagine what they will do for fresh water.

There is a very interesting article in the June, 2015 issue of Canadian Geographic by Nick Walker entitled "Water Lies Beneath." This article is about Canada's plentiful groundwater resources. Walker says that one third of Canadians (a little over 10 million people) rely on groundwater on a daily basis. The amount of water moving under our feet is mindboggling. According to Alfonso Rivera, chief hydrologist for the Geological Survey in Canada, we have about three times more water moving beneath our feet than all the water in the Great Lakes, 70,000 cubic kilometres at a conservative estimate.

In his article, Walter shows us the map of Canada with each province's water sources, either groundwater or above the water table (which people see in the form of snow, streams, rivers, and lakes). If we consider all the provinces, the weighted average of Canada's water comes 42.23 per cent from underground sources and 57.77 per cent from above the surface (water-table) water. This data was sourced from Rivera's book, Canada's Groundwater Resources. Groundwater (sub-surface H_2O) is usually free of dangerous micro-organisms compared to our above-surface water, but it can easily be contaminated by irresponsible human activity in the form of industrial and agricultural contamination if chemicals and other hazardous materials are not dealt with properly during cleaning processes.

In his book, Rivera says that groundwater is constantly being replenished by a phenomenon called recharge, which is calculated by subtracting the evapotranspiration (H_2O evaporation) from precipitation (rain and snow) on an annual basis. Yes, we have abundant water sources in Canada in frozen and liquid state, but the question is: Are we taking care of them? Citing Rivera, Walker writes:

The aquifers are vulnerable to pollution, "and," notes Rivera, "they're in contact with rivers, lakes, wetlands, and whole ecosystems." Contamination can stem from landfills, septic systems, road salt, agricultural and industrial products and waste, and many other sources.

At the end of Walker's article there is a note on how to protect groundwater for our future consumption and security. Among Walker's and Rivera's most important suggestions are:

- Use native plants that are adapted to the water needs and availability of the area.

- Manage chemical waste and toxic materials properly. Do not just dump them in landfills or, worse, in people's back yards. All hazardous materials need strict control, because they can easily end up in our streams, rivers, lakes, and groundwater.

- Do not let the water run, regardless of where it is taking place, whether from the faucets while shaving or brushing your teeth, to the hose in the garden when doing something else.

For more detailed information and suggestions, visit: canadiangeographic.ca/magazine/jun15/guide-to-protecting-your-groundwater.asp

Water Wealth Project

There is a website (waterwealthproject.com/) run by Ian Stephen, who is the campaign director of The Water Wealth Project, based in Chilliwack, British Columbia. Stephen is not only a reasonable and accessible individual, but he is a person who is down to earth and tackles The Water Wealth Project head on with decisive force, tenacity, and focus. On his website, he describes the relevance of the invisible power of our most valuable resource as follows:

> We believe that water is precious, and that ordinary people can protect it. We believe that our wealth is in our water. Many local people – especially in the agriculture, fishing, and tourism sectors — depend on water for their livelihoods. But our waters give us more than financial revenue. Water wealth is also about the physical, spiritual, cultural, and ecological prosperity that water makes possible. All living things depend on healthy water. Our land, food, and life-support systems are all powered by fresh, clean, flowing water. But right now, the protection of our shared water faces grave challenges. Industrial developments such as oil pipelines, agricultural pollution, and large-scale gravel mining can all put the waters we depend on at risk.
>
> The Water Wealth Project is about taking a fresh approach to economic well-being, one that respects the needs of all living beings and provides the foundation for healthy, thriving communities. It recognizes that the actions of today drive the outcomes of tomorrow. Unless ordinary people work together to protect their water now, the future will be uncertain. Our wealth is in our water. Let's work to protect it.

Immediate action required

What good is it to be rich in natural resources (and especially in water), if we do not know how to protect them and keep them clean for present and future generations? There are various organizations in Canada (and worldwide) that exhort us not to threaten our precious liquid commodity with indiscriminate and rampant industrialization, agriculture, and continued creeping urbanization. According to Ian Stephen, the Council of Canadian Academies (CCA) listed 28,000 contaminated sites in Canada. Since then, more contaminated sites have been added to the list. The CCA says that groundwater moves slowly through porous rock. The impact of contamination will take decades to be revealed. Ban Ki-Moon, Secretary General of the United Nations (from January 1, 2007 to December 31, 2016) once said:

> There has been a widespread failure to recognize water's vital role in providing food, energy, sanitation, disaster relief, environmental sustainability, and other benefits. This has left hundreds of millions of people suffering from poverty and ill health and exposed to the risks of water-related diseases.

The United Nations is correct in their view of our need for water and the problems some countries are going through. The question is: Are they doing anything substantial, concrete, and immediate about it?

Water desalination technology

It has long been a goal of humans to desalinate the ocean waters and turn them into fresh drinkable water. Desalination has always been a challenge due mainly to biofouling during the desalination process. Biofouling is the accumulation of algae, plants, microorganisms and animals on wet surfaces, which affects the overall process to obtain fresh water from our oceans during the desalination. This is one of the main reasons why desalination has been one of the last resorts to obtain fresh water. With the latest research and technologies, scientists have developed new coatings and materials to prevent biofouling on wet surfaces.

After many years of research and billions of dollars of investment, one of the driest countries in the world is now making abundant fresh water. An article published by Rowan Jacobsen in Scientific American (July 29, 2016) entitled "Israel Proves the Desalination Era Is Here," reports that Israel now obtains 55 per cent of its water needs from desalination. The new technology, says Jacobsen, uses porous stone to prevent microorganisms from blocking the membranes through which the saltwater gets filtered. This is a chemical-free process, which is a lot more cost-efficient than anything used before.

Jacobsen confirms that the only country in the Middle East that is not stressed for water is Israel. Their Zuckerberg Institute for Water Research has developed breakthrough technologies in many areas such as drip irrigation, water treatment, biological digesters, desalination processes, wastewater management, and others. Over many years, Israel has worked on an innovative water treatment system to recapture for irrigation over 85 per cent of all the water going down their drains and ultimately, into their irrigation system. Israel is by far the most efficient country in the world in recycling their water. Spain is a distant second with only 19 per cent recycled water.

According to the article, Israel's progress has been driven by pure necessity. Jacobsen then stated in his article:

> In 2008, Israel teetered on the edge of catastrophe. A decade-long drought had scorched the Fertile Crescent, and Israel's largest source of freshwater, the Sea of Galilee, had dropped to within inches of the "black line" at which irreversible salt infiltration would flood the lake and ruin it forever. Water restrictions were imposed, and many farmers lost a year's crops.

> Their counterparts in Syria fared much worse. As the drought intensified and the water table plunged, Syria's farmers chased it, drilling wells 100, 200, then 500 meters (all the way to 1,600 feet) down in a literal race to the bottom. Eventually, the wells ran dry and Syria's farmland collapsed in an epic dust storm. More than a

million farmers joined massive shantytowns on the outskirts of Aleppo, Homs, Damascus, and other cities in a futile attempt to find work and purpose.

The rapidly growing urban peripheries of Syria, *they wrote*, are marked by illegal settlements, overcrowding, poor infrastructure, unemployment, and crime, were neglected by the Assad government and became the heart of developing unrest. Similar stories are playing out across the Middle East, where drought and agricultural collapse have produced a lost generation with no prospects and simmering resentments. Iran, Iraq, and Jordan all face water catastrophes. Water is driving the entire region to desperate acts. But even with those measures, Israel still needed about 1.9 billion cubic meters (2.5 billion cubic yards) of freshwater per year and was getting just 1.4 billion cubic meters (1.8 billion cubic yards) from natural sources. That 500-million-cubic-meter (650-million-cubic-yard) shortfall was why the Sea of Galilee was draining like an unplugged tub and why the country was about to lose its farms.

Enter desalination. The Ashkelon plant, in 2005, provided 127 million cubic meters (166 million cubic yards) of water. Hadera, in 2009, put out another 140 million cubic meters (183 million cubic yards). And now Sorek, 150 million cubic meters (196 million cubic yards). All told, desalt plants can provide some 600 million cubic meters (785 million cubic yards) of water a year, and more are on the way. The Sea of Galilee is fuller. Israel's farms are thriving. And the country faces a previously unfathomable question: What to do with its extra water?

Thanks to technological advances, the desalination process now costs a third of what it used to. More technological advances are continuously bringing the cost of desalination down considerably. More people are going to be getting their water from desalination and less from underground sources, which required deeper drilling and a great number of wells are all drying out. For more details about the desalination process, I encourage the reader to read the whole article in Scientific American.

Current water shortages are a big problem worldwide, but new technology is closing the gap between our needs and future supply. Unfortunately, some questions still stand regarding the needs of a continued population growth. Can technological advances solve all human needs and ensure our long-term survival? What is the future tipping point when our planet will stop providing what humans need, regardless of technological breakthroughs?

Fossil fuels, CO_2, and the economy

I could write about this subject until I am over 95 years old, but I will just venture to say something brief tying together the correlation between the impact of fossil fuel exploitation and climate change. Even the most incredulous and least educated people on the planet know that the correlation between the two is direct, profound, intense, and undeniable. The more we use oil and all its industrial derivatives for energy and other uses, the more we damage our atmosphere. On December 1, 2015, The National Post published a list of 12 points on page A4 that we should all know about climate change. Two points particularly caught my attention due to their alarming urgency:

> 1. "97,000 kilotons of carbon dioxide [are] pumped into earth's atmosphere every day by the burning of fossil fuels. That's a substantial primordial forest going up in smoke every 24 hours. And every four days, humanity emits enough carbon dioxide to equal the weight of all

7.3 billion humans on earth."

2. "CO_2 emissions have risen 42 per since 1990, the baseline year for the 1997 Kyoto Protocol. Several signatories – mostly former Communist states in Eastern Europe – were able to reduce their emissions below 1990 levels, but overall the agreement did little to stop the global rise in fossil-fuel consumption."

These are strong statements based on facts, which in general, the average person has no knowledge about. But if we read carefully, shouldn't we completely perceive and understand the depth of the real impact of burning fossil fuel to satisfy all human needs? I trust one day we all will.

If these figures are accurate, which they are, what hope can we have for our future? Power, profits, growth, development and the bottom line seem to be more important than human health and the well-being of communities everywhere in the world. This sounds absurd and irrational, but it is the cruel reality. Oil companies keep exploiting fossil fuels because that is how all the stakeholders and their employees (in the millions) make their livelihoods. They all depend on the exploitation of this environmentally damaging and finite resource.

Thanks to fossil fuels, humankind has evolved and progressed enormously. Due to the income derived from the use of crude oil and natural gas, tens of millions of people put food on the table, pay their monthly bills, send their kids to school, cover medical bills, go to the movies, celebrate birthdays, feed their dogs and cats, contribute to their pension plans, pay taxes, sit on their back deck to have a drink, go to restaurants, etc.

Unfortunately, their daily lives depend on their lack of solidarity with the rest of humanity that does not work in the oil industry. Having said that, almost every product we touch on a daily basis, such as the laptop I am writing this page with, is a derivative of fossil fuels.

The need for all humans to work together for benefit of our common environment is urgent, but we also need to be realistic in our efforts to go green and protect our ecosystem. We must be realistic about the extent and speed with which we proceed. Preferences and consumer needs require changing, but within the boundaries of logic and common sense, keeping always in mind our ultimate duty to safeguard planet Earth. It is imperative to adapt to new ways of life and new technologies slowly but surely (or should I say, rapidly *and* surely). We should all feel compelled to reduce, re-use, and recycle, and we should feel embarrassed about our lack of vision and sense of responsibility. We are all what some call "oilholics", and we need to do our best to reduce our dependency on crude oil.

On a personal basis, we can start by doing the following:

- Use our cars less, while biking and walking more.

- Use less electricity by turning lights off when leaving a room.

- Conserve our water and use it in a considerate and smart way.

- Buy fewer products based on oil derivatives (plastics, for example).

- Purchase locally produced meat and, if we can reduce our consumption, even better.

- Try as much as possible to consume vegetables and

fruits that have been locally produced and within the agricultural possibilities of our specific geographical area.

- In the construction or renovation industry, try consuming more locally manufactured products and fewer imported ones.

- Look for alternative sources of energy such as solar.

- Change your light bulbs to LED, leaving all the rest behind. You need not to change them all overnight, but start now.

- Use high-efficiency appliances.

- Improve your home insulation.

- Install more efficient double-pane windows and better-insulated doors.

- Reduce waste as much as possible.

- Seal your windows and doors properly if you cannot afford changing them to more efficient ones.

- Try to expand and improve based on your savings and gains, not on debt.

- Next time you purchase a car, buy a "smarter" and more efficient vehicle.

- Let go of pride and good looks by letting go of your gas guzzler in any form of pick-up truck, SUV, big van, Hummer, and any V8 motor, if you do not need it for work. If you do not need the power, then power down.

- Participate in local community initiatives to improve transportation in your city.

- If you live in a concrete jungle, make an effort to understand that, for you to survive in a big city, you need all the help you can from the rural areas.

- Plant more trees and flowers while making a conscious effort to appreciate and enjoy nature more. Get the family involved. Go hiking with your family and smell the flowers.

- Respect your surroundings and love your planet.

- Be creative and help sponsor change by spreading the word and the good will for our environment.

- Drive smarter and more efficiently.

For more information on what you can do, refer to any of the following sites:

nrdc.org/air/energy/genergy.asp
alwayswellwithin.com/2010/06/06/reducing-personal-oil-use/
greenpeace.org/international/en/campaigns/climate-change/10-simple-ways-to-use-less-oil/blog/12883/

The Arctic and Antarctic

According to research done by private companies and government agencies, it is estimated that the Arctic has the largest untouched reserves of oil and natural gas. Unfortunately, we know that, if private companies decide to explore and exploit those reserves, the rest of the world will pay the environmental impact, starting with drastic climate changes.

Why not invest those billions of dollars in research into new clean-energy technologies? I know this is a brilliant and, at the same time, a dumb question, so I will let readers arrive at their own conclusions. Why? Because there is no wrong or right answer. It all depends on which side of the negotiating table we are sitting on. But I insist that moderation is the key. Focusing our growth and our future only on fossil fuels is not just an archaic and obtuse strategy, it is a total betrayal of the human race. A moderate combination of fossil fuel consumption along with new technologies for environmentally clean energies should be imposed by government regulations in coordination with private enterprise.

Fortunately, many companies are now giving the Arctic the cold shoulder and backing off. The trend started with Shell International, which evaluated the feasibility of exploring and drilling in the Arctic and decided to step back, at least for now. Since then, BP, Exxon, and Chevron have made the same decision. The main reasons for their reluctance to proceed are strict government regulations, the extreme and unforgiving climate, and recently, the steep drop in the price of oil.

Personally, I am happy they are backing off, not just because I am pro-environment, but because I know very well that nature does not bargain or accommodate our needs. I am glad it is finally sinking in that, if we keep pushing nature to its limits, it will bounce back in revenge and with pure force, causing devastating natural disasters hurting humans throughout the world. It is also our moral and ethical obligation to protect those last frontiers that are still pristine and should remain so.

Wherever humans walk, we leave a trail of disruption behind us. But I admit that, economically, we cannot let go of fossil fuels suddenly and, much less, completely; not yet. What worries me is that, with global warming, the Arctic is not the only region at risk. Antarctica is already being explored by China, which, in coordination with Australia, is planning its strategic moves in favour of its own nation and people, regardless of what it might mean for the rest of the world. Jane Perez wrote an article in the New York Times last May 3, 2015 entitled "China, Pursuing Strategic Interests, Builds Presence in Antarctica," in which she reported:

> Xi-Jinping [the current Chinese president] signed a five-year accord with the Australian government that allows Chinese vessels and, in the future, aircraft to resupply for fuel and food before heading south. That will help secure easier access to a region that is believed to have vast oil and mineral resources; huge quantities of high-protein sea life; and for times of possible future dire need, fresh water contained in icebergs.

I certainly do not have anything against the Chinese culture that has given so much to humanity, but I have to admit that in the area of human rights and overpopulation, I prefer Canada over China any day of the week. The Chinese are known to embrace their environment in many parts of their country, but they are also well known for destroying their surroundings in the name of development, progress, and profit. In Canada, we have a better environmental reputation, but is it really deserved? The mining, oil, and logging industries certainly don't help to make this reputation a reality.

What will happen to the Antarctic if nobody looks in detail at what other countries will or will not do in their pursuit of natural resources? If the Chinese do not take care of their own environment and people in many areas (for example, cities like Baoding, Xingtai, Shijiazhuang, Handan, Shanghai, Zhengzhou, Cangzhou, Chengdu, etc.), what guarantees that they will take care of the beautiful and still pristine Antarctic region? Answer: Absolutely nothing!

Regarding the Arctic, the main international concerns have always been in relation to the following:

- The excessive noise during exploration and drilling will affect marine life in a very direct and deep manner. Noise pollution in the Arctic could be devastating to many species, such as the beluga whale.

- Oil spills in pristine waters will not just affect marine and bird life but could be almost impossible to clean up due to the extreme climate and a lack of people willing to work so far north.

- Oil rig and shipping accidents are bound to happen. It is only a matter of time. (i.e.: An Iranian oil tanker collided against a Chinese freight ship in the East China Sea the night of January 07, 2018. All the crude oil was spilled into the ocean).

Alberta Tar Sands

We do not need to go all the way across the world to find a bad example. We have one here in our own back yard. The more I research about the tar sands in Alberta, the more I feel frustrated about not being able to do something about them, so I decided to include a brief account of the reality of this massive, ongoing disaster.

The well-researched website oilsandtruth.org makes two very strong statements worth quoting:

> The Tar Sands "Gigaproject" is the largest industrial project in human history and likely also the most destructive. The tar sands mining procedure releases

OUR RUNAWAY GLOBE   *- The Runaway Trilogy -*

at least three times the CO_2 emissions of regular oil production and is slated to become the single largest industrial contributor in North America to climate change.

The tar sands are already slated to be the cause of up to the second fastest rate of deforestation on the planet behind the Amazon Rainforest Basin. Currently approved projects will see three million barrels of tar sands mock crude produced daily by 2018: for each barrel of oil up to as high as five barrels of water are used.

Human health in many communities in the region has taken a serious turn for the worse, allegedly as a result of the exploitation of the tar sands. Tar sands production has led to many serious social issues throughout Alberta, from housing crises to the vast expansion of temporary foreign worker programmes. New pipelines and the expansion or creation of new refineries place at risk our land and our ecosystem. The use of more supertankers crossing our vast oceans in every direction to transport the crude oil to its final destination, are also placing our oceans and its marine life at risk.

We all know that the Alberta economy, and that of Canada as a whole, depends to a great extent on the "three Es": exploration, exploitation, and export of fossil fuels, supposedly for the benefit of our economy and our people. According to the Canadian Association of Petroleum Producers (CAPP), Canada exported over $68 billion of oil in 2011 alone. The CAPP also acknowledges that oil sands pollution "is clearly evident." Added to that fact, NASA's data showed that oil sands pollution is comparable to a "large power plant."

Josh Wingrove's article published January 07, 2013 entitled "Oil sands development polluting Alberta lakes" explains that a peer-reviewed study published by a team of researchers, which includes some scientists from Environment Canada, has confirmed that polycyclic aromatic hydrocarbons (PAHs) have polluted all six lakes in the area. The use of some PAHs has serious side effects on the environment and has been linked to immune disorders, fish mutations, and infertility. Wingrove goes on to note that both industry and government have accepted the findings of this research as facts, but industry insists that we are still at low and manageable levels, given the scale of economic development in the area. Wingrove's conclusion is that "oil-sands development is polluting nearby ... lakes with rising levels of a toxic carcinogen, refuting long-standing claims that waterway pollution in the region is largely naturally occurring." This underlines the fact that as long as industry keeps making money and the Alberta government keeps receiving taxes, they will both turn a blind eye to the damage being caused.

David Biello published an article in Scientific American in January, 2013 entitled "More Oil From Canada's Tar Sands Could Mean Game Over for Climate Change." Biello confirms that the northern corner of Alberta, where the tar sands are located, contains huge, and easily accessed, deposits of thick, heavy oil that are "among the most greenhouse gas-intensive forms of petroleum to produce." Biello adds: "In the past decade Canada has become the US's primary supplier of imported petroleum – ahead of Saudi Arabia. Sourcing more oil from Canada achieves the politically desirable goal of making the US less dependent on OPEC."

Again, the more research I do, the more I find scientific evidence against the tar sands, so I decided to cut it short because my blood pressure was reaching dangerous levels. I exhort every North American to look at the devastation of the Canadian environment in Alberta as a result of the tar sands. Yes, I can easily be criticized for writing this, but the facts remain, and the truth is undeniable. In the future, when the pockets of many local Albertans are full of money, their environmental damage will be done. They will then leave behind contaminated water and soil along with destroyed forests. They will pack up their suitcases and go live somewhere else, such as in beautiful British Columbia or abroad.

Their actions certainly indicate that some do not care about the condition of what they will be leaving behind. The real shocker is that the federal government is not doing anything about this; it is silently endorsing their actions by not shutting them down or fining them billions of dollars. What is even worse is that, after the price of oil went to extreme lows in 2015, Alberta asked for billions of dollars from the federal government to assist their economy. Where are the billions and billions of dollars they should have saved for rough winters? It reminds me of the story of the jolly grasshopper and the hard-working ant. The latter survived the winter, while the grasshopper starved as a result of not working and saving during the summer.

The June 11, 2015, Globe and Mail Business Report published an article by Shawn McCarthy entitled "Alberta's oil sands take a hit as scientists, academics call for halt to development," in which he reports that Wendy Palen, a Simon Fraser University ecologist, confirmed that, after research on the oil sands in Alberta, the consensus of scientists was that "we offer a unified voice, calling for a moratorium on new oil sands projects." She added that "decisions on oil sand developments add up to a social and environmental legacy that will last for generations." That legacy is detrimental to the children of those destroying Alberta's forests, lakes, and wildlife in search of more profits, but with absolute neglect and disrespect for their own environment.

In July 2013, Scientific American published another detailed article by David Biello entitled "Greenhouse Goo – The Fate of Alberta's Tar Mines – and the Climate – may come down to the Keystone XL pipeline." He confirms that what makes Alberta's tar sands region so profitable is that the oil can be dug right out of the ground. The ground consists of a special type of mud that is mainly composed of water, metals, and minerals, from which bitumen (tarlike oil) is extracted. The majority of the bitumen in Alberta's northern region is between 10 and 40 feet thick. Considered by many, and referred to by Biello, as underground treasure, the rest of the world sees it as another threat to the survival of our species due to the pressure inflicted on the atmosphere.

Biello confirms that, with today's technology and potential advances in the future, Alberta will be able to extract over 170 billion barrels of oil from the tar sands, which would, in turn, pump about 25 billion metric tons of CO_2 into our atmosphere, if it was all burned. But Biello adds that, if the technology were improved, engineers could extract 1.63 *trillion* more barrels, with a corresponding impact of another 250 million metric tons of CO_2 on the atmosphere. This in itself would affect planetary warming by another 0.4 degrees Celsius just from Alberta's tar sands oil alone!

Why is bitumen from the tar sands more polluting than any other crude oil? Biello explains:

> At Christina Lake, engineers injected roughly two barrels of steam to pump back out one barrel of bitumen. All the steam – and the natural gas burned to heat it – means melting bitumen results in two and a half times more greenhouse gas pollution than surface mining, itself among the highest emitters for any kind of oil production. Greater production by this melting method has caused greenhouse gas emissions from Alberta's tar sands to rise by 16 per cent since 2009.

Now imagine, if Alberta were able to extract all the bitumen reserves mentioned above, what would the final impact on our environment and ecosystem be? To my mind, some Albertans do not seem to grasp that this planet is where we all live. We cannot go and hide somewhere else to avoid future extreme weather conditions. We are going to have to take it on the chin, and I guarantee we are going to be no match for nature's vengeful wrath.

Biello goes on, in this article, to make a very interesting, fair, and wise comparison of Alberta's impact on the world with that of other notorious cases of uncontrolled extraction of oil in countries such as Venezuela, Mexico, and Nigeria, which produce, in many instances, similar pollutants to the tar sands bitumen. Worst of all is California's CO_2 pollution from their own oil extraction, which critics say is even greater than that of our tar sands, though this does not justify our inaction. Biello quotes engineer Murray Gray, director of the Centre for Oil Sands Innovation at the University of Alberta, who points out that, "if you think that using other petroleum sources (than tar sands) is much better, then you are delusional."

Gray's point does not justify the irresponsibility of the tar sands project, of course. It is worth reminding everybody that the main reason for President Obama's rejection of the Keystone XL pipeline (about 2,700 km of proposed pipeline from Alberta to the US) was the likely environmental impact. He listened to what a group of scientists wrote in a report, which concluded that "allowing more tar sand oil into the United States is counter to both national and international interests."

In fairness to the tar sands, Biello gives an example of another environmental impact that is even worse than that of the tar sands, Australian coal extraction and exports. The expansion of Australia's coal exports to Asia, which puts at extraordinary risk the Australian Great Barrier Reef (the biggest coral reef on the planet), could add 1.2 billion metric tons of CO_2 to the atmosphere each year that the coal is burned. That amount dwarfs emissions from even the most optimistic tar sands expansion, according to Biello.

But although there are many other projects out there that are as bad or worse than the tar sands, this does not justify our inaction. As a developed country, we need to be an example for others to follow, yet we are still acting against our environment for the sake of profits, big dividend payments, and the government's desire to collect billions of dollars in taxes.

Unfortunately, US President Donald Trump does not seem to care about the environment as Barack Obama did. On April of 2017 he authorized the Keystone XL and Dakota Access Pipelines. He wants to create jobs regardless of its detrimental impact on the environment and ecosystem, focusing in the wrong energy industry.

But what is really sad and embarrassing, is that Prime Minister Trudeau and Alberta's Premier Rachel Notley applauded Trump's decision, while breaking Trudeau's promise to keep CO_2 in the atmosphere at bay. The National Observer published in Dec 01, 2016 the following: "Prime Minister Trudeau approved two giant new bitumen pipelines at once -- Kinder Morgan's tripling of Trans Mountain and Enbridge's doubling of Line 3. Combined they will allow an additional 200 million tonnes of climate pollution (CO_2) to come out of Alberta's soil every year. That exceeds the combined annual emissions from 100 nations." Then, in April 25, 2017 Toronto Star (thestar.com) published "Justin Trudeau's troubling broken promise on methane. Once again, there seems to be a worrying gap between Ottawa's rhetoric on the environment and its willingness to act." Money talks louder than nature and there is "nothing we can do", unless we stop being passive aggressive and get actively involved. Otherwise, mother nature will take care of itself and react violently against humans with its impact on climate change.

Now, to make matters worse from the environmental point of view, in April 28, 2017 US President Trump signed an executive order allowing the expansion of offshore drilling in the Arctic and Atlantic oceans. Is the Arctic at risk now? Absolutely! Regardless of technological advance the oil industry says they have achieved, accidents are always bound to happen, and make no mistake, will happen. As humans, we should never place at risk areas like the Arctic and the Antarctic. But again, power, politics, and greed ("money makes the world go round" - Liza Minnelli). Close to 94 per cent of offshore exploration and production were kept closed by previous administrations for environmental and political reasons.

Oil industry accidents and environmental contamination

Let's forget for a moment all the previously mentioned facts and focus only on the potential for future accidents in the fossil fuel industry. The damage and contamination to international waters and marine life from such accidents could be totally devastating. The exact same scenario can happen in the Arctic or Antarctic regions. It does not matter how advanced or sophisticated our technology becomes, we are no match for the caprices and demands of nature. When nature gets angry, you better get out of its way and hide until it calms down. An atomic bomb is like playing with marbles or a yoyo compared to this scale of natural disaster. Any state-of-the-art technology will be insufficient against massive waves, pounding hurricanes, racing ocean currents, and freezing temperatures beyond the capacity of human technology to handle.

As a friend of mine used to say, "you need not believe me, the proof is in the pudding!" Why? Let's just look at five short and simple examples of each of the following three disaster areas or categories where our state-of-the-art technology, which was supposed to protect us, failed, and failed profoundly. This is why events like these are called accidents waiting to happen. It is not a matter of if, but just a matter of when and where. The three main areas of potential disaster waiting to happen are offshore rigs, ocean oil spills, and oil pipeline and ground transportation disasters.

Offshore rig disasters

There have been so many offshore rig disasters (just Google the topic) that I will list only the five I consider the most significant, which are:

Piper Alpha Disaster: 167 workers lost their lives in 1988 when their platform (oil rig) exploded and caught fire. This rig was producing both gas and oil at the same time. It was manufactured, and managed by Occidental in alliance with other companies. The disaster started in a pressure safety valve and ended up as the worst oil rig disaster known to man, not just because of the 167 human lives lost that day, but also because of the environmental damage to the area.

Ocean Ranger Disaster: This rig capsized in the middle of a fierce storm in the cold waters of the North Atlantic, causing the deaths of more than 80 people. It was originally built in Japan and managed by Mobil Oil of Canada. One of the biggest semi-submersible oilrigs of the time, it was situated about 265 kilometres east of Newfoundland. The rig was no match for 190 kilometre/hour winds and waves over 60 feet high. The disaster started in the ballast room on February 14, 1982. The storm was so strong that there was nothing anybody could do. Heavy damage was caused to the environment, seriously affecting marine life in the area.

Alexander L. Kielland Disaster: This happened in 1980 on the Norwegian Continental Shelf. Phillips Petroleum managed the rig at the time. More than 120 people lost their lives that afternoon of March 27. Due to very strong winds, once the braces attached to a leg supporting the rig failed. This caused the rest of the legs to fail almost in a synchronized manner, tilting and capsizing the rig, causing not just loss of human life but serious ecological damage in the area as well.

Seacrest Drillship Disaster: Typhoon Gale capsized the drillship, causing a loss of 91 crew members on November 3, 1989, in the Gulf of Thailand. Communications with the drillship were lost, and it was only discovered a day later floating upside-down in the gulf. Known also as the Scan Queen, the drillship was working for Unocal. Only six crew members were found alive by local fishermen.

Bohai 2 Oil Rig Disaster: This rig was being towed in the Gulf of Bohai (between Korea and China) when a strong storm with high winds hit the area, capsizing it. Out of 74 crew members, 72 lost their lives that November 25,1979. The rig also caused ecological and marine damage in the area after it ended up sinking to the bottom of the ocean.

Ocean oil spills

There have been over 200 ocean oil spills (just Yahoo to confirm), but again I will limit myself to a few of most important yielded by my research:

Torrey Canyon Oil Spill: This huge spill took place on March 18, 1967, in the Scilly Isles of the United Kingdom, discharging over 30 million gallons of crude oil. According to Laura Moss in Mother Nature Network (July 16, 2010), it was the worst oil spill in history up to that time. She wrote: "The spill created an oil slick measuring 270 square miles, contaminating 180 miles of coastland. More than 15,000 sea birds and enormous numbers of aquatic animals were killed before the spill was finally contained." The Torrey Canyon was the first super tanker and boasted what everyone considered state-of-the-art safety technology (as was said of the Titanic just before it sank). Originally built to carry 60,000 tons of crude oil, the tanker was later renovated and its carrying capacity doubled.

It was sailing at full capacity when it hit a reef off the coast of Cornwall. The Royal Navy used toxic solvents in their efforts to disperse the oil but only caused worse ecological damage in the area, says Moss. It took years to bring the area back to normal and thousands of volunteers to bring it under control. The damage to sea birds and marine life was extensive and tragic and is still being felt today. More than 270 square miles and over 280 kilometres of coastline were contaminated with gooey, sticky oil.

Arabian Gulf/Kuwait: This happened on January 19, 1991, in the Persian Gulf and was deliberately caused by Iraqi forces during the Gulf War. Over 4,000 square miles were covered with a 4-inch thick layer of oil that caused extensive damage to the coastline and a severe ecological punishment of the whole area. Over 500 million gallons of oil were dumped, by far the largest oil spill ever.

Ixtoc I Oil Spill: This was an exploratory drilling rig located in the Bay of Campeche, Mexico, an area full of beautiful marine and bird life, various types of coral, coastal lagoons, and extremely diversified marine species. Among the most important were a wide variety of molluscs, exotic fish, and crustaceans, along with amazing coastal birds. On June 3, 1979, a semi-submersible drilling rig, the Ixtoc I, was drilling a well when an explosion and fire destroyed it, mixing gas and oil in the process and sending the Ixtoc I to the bottom of the sea. Oil was expelled into the Gulf of Mexico at an average rate of nine million gallons per day, a rate never experienced before.

Deep Water Horizon: This disaster took place in the Gulf of Mexico under the management of BP (British Petroleum) on

April 22, 2010. It has been estimated that over 205 million gallons of oil (about 1,400,000 tonnes) were dumped into the gulf, causing serious damage to the US and Mexican shorelines along with a huge detrimental impact on sea birds and marine life. It is estimated that about 2.5 million gallons gushed into the Gulf of Mexico per day before the spill was contained. The well spilled close to 5 million barrels of crude oil in total and is considered the largest marine oil spill in history to date. It seriously affected the livelihoods of many people in the fishing and tourism industries for many years. The oil well exploded, and this caused the drilling platform to catch on fire. It took BP many attempts before they managed to plug the well after 85 days and after contaminating more than 900 kilometres of coastline. Eleven men died in the explosion and BP lost their $560 million-dollar rig, which ended up at the bottom of the sea, a scorched and distorted pile of metal.

Both the Ixtoc I and Deep Water Horizon oil spills occurred in the Gulf of Mexico, but it is obvious we have not learned our lesson from them. Three new oil reserves were recently discovered in the gulf, and already a new "high-tech, state of-the-art" rig called the Perdido Rig (Lost Rig in Spanish) has been built only three kilometres offshore in the Gulf of Mexico. This rig, a project of Shell Global, is the deepest offshore oil drilling and production platform in the world and promises "a new frontier in deep-water oil and gas recovery."

<u>ABT Summer Oil Spill</u>: This took place about 700 nautical miles off the coast of Angola on May 28, 1991. The ship exploded, releasing about 80 million gallons of oil into the ocean. Over 125 square kilometres were contaminated along with the damage to every living species that got into contact with the thick spill, which ended up burning. The tanker was travelling from Iran to Rotterdam when it leaked oil and then caught on fire, with subsequent explosions that ultimately ended up sinking it.

<u>Castillo de Bellver Oil Spill</u>: This took place on August 6, 1983, in Saldanha Bay in South Africa (about 110 kilometres from Cape Town). Close to 80 million gallons of oil (about 1.9 million barrels) were lost to the ocean waters. The Spanish tanker was loaded with 250,000 tons of oil and was travelling in a very sensitive environmental area with a rich marine ecosystem that was also a very productive fishing area. Needless to say, the damage was very extensive. The vessel broke apart after burning for days.

Pipeline and ground transportation oil disasters

There have been thousands of accidents with oil pipelines and oil transportation by train. The following are the six that impressed me the most:

<u>Lac-Mégantic Derailment</u>: Over six million litres of oil were spilled in Lac-Mégantic, Quebec, and 47 people lost their lives when a train carrying crude oil derailed on July 6, 2013, near this small lakeshore town. The oil rushed all the way to the St. Lawrence River through the crystal-clear waters of the lake.

The derailment happened very close to downtown. More than 30 buildings were destroyed, wiping out half of the downtown core. Many people also went missing and eventually were presumed dead. This accident put at serious risk the health of local people, and the contaminated water and air seriously affected the local ecosystem as well.

<u>Kolva River Oil Spill</u>:   This disaster happened in northern Russia close to the city of Usinsk starting in early 1983 (though it was not properly reported until August of that year). The oil pipeline running through the area was heavily corroded and not well maintained and is said to have leaked for at least eight months. The escaping oil was contained by a dam, which then collapsed, causing severe damage to the

Russian tundra all the way to the Kolva River. The ecological damage to all the surrounding marshlands, grasslands and wild life was substantial. More than 180 square kilometres were affected.

Yellowstone Oil Pipeline Rupture: This oil pipeline, built in the mid-1950s, breached its integrity and split open due to poor welding materials. The pipeline, which goes through a vast area of Yellowstone National Park, suddenly ruptured, spilling over 45,000 gallons of oil into the Yellowstone River and affecting the surrounding natural habitat in one of the most pristine and beautiful national parks in the world. Some critics claim that it was not manufacturing flaws or poor-quality welding materials that caused the rupture. Whatever the cause, the bottom line is that it affected the ecosystem of one of the most admired places on earth. If that were not enough, in 2011 Exxon's Silvertip Pipeline also failed and poured over 63,000 gallons of oil into the Yellowstone River, damaging the environment and putting the local wildlife at risk.

Derailment in Lynchburg, Virginia: In April, 2014, a train was travelling at low speed when it suddenly derailed and ended up spilling thousands of gallons of crude oil into the James River. Dirt and stone gave way under the train tracks, causing more than 14 tankers to derail. This happened very close to downtown Lynchburg. The oil caught on fire and sent many pollutants into the air, affecting people's health in the area. It seriously impacted their environment and put at risk the wildlife along the James River and beyond.

Pennsylvania Derailments: Two consecutive accidents happened in the state of Pennsylvania, one after the other. The first took place in January, 2014, and the second in February. In the first derailment, 19 cars were carrying crude oil, but, luckily, only four cars spilled about 4,000 gallons. Other cars were carrying liquefied petroleum gas and, fortunately, did not leak. The second derailment in February did not result in any leaks but left an oil tanker dangling over the bridge. It was pure luck that it did not fall into the Schuykill River, which would have caused severe ecological contamination and damage.

Prince Albert, Saskatchewan oil spill (July 2016): Over 200,000 litres of oil from the Husky Energy pipe leaked into the North Saskatchewan River. I decided to bring to the attention of the readers this recent Saskatchewan oil spill case, because it does not matter how advanced and high tech the new production, distribution, and transportation policies, methods and procedures are, or how advanced the technology is. Why? Because such systems and structures are still, and always will be, dangerous and prone to accidents. Pipelines will always be subject to technical failures and human mistakes that cause oil spills.

The situation in Prince Albert turned out to be so critical that the city council declared a local state of emergency and had to install a 30-km water pipe in order to bring clean water from the South Saskatchewan River into the city. Many businesses had to close and prohibitions were imposed on watering and irrigation subject to a $1,000 fine if caught doing so. The environment and the local ecosystem were seriously affected and required immediate costly cleaning that, in many cases, will never be totally effective. The area is unlikely to ever be as environmentally clean as it was before the accident, at least in our lifetime.

Alarming disassociation: Greed and betrayal vs. balance in life

It seems that almost nobody cares about accidents beyond their own back yards. If it does not affect them, people do not seem to register the real depth of the damage caused by an accident. But what is really mindboggling is the fact that people believe that everything happens to others but will not happen to them or someone close to them. Others think that, if it happens, there is nothing they can do or could have done. In either case, the average person fails to try and prevent things from happening. However, prevention techniques are crucial for survival anywhere in the world, and so we need to be conscious and proactive at all times.

We have a very wise saying in Spanish: "*Si vez a tu vecino rasurar, pon tus barbas a remojar, porque después sigues tú*", ("If you see your neighbour shave, place your beard in hot water; you are next"). In other words, the odds are that you might be next. Nobody is exempt from things happening to them. Nobody!

Please feel free to Google or Yahoo the World Wide Web about crude oil accidents. I am confident it will blow your mind to realize how many thousands and thousands of these accidents have happened just on the American continent alone. Now imagine for a moment if we were to add all those accidents that have occurred around the world, along with their devastating impacts, to earth's delicate ecological balance. It is hard to fathom the accumulated damage and all that has been lost forever.

It is normal for accidents to happen, and it is normal for companies to want to make a profit and protect the interests of their shareholders as much as possible. However, we seldom hear about these types of accidents, either because the companies involved do not want people to know or because we simply consider such accidents part of daily life that we need to get used to, because it represents the cost of doing business. In either case, what is alarming is the absolute disassociation and lack of responsibility between the shareholders and their families, between the employees of these oil companies and their children, between the government officials and the people who elected them, and so on.

Yes, we need to keep exploiting fossil fuel for many human needs, but we can drastically slow down its use as an energy source if we all put our minds and efforts together. However, this demands consciousness, desire, and sacrifice. Nothing comes easy. If it does, it is not worth it, simple as that!

The disassociation between profit and the company's greed to make more and more money versus having some consideration for the environment and the future well-being of their own children is staggering, astonishing, and totally hypocritical. This brings to mind the seven cardinal sins – lust, greed, gluttony, laziness, wrath, envy, and pride. Regarding greed and gluttony, it is like seeing the Roman emperors going to the vomitorium, where they used to throw up the contents of their stomach after feasting and gorging themselves with all sorts of exotic foods and drinks. Their gluttony and greed to consume more and more was so extreme that they needed to release their stomach pressure by vomiting the contents so they could go back and do it all over again. By the way, the exact definition of a vomitorium is "amphitheater passageways," but the word has been used for what I have just described above as well. The same degree of greed and gluttony (metaphorically speaking) for more and more food and or profits, whichever the real cause might be, is what is affecting our environment and putting the future of mankind and all other species in jeopardy.

We all understand the need for expansion, growth, and development. What I neither agree with nor understand is the level of profits these oil companies make, in absolute disregard for their surroundings and of the future of their employees and their own families. Money will fail to provide their families a bubble of protection when disasters happen in the future, regardless of how much money they have accumulated and how advanced the technology they use at the time. As just one isolated and random example, consider what Jeff Lewis from Calgary, Alberta, published on July 29,

2015, in the Globe and Mail regarding Husky Energy Inc. Lewis used a graphic that shows that during the second quarters of 2014 and 2015, Husky made over $600 million and over $100 million respectively in their exploration and production business alone. And Husky has moderate profits compared to other giants in the oil industry. How much profit is enough?

To finish this section (I could easily go on forever), I want to bring to the reader's attention two brief anecdotes:

1. A friend of mine once sarcastically remarked, concerning all those oil business corporations in North America (and around the world): It is like what Jack Nicholson once screamed in a film called A Few Good Men – "You can't handle the truth!" By this, my friend was referring to all those oil corporations denying the damage they are causing to our ecosystem and their direct and heavy participation in global warming. They cannot or do not want to handle the truth! It is not economically feasible to accept fault, or else ….

2. I just finished taking an on-line course on Project Management from a well-known Canadian university whose name I will not mention for reasons of confidentiality. During this course, we had to participate in on-time and intelligent discussions of certain concepts and topics. What Jack Nicholson said in the movie reverberated in my mind when I asked about the motivation behind working for companies involved in the Tar Sands of Alberta. It is true. People cannot handle the truth and always try to provide excuses or justifications for what they do or avoid doing. Here is how my question was responded to by one of my classmates:

Question:

Rafael Carreras - *RE:* Team Motivation - Personal Values

Professor, I like how you phrased it and completely concur

that our own values and goals need alignment with those of the companies. Isn't that the way we all look for a project or even employment? A person needs them properly aligned and directly correlated to feel motivated and eager to go to work. Even a distant parallel, but good examples of the above, are all those non-profit organizations such as Green Peace, where the values and goals of their members go hand in hand with those of the organization. It does not matter if it is for profit or non-profit. We are just emphasizing on the motivational fact and values.

But what about those pro-environment people that work for oil companies in the Tar Sands? Are they working there for the same values and goals of the oil company or just for the money? How can team motivation relate to this scenario?

Answer:

Tania Ho - *RE:* Team Motivation - Personal Values

Quote:

> *I agree Rafael! One of my favourite work experiences was working for the Canadian Parks and Wilderness Society because my values regarding environmental stewardship echoed that of the companies! It was extremely motivating to work for a cause you believed in! Regarding environmental employees working for oil and gas (includes me :-) !). In my experiences our work strives to be innovative to find better solutions for the environment regarding oil and gas development. That's a huge motivation! What can we do better? How can we save water? How can we have a minimal or no impact? These are all questions we face in our projects in order to do better for the environment and in turn our communities.*

Her answer sounds very nice and altruistic, but the truth and bottom line is that the Tar Sands still use enormous amounts of water per barrel of oil and, above all, are still destroying everything in their path while contaminating the soil, rivers and lakes, and killing local species. It is clear to me that they have not found better techniques to responsibly protect the environment while exploiting the oil Tar Sands. Again, that is the bottom line! The lack of understanding (and refusal to admit their guilt) of the oil corporations in Alberta is so extreme that some oil companies are even suing the United States government after President Obama rejected the Keystone XL Oil Pipeline project. The reader can attest to this by referring to an article published by Laura Wagner in The-Two-Way (breaking news – nrp.org) last January 7, 2016, entitled "Company Behind Keystone XL Oil Pipeline Sues US Government." According to Wagner: "The Keystone XL pipeline was intended to connect to this pumping station in Steele City, Neb. Keystone's parent company is suing the US government because President Obama blocked the project." For more information, please refer to: npr.org/sections/thetwo-way/

Oil companies are not putting their money where their mouths are, but they are still making billions for their shareholders. Why not reduce those dividends and put more into the development of alternative clean energy sources, instead of sticking to fossil fuel dependence just to provide their shareholders with a lucrative income? They can recover those dividends with future renewable energy profit sharing in a stronger market where Germany is now the current leader.

Critical scientific confirmation

National Geographic's issue of April 2017, has a dedicated chapter to water and seven important things we need to understand about climate change. A lot of people still doubt the reality of climate change, but no one should ever doubt "leaving your family a better world." This is one of National Geographic's mottos, with which I fully agree. Catherine Zuckerman published an article in this issue entitled "Garbage Swell." Zucherman says that when she was assigned a job in a remote spot on the coast of Java, she met an Indonesian surfer who was literally swimming in a sea of garbage. The surfer (Mr. Dede Surayana) stated: "It was overwhelming. I really thought we were going to see a dead body in the water." Zuckerman confirms that roughly 8 million tons of plastic end up in the ocean every year.

Plastic brings with it devastating effects to marine life and therefore, to the ocean's natural balance. She says that this is a rising problem worldwide, especially in developing countries with the expansion of the middle-class population along the coasts. Fortunately, she ends her brief report by saying that proper awareness and actions are required, and apparently, it is slowly starting to happen, and as she stated, "the tide might be turning."

With population growth worldwide, immediate needs for food, power and fuel are increasing exponentially. National Geographic insists that the way we supply and consume our energy "is changing the world we are living in." They proceeded to confirm that in 2016, we exceeded the threshold of 400 parts per million of CO_2 in our atmosphere. The safe level of carbon dioxide in the atmosphere is 350 parts per million. There is no scientific doubt that the planet is undergoing a serious and formidable climate change. We are already experiencing the deadly effects of extreme weather of all kinds, such as aggressive wildfires, rising sea levels, devastating mudslide, and powerful and destructive storms. The heavy dependency on fossil fuels is mainly to blame, along with population growth, which needs this form of energy source. Therefore, National Geographic issue of April 2017 wants its readers to understand and hopefully do something, about the following points:

- The world is warming - *period!*
- It is because of humans - *without doubt!*
- We are sure - *almost 100 per cent certainty!*
- Ice is melting fast; *it is undeniable!*
- Weather is getting intense - *there is worldwide proof!*
- Wild life is already hurting - *confirmed the Polar bear's loss of habitat!*
- We can do something about it - *with co-ordinate worldwide solutions!*

But to the above, I would add another factor, which I consider crucial:

- We must not procrastinate. Individual and collective action is desperately required ASAP – *a call to immediate action*!

Put it this way, if scientists are accurate in their calculations and predictions, then we must act as quickly as "yesterday", and if they are not, there is no harm done. Regardless, it is our moral and ethical responsibility to protect the only planet we have for future generations to enjoy, as well as all other species in planet Earth. How wrong is that?

CONCLUSION

Our planet is all we have. As human beings, if we want to move from one state or province to another, or from one country to another, we could most likely do it, if need be, but, for very obvious reasons, we certainly cannot, for the foreseeable future, move from planet Earth to another planet in our galaxy or beyond. Therefore, shouldn't we be taking care of our globe with absolute devotion, legitimate interest, and unbreakable spirit and dedication?

If our planet is not healthy, balanced, and happy, it can make our existence extremely bitter, difficult, painful, and close to impossible. Humans are going too far in mistreating and exploiting the planet's natural resources, and this exploitation does not seem to be slowing down, in fact, just the opposite. We are undeniably destroying the peace, harmony, and balance we all need in order to coexist in harmony with our planet, but, I insist, we do not seem to fully understand this, or if we do, we are refusing to accept it and much less, care about it. To save this planet from irreparable damage, we need to start acting responsibly in every corner of our world. Our attitude has to change dramatically before it is too late. We need to stop demanding more and more from our natural resources and focus more on the protection of our environment and our overall ecosystem. To achieve productivity and real happiness in this world we need to be honest, sincere, and authentic in our principles, and our principles need to "hold hands" in absolute harmony with our environment worldwide.

In our search for success and real happiness, we sometimes have to cope with circumstances that we may not like. It is of utmost importance to adapt and to at least look comfortable, as chameleons do during their lives. We need to choose our battles. We need not sweat the small and insignificant matters, but do need to let go of those superficial situations and try focusing on the big picture, the end result, and what is really important to us – our environment and ecosystem, which provide us with everything we possess. We should strive to focus on what matters the most without being stubborn, careless, and greedy, and without focusing only on personal gain. We need to centre our attention on the ultimate balance of the overall big picture that surrounds us in the world where we live. That should be our utmost goal. If we accept this with good will and harmony, we stand better chances to retain what we still have before it disappears.

Humanity's biggest sin is taking things for granted! Yes, humans have been taking this planet for granted, as if it had unlimited resources. Some valuable reminders are:

- "The things you take for granted someone else is praying for" – staypositive.me.
- "When you take things for granted, the things you are granted get taken" – pinterest.com and livelifehappy.com.
- "People say you don't know what you've got till it's gone. Truth is, you knew what you had, you just never thought you'd lose it" – Anonymous.
- "We often take for granted the very things that most deserve our gratitude" – Cynthia Ozick.

It does not matter if we are poor or rich, the colour of our skin, the geographical location where we live, our age, or the type of faith we have. Every one of us somewhere or somehow has taken this planet and its resources for granted. Shame on us! It is time to learn to be humble and appreciative, or we will live to regret it.

There is an old expression that says: "things happen for a reason." To my mind, this lacks accuracy. I believe certain things just happen because they happen (no specific reason involved), but, most importantly, they happen because we make them happen! They do not happen for an unknown, unplanned, or celestial reason. When some people say that it "happens for a reason," it is just an excuse without a firm foundation on facts. Why? It is most likely because they ignore the real reason or because they do not want to be honest with themselves, accept the truth, and take responsibility. The latter implies admission of guilt and true effort and commitment to solve the problem, and that is certainly a challenge. Before the treasures provided by our only globe are gone, please always keep in mind that we owe our respect and total appreciation to the following:

- To planet Earth and its infinite beauty.
- To nature and its boundless wisdom.
- To water and its calming and refreshing power, essential for both our happiness and our survival.
- To the soil and its generosity in giving.
- To fire and its ability to provide warmth and protection.
- To fresh air and the health, it brings with it.
- To the flora and fauna and their beautiful, stable integration on the planet.
- To the environment and its efforts to maintain its balance.
- To future technology and renewable resources.
- To human wisdom, inventiveness, and ability to adapt.

There is a very wise native American proverb, which people do not seem to understand. It is definitely worth quoting in bold and italic letters, and it goes like so:

Treat Earth well: it was not given to you by your parents; it was loaned to you by your children. We do not inherit Earth from our ancestors; we borrowed it from our children.

APPENDIX 1: ALARMING WILDLIFE EXAMPLES

The idea of this appendix is to bring to the attention of the reader only some of the most alarming cases of animal species in danger of extinction due to the following main reasons:

A) Illegal hunting (killed for their skins or body parts)

B) Illegal trade (captured and traded)

C) Loss of habitat (human population invasion).

The information included here is widely and readily available in libraries and on the Internet.

We humans are the most dangerous species on earth. We kill for both need and greed, contrary to all other animals, which only kill in order to survive. As humans, we are reshaping our world, but not necessarily for the better. Wild animals, exotic forests, clean oceans, lakes, and rivers are being damaged and even disappearing at an alarming rate in the name of progress and development. As humans always justify what we do or do not do, regardless of the results and repercussions. We are seriously affecting many species and pushing them to extinction. Some examples of species endangered by illegal hunting, which are already on the brink of disappearing forever, are summarized below, with hopes that more people join efforts to stop it.

Whale massacre

According to various sources, most notably, the Sea Shepherd Conservation Society, the Danish people allow a hideous massacre of whales in the Faeroe Islands, a North Sea Danish protectorate, in a horrendous and cowardly manner. Denmark practices a savage whale slaughter every year, mostly of long-finned pilot whales. The Faroese authorities, in a long tradition, have apparently regulated this aggressive act since these islands were first settled. It is also reported that some dolphins fall victim to this event every year, when they are captured or cornered as well.

The Sea Shepherd Conservation Society has been a strong advocate of stopping illegal whalers, mainly from Iceland, Norway, and Japan. These three nations are well known for practicing illegal hunting of various other species in international waters.

In Denmark, the whales are collected and driven into specific bays in the islands and forced into shallow waters, where they are slaughtered by targeting their spinal cords with anything handy, such as swords, knives, spears, harpoons, stones, etc. After the massacre (or ritual) is finished, the ocean in the bay is not blue or green anymore. It is absolutely and gruesomely blood-red. Sea Shepherd Conservation Society says: "This slaughter is particularly gruesome, since the killing is conducted as a community sporting event, with young children often participating in the killing of the visibly and audibly terrified whales."

Honestly, in today's world, can deep traditions or religious beliefs justify slaughtering whales as part of your cultural heritage? Why are the responsible authorities not doing anything serious and definite about this massacre?

Not every country that has access to whale hunting does it to the full extent of its possibilities. A good example is Norway, where they have hunted whales for generations. Today, however, the number of hunted whales has fallen drastically, mainly for the following reasons: Norwegians prefer to become cod fishermen rather than whalers; the cost of whaling is high, and its profit margins are lower than the cod industry; and they want to avoid stormy winter seas during whale-hunting season. The reason whales are being hunted less is not due to social and moral changes, but to economic and practical reasons, as well as alternative catches that are more profitable than whaling. It is uncivilized and sad but true.

There is an interesting article by Roff Smith (pictures by Marcus Bleasdale) in National Geographic's issue of June 2013 entitled "Last of The Viking Whalers." Smith writes: "There are restrictions imposed by the Convention on International Trade in Endangered Species (CITES) in the export markets and although Norway's government sets an annual quota of 1,286 Minke whales, in practice whalers take far fewer (only 533 in 2011)." The quotas being achieved in 2014 and 2015 by the whalers are still below those authorized by the government of Norway.

The main real threat to the whales are those Japanese factory ships that stay in high seas for months hunting whales with explosive harpoons, giving no chance of survival to the whales they hit. The International Whaling Commission (IWC) imposed a moratorium on commercial whaling in 1986, but the hunt continues. Among the most hunted whale species are the Minke and Grey whales, although the Minke is hunted nine times more than the grey.

Turtle egg poaching

In Costa Rica the poaching of sea turtles takes place with total disregard for their healthy natural balance and their future preservation. This is risking not just their natural balance but also their potential extinction from the shores of Costa Rica. But what is really alarming is that, instead of promoting tourism during the turtle's hatching season, the government has gone ahead and legalized this activity. For more details, visit: coastalcare.org/2011/07/legalized-poaching-turtles-eggs-and-playa-ostional-costa-rica/

There is an article on the Coastal Care Website by Claire Le Guern Lytle entitled "Sea Turtle Egg Poaching Legalized In Costa Rica: The Debate." Lytle reports that the Costa Rican government has legalized poaching using the following rationale:

> Circumventing a global conservation effort is to sustainably maintain the local population of the Olive Ridley sea turtle, while concurrently providing a consistent income stream for the economically challenged local community of Ostional that may harvest the turtle eggs from the beach to sell locally.

The debate continues about whether the harvesting will be beneficial or not for the survival of the species in the long run, but for now the number of turtles and eggs seems to be declining.

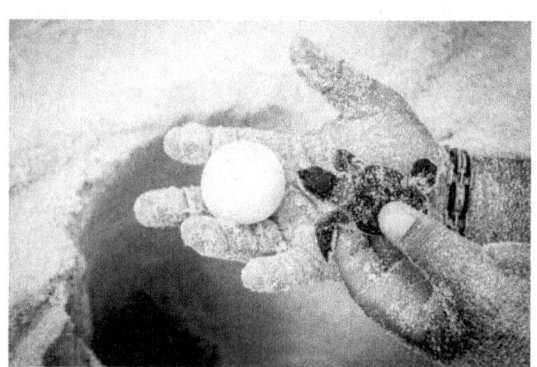 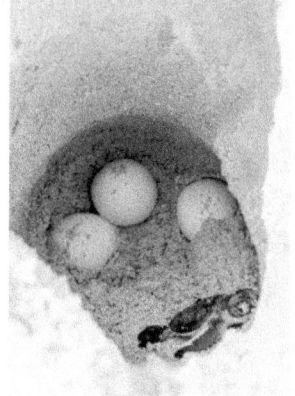

Source: iStock

All types of turtles play a key role in our oceans and beaches. For millions of years, they have roamed the oceans freely, and they still do today. Victims of egg poaching and indiscriminate and accidental fishing, some types of turtles are now on the endangered species list of the WWF. Such is the case with the Hawksbill turtle (mainly found in coral reefs around the world), the Loggerhead turtle (mainly found in the

Mediterranean Sea) and the Green turtle.

Turtles have been in existence for over 100 million years and, here we are, in the twenty-first century, about to exterminate various species. What on earth gives us the right to do so? Such is the case of the Southern River Terrapin turtle (from the Batagur family), which is now critically endangered. According to Patricia Edmonds in an article published in National Geographic of July, 2015, entitled "Too Hot To Handle," the Terrapin turtles are losing habitat mainly to sand mining and also fall victim to by-catch in fishing nets. River Terrapin turtles are a delicacy on Chinese menus, so they are being fished illegally and their eggs poached from beaches and rivers, especially in Malaysia, Indonesia, and Cambodia, which export them to China.

Other turtle species in danger of extinction, according to the Canadian Wild Life Federation (CWF), include the Eastern Musk and the Leatherback sea turtle. The first has a skunk-like musky scent to keep predators away, while the latter reaches a length of close to two meters and can weigh close to a ton.

Dolphin killing

Japan is not all beautiful rose gardens. It also has a tradition of slaughtering dolphins in a hidden cove near the village of Taiji. It happens every year and is not just gruesome but also cowardly, archaic, barbaric, and ignorant. If readers surf the World Wide Web for information, they will be shocked by the data and images on this horrific event. An organization in the United States called People for the Ethical Treatment of Animals (PETA) has published very important data on this matter and summarizes the hunt as follows:

> In Japan, fishers round up and slaughter approximately 23,000 dolphins and small whales each year. In the

small fishing village of Taiji, entire schools of dolphins are driven into a hidden cove after a prolonged chase. Once trapped inside the cove, the fishers kill the dolphins by cutting their throats with knives or stabbing them with spears. The water turns red with the dolphins' blood, and the air is filled with their screams. This horrific massacre goes on for six months every year.

As shocking as it sounds, dolphins are viewed as "pests" and are eradicated in huge numbers in order to preserve the ocean's fish for human consumption. What's even more scandalous is that members of the international dolphin-display industry take advantage of the slaughter to obtain animals for use in captive-dolphin shows and swim-with-dolphins programs.

How obtuse and narrow-minded somebody must be to consider dolphins a pest. To my mind, some Japanese have a distorted idea of what pests are, and I sometimes wonder, who is the real pest? Dolphins assist in maintaining the overall balance of the ocean and are a vital part of our marine ecosystem. The Japanese are the ones who are exterminating various species of fish through irrational hunting to satisfy their culinary preferences. They pay extreme top dollar for certain types of fish (such as tuna). This is why there are fewer and fewer tuna in the oceans.

Although the Bottlenose dolphin, which lives in the open sea, is not considered an endangered species, other types of dolphins are. This is the case with the Ganges River dolphin, the Hector's dolphin, and the Indus River dolphin. According to the WWF, the Ganges River dolphins were once located in the Ganges-Brahmaputra-Meghna and Kaqrnaphuli-Sangu rivers of Nepal, Bangladesh and India. These are blind dolphins that live in freshwater and hunt similarly to bats with the use of ultrasonic sounds.

Hector's dolphins live on the western shores of New Zealand's North Island. According to the WWF, there are estimated to be only about 55 Hector's dolphins remaining. It is the smallest and rarest of the dolphin family. The Indus River dolphins from Pakistan are freshwater dolphins and there are only an estimated 1,100 still alive, according to the WWF.

Source: iStock

But let's face it. Who has swum with the dolphins and not said "Oh, what a great experience!" Many countries are guilty of having dolphins in captivity. That is cruel and heartless, but hey, you get to say: "I have swum with and touched the dolphins." Imagine being kept in captivity in a glass room 25 feet by 25 feet. Would you like that? What is the difference? In fact, dolphins swim and cover distances ten times faster than an average human being. Are humans cruel by nature? Why do we pretend not to see and acknowledge what really goes on? Why do we turn a blind eye? Shouldn't we all get together and do something about this? For more information, see:

secure.peta.org/site/Advocacy?cmd=display&page=UserActio n&id=803

Bluefin tuna overfishing

Japanese and Spanish high-tech ships using impressive, strong meshes that are several kilometres long and hundreds of metres deep are catching anything in their path while trying to hunt for the famous Bluefin tuna. Some of the drift nets used in international oceans during the 1950s were as long as 50 kilometres, until the United Nations stepped in and banned the use of drift nets longer than 2.5 kilometres in 1992. But please just stop and think for a minute. Can you imagine kilometres of fishing net laid in the oceans to catch whatever crosses their path? But if this is not enough, some fishermen discard or carelessly lose these nets in the oceans, posing a fatal risk to marine life. There is an alarming final project report published in October of 2105 by the World Wildlife Fund (WWF) entitled "Removal of derelict fishing gear, lost or discarded by fishermen in the Baltic Sea". For further detailed information about the findings and conclusions of this project, please contact WWF Poland or Marta Kalinowska: mkalinowska@wwf.pl

Source: iStock

Atlantic Bluefin tuna

Even with the smaller drift nets of today, the Atlantic Bluefin tuna (known as Bluefin or giant Bluefin) is already on the endangered list and being pushed slowly but surely to extinction. The number of Bluefin tuna in the oceans is decreasing rapidly, and they are expected to disappear relatively soon. Their biggest consumption markets, in priority sequence, are Japan, then other Asian and European markets. Spain and France are among the leading tuna fishing nations in Europe pushing them to extinction.

The scientific name for the Atlantic Bluefin tuna is Thunnus thynnus. It achieves an average weight of 380 to 400 kilograms at adult stage and, with an average length of about six feet and a smooth streamlined shape, is one of the largest and fastest fishes in the ocean. It has beautiful colours and lean meat rich in Omega 3 fatty acids and is also, unfortunately, a very delicious fish as steak or sashimi-style slices, the main reason it is in great demand by various countries around the world.

They are a warm-blooded fish, which swim peacefully in the cold waters of Iceland and Newfoundland, as much as in warm waters such as the Mediterranean Sea and the Gulf of Mexico, where the Pacific tuna is being caught in excess. Kumi Naidoo wrote an alarming article entitled "Pacific tuna fishing out of control" in his blogpost for Greenpeace last August 4, 2015, in which he confirms that the way the tuna business operates is putting the whole system at risk. Ships from many parts of the world (in his article he shows a Taiwanese ship in international waters fishing indiscriminately) are pillaging the Pacific Ocean while taking too many fish, in absolute disregard of international laws and with nobody to police them, while storming and assaulting the coastal zones of small countries that lack adequate Coast Guard protection for their own waters. These illegal fleets are not just affecting our oceans and their marine ecosystems, they are also damaging the societies where the fishermen come from. Naidoo writes:

> Recent stories of labour abuse, terrible bullying, slavery, and human trafficking are exposing serious problems in global fisheries. Similar stories – too many to ignore – are starting to emerge from the tuna fleet. Long liners catching albacore for the canned tuna markets of the West can be like floating sweatshops,

taking young men desperate for work away from their families, locking them into contracts that can last for years, and saddling them with debt if they try to break those contracts early.

Out on the high seas, with no means of escape, it must seem to some of these young fishermen as if they are serving a prison sentence. And with less than one per cent of fishing activity by long-line fleets witnessed by on-board independent observers in the Western Central Pacific, there is no one to turn to and nowhere to go. It is the perfect environment for exploitation – a captive workforce.

Last week, Greenpeace released a series of videos linking bullying and labour abuse to Pacific tuna boats. The stories of violence and exploitation we have heard about tuna fishermen are heartbreaking.

For more information, visit:

greenpeace.org/international/en/news/Blogs/makingwaves/pacific-tuna-fishing-is-out-of-control/blog/53670/

© Paul Hilton / Greenpeace
Taiwanese longline fishing vessel, just one of thousands of tuna boats fishing the Pacific Ocean.

What is tuna transshipment?

Also, known as trans-loading, this is the transfer of goods from one ship to another ship for transport to a final destination. In the fishing industry, it means to load the catch of the day or the month from one ship to another.

As Alex Hofford of Greenpeace comments on the above photo:

> Tuna on the ship "Heng Xing 1" in an area of international waters near the exclusive economic zone of Indonesia. The Cambodian flagged vessel was caught illegally transhipping frozen tuna from a Philippine fishing vessel and two other Indonesian vessels in the Pacific high seas, where none of the ships have licenses to operate. Under international law, the lack of a valid license means the vessels are forbidden to engage in any fishing activities – including fish transfer. The transshipment of fish from one vessel to another is prohibited in international waters under international law, as it has been proven to aid illegal, unregulated, and unreported fishing activities.

Source: iStock
Transshipment 'Style' Ships

For more information, please visit:

(greenpeace.org/eastasia/multimedia/slideshows/oceans/ocean-to-market-fish/Illegal-Pacific-Tuna-Transhipment/).

Due to its great demand in the diets of Japan and other Asian countries, the Bluefin tuna is being fished rampantly to the extent that fishermen are not allowing this giant tuna to reach full growth. The tuna are not being allowed to reproduce and spawn as nature intended, which means extinction in the short to medium term. It is rare to find a full-grown Bluefin tuna nowadays. If caught, a single specimen can be sold for over $1.2 million USD.

The tuna from the Pacific Ocean are also being fished in excess, and to make matters worse, they are being hunted right on their spawning grounds with total disregard to the future survival of the species. Fishermen want to make their money and retire, without caring if the tuna goes extinct. Don't they want their children to be able to earn a living by fishing for tuna for generations to come, as their ancestors did? Soon, there will be no more tuna of any kind to catch. Yet, according to The Guardian (November 18, 2014), governments have agreed to a 20 per cent *increase* in the allowed Bluefin tuna catch:

> The tuna decision came against the backdrop of an apparent recovery in stocks of the species…. This year's quota of 13,500 tons will rise to 16,142 tons in 2015 and 19,296 tons in 2016, according to green groups, who attended the meeting as observers. The 2017 quota has been provisionally set for 23,155 tons, but will be reviewed in the light of a stock assessment to be carried out in 2016, they said.

For more information, see:

theguardian.com/environment/2014/nov/18/   governments-agree-20-hike-in-bluefin-tuna-catch

We need to fight harder for the protection of our Bluefin tuna and whatever other species are being caught with total disregard to their future survival. I strongly encourage the reader to join groups fighting for specific animal protection or environmental causes. They need our help. For information, specifically on the now-critical Bluefin tuna crisis in Spain, visit the following link:

hnewshub.co.nz/environmentsci/uneasy-times-for-spains-bluefin-tuna-fishing-2011050309#axzz477xF9kKB

Elephant poaching

In Africa and Southeast Asia, elephants and rhinos are being killed every year for their tusks and horns. According to Hanna Osborne in an article in International Business Times on January 9, 2013 entitled "Family of Elephants Slaughtered in Kenyan Massacre":

> The Kenya Wildlife Service (KWS) says the massacre took place at the weekend in the Bisadi area of Tsavo East National Park, and all 12 elephants were found with their tusks hacked off. We have not seen such an incident in recent memory. All of the elephants had been shot. The youngest was a juvenile, just two months old. It's the worst single loss that we have on record, and our records go back almost 30 years. These were professional killers. The attack was targeted and efficient.

That year, Kenya lost approximately 360 elephants to

poaching. In 2012, they lost 289 elephants, a 25 per cent increase in fatalities. Even though park rangers killed at least 40 poachers, the poaching is still increasing due to the high price paid internationally for elephant tusks by Asian countries alone. In previous encounters, some rangers have lost their lives as well.

[Tsavo National Park] spans 22,000 square kilometres and was home to an estimated 13,000 elephants. The number of elephants killed for their tusks has increased dramatically in recent years; in 2010 178 elephants were killed, while 360 were killed last year.

According to a KWS spokesman, the poachers in this massacre killed the matriarch elephant first, meaning the rest of the family had to mill around, so it was very easy to kill them. In order to combat poaching, some have suggested a "shoot to kill" policy for poachers, and, in another incident in Kenya, two suspected poachers were gunned down in Isiolo County in northern Kenya. Afterwards, according to Osborne, "the KWS said it recovered eight pieces of ivory after the battle. They also found a G3 rifle, 12 rounds of ammunition, assorted weapons and a weighing scale."

Source: conservationaction.co.za

Meanwhile, Peta Thornycroft and Aisilinn Laing (The Telegraph October 20, 2013) reported on poachers killing 300 elephants with cyanide in Hwange National Park in Zimbabwe. The carcasses were left there to rot in a devastating and horrific scene.

Question:
Is the artistic ivory work made from elephant tusks something to feel proud of owning? A magnificent animal was killed, and you want to brag about it? What kind of human being are you?

Answer:
It is definitely not worth owning ivory art, no matter how fine! Not at the expense of the life of a single elephant! In my opinion, owning "artistic" ivory is denigrating, revolting, and humiliating. It should be legally penalized.

For sad examples of "artistic" ivory images from slaughtered animals and illegal trading please visit:

dailymail.co.uk/news/article-2140734/Intricately-carved-Chinese-elephant-tusks-biggest-sale-set-fetch-mammoth-250-000-British-auction.html

Source: iStock

Source: iStock

Although many countries are taking measures to stop the killing of elephants, the slaughter continues. On October 22, 2015, Aisilinn Laing reported in The Telegraph on "South African conservationist shock over surge in Kruger elephant poaching." In Kruger National Park, 19 elephants were killed in 2015, proving, according to Laing, that there is still high demand by Asian countries (mainly China) for African ivory. And also in October 2015, a German hunter paid $60,000 to "legally kill an elephant." Critics say that it was the largest elephant hunted in the past 50 years, at least legally. The elephant was about 45 years old, and his life was terminated in less than 10 seconds, erasing forever his past and the still beautiful future he had ahead of him with his family group.

Ethical restraints on killing these beautiful animals are overridden by the power of the profits to be made. Money always has the last word, and always will. *"Poderoso Caballero, Don Dinero"* (Powerful Gentleman, Mr. Money!). When are we going to get smarter and stop this relentless killing just to justify the ridiculous personal needs of one hunter? I cannot fathom hunting down a magnificent elephant for some twisted "trophy" satisfaction. It is a cowardly, degrading action against a peaceful and defenseless animal!

Illegal rhinoceros hunting

According to scientists, rhinos have been around for over 40 million years, but now they are in danger simply for their horns. Asian markets demand the horn mainly for medicinal and aphrodisiac purposes. As Aisilinn Laing reported in an article entitled "Last Rhinos in Mozambique Killed By Poachers" in The Telegraph in April, 2013:

> Poachers apparently working in cahoots with the game rangers responsible for protecting them have wiped out the last known rhinoceroses in Mozambique. The 15 threatened animals were shot dead for their horns in the Mozambican part of Great Limpopo Trans-Frontier Park, which also covers South Africa and Zimbabwe.

> They were thought to be the last of an estimated 300 that roamed through the special conservation area when it was established as "the world's greatest animal kingdom" in a treaty signed by the three countries' presidents in 2002. The latest deaths, and Mozambique's failure to tackle poaching, has prompted threats by South Africa to re-erect fences between their reserves.

> Wildlife authorities believe the poachers were able to track the rhinoceroses with the help of game rangers working in the Limpopo National Park, as the Mozambican side of the reserve is known. A total of 30 rangers are due in court in the coming weeks, charged with collusion in the creatures' deaths, according to the park's administrators.

In Asian culture, rhino horn is considered very effective for healing purposes, although they are also prized for carving. Malaysia, India, and South Korea follow similar medicinal traditions regarding the properties and healing purposes of the rhino's horn. The ancient Persians and Greeks used rhino horns to detect poison. Many poisons are alkaline and react to the rhino horn's keratin protein. The center of the horn also contains strong deposits of melanin and calcium. Other cultures utilize the rhino horn as an ornamental handle for the daggers used during important cultural and religious events.

There are five types of rhinos: the Black rhino, the White rhino, Greater On-Horn rhino, Java rhino, and Sumatra rhino. The Northern White is a subspecies of the White. In Kenya, there is a rhino named Sudan that has no horn and is being guarded 24/7 by armed rangers. They also guard two female rhinos of his subspecies 24/7. Sudan's horn was intentionally removed to deter poachers. He is the only male alive from the Northern White rhino subspecies, and apparently, he is breeding successfully with the other two females in the Ol Pejeta Conservancy in Kenya.

Source: iStock

The poaching of rhinoceros is so bad and alarming that the night of Mar the 6th of 2017, poachers broke into a French zoo to kill a four-year-old white rhinoceros, cutting of his horn with a chain saw. It is one of the most aggressive actions ever experienced in Europe against an endangered species, especially when they were five security staff members living in the zoo, along with many security cameras. His second horn was partially cut because they apparently ran out of time. Countries like Zimbabwe, believe that to save the rhinoceros they need to remove their horns to avoid poaching attacks against the species in the wild and now in zoos. They are acting accordingly.

As per the WWF's species directory of endangered or critically endangered species, the rhinos considered most critically endangered are the Black rhino, the Java rhino and the Sumatran rhino. At present, there are fewer than 100 Sumatran rhinos and less than 65 Java rhinos.

Tigers

There are nine well-known and documented types of tiger (Panthera Tigris) still roaming our world. These are: the Caspian tiger, Amur or Siberian tiger, Sumatra tiger, Bengal tiger, South China tiger, Java tiger, Indochinese tiger, Malayan tiger, and Bali tiger. Some of the species in the tigers' population are at a dangerously low tipping point towards extinction. Not all the above-mentioned tigers are on the endangered species list though. But according to Greenpeace, the critically endangered tigers are the South China and Sumatran tigers. The endangered tigers are the Indochinese, Bengal tiger, and Amur tigers.

Tigers are carnivores and are known to be the largest cat species. They can reach over three metres in length and weigh close to 400 kilograms of pure lean muscle. They are fast, silent, and skilled hunters, as well as amazing swimmers and patient while waiting for their prey. They are one of the most majestic animals in the world. Their habitat is constantly threatened and has been reduced by the advancement of human encroachment into their territory due to continued human development. This has reduced their hunting grounds and put them more and more at risk. They are very independent animals known to reach an average of 23 to 24 years of age. They give birth to about three cubs every two to three years. Females reach maturity one or two years earlier than males (about three to four years for female breeding stage).

Unfortunately, tiger parts are a delicacy in the diet of many Chinese people, who also use them for medicinal purposes. These are the main reasons tiger poaching has been (and still is) practiced so extensively throughout human history. For years, the WWF has been promoting zero tolerance for tiger hunting in the interest of what they call "TX2," a target of doubling the tiger population as quickly as possible.

There are no precise numbers or statistics out there on the exact number of tigers roaming their various habitats, but many say there are probably no more than about 3,200 tigers, down from over 100,000 at the beginning of the twentieth century.

An interesting article from The Associated Press published on the website of The New York Daily News on April 17, 2015 (*nydailynews.com/life-style/india-tiger-population-increasenot-real-scientist-article-1.2188712*) entitled "India's tiger population may not have increased despite government claims, scientists say," reports that the Sundarban Tiger Reserve in India claimed their tiger population had increased 30 per cent in only four years, allowing the Indian government to boast that they were being very successful in the conservation of the tiger population in India. However, according to experts, it is mathematically impossible that the tiger population could have increased by that amount in such a short time.

Source: iStock

According to the government of Prime Minister Narendra Modi, the tiger population increased by 2,226 large felines, a figure which scientifically is not possible in that period of time and with the number of existing tigers to start with. To make matters worse, the Environment Minister Parkash Javadekar confirmed the 30 per cent increase, and then, immediately thereafter, Modi said that the increase had been 40 per cent! Tiger expert K. Ullas Karanth, the science director for the Wildlife Conservation Society in Asia (WCSA), said that both figures are improbable. Such playing with figures can hurt (instead of helping) the tiger population in the long run.

The Wild Life Conservation Society of India (WLPI) observed "a 30 per cent increase within four years is implausible. Though tigers have high birth rates, they also have high natural death rates, and factors such as habitat loss and poaching haven't slowed. At least 110 tigers per year were killed in 2011-14, barely a drop from the 118 poached in 2007-10." In 2011-17 over 100 tigers per year were killed and trafficked illegally. Sadly, by Feb of 2018, they are still doing it.

In the Europe edition of the FT Weekend of Saturday June 11, 2016, there is an article entitled "Tiger Scandal - Temples deny 'selling heaven' as monks face fraud claims." Thailand's venerable monks, as the author Michael Peel puts it, are being accused of fraud, animal smuggling, and of committing macabre acts with the Tigers. Buddhist monks are being accused of trading body parts while taking advantage of their so-called tiger sanctuary, which is visited every year by thousands of tourists, who have no idea of what really is going behind those doors at night. After gruesome discoveries, the government removed over 130 tigers from the monks' care. Sometimes those that portray the most positive and peaceful image are worse than the devil themselves.

Gorillas' delicate balance

The most endangered of these magnificent animals are the Cross-River gorilla, the Western Lowland gorilla, and the well-known Mountain gorilla.

When the Mountain gorilla was first discovered in 1902, hunting for gorillas started immediately, and there was a sharp decline in their population, which drove them almost to extinction. But thanks mainly to efforts over many years by Dian Fossey, an American zoologist and primatologist (known as "the woman that lives alone in the mountain"), gorillas as a species were put on the world map as noble, independent, and family-oriented animals that required protection. Fossey started several conservation organizations in Congo and Rwanda for the protection of the species. Her efforts paid off, even though poachers ultimately killed her.

It is believed that the gorilla population, and specifically that of the Mountain gorilla (known scientifically as Gorilla beringei beringei), has made a comeback in numbers thanks to the strong conservation efforts of various organizations. The Mountain gorilla is found mainly in three national parks in Rwanda, the Democratic Republic of Congo (DRC), and Uganda. They live in clans or families usually made up of three females, with their babies, and one silverback male who is the dominant member of the group and protects it from threats or dangers.

According to the last WWF monitoring report, the Mountain gorilla population has increased by 41.94 per cent since 1989, from 620 to 880. This is definitely the result of intensive monitoring and support by private non-profit organizations and government agencies. Cooperation between both groups has been essential in reducing poaching and human encroachment. Again, if there is a will, there is a way.

Lions still at risk

In Scientific American (October 27, 2014), an article John R. Platt entitled "African Lions Face Extinction by 2050, Could Gain Endangered Species Act Protection" reports that the African lion population fell by 50 per cent over the past three decades, from 68,000 to 34,000 lions by the end of 2014. He lists three main causes for the downward trend: habitat loss, human-lion confrontations, and loss of the lions' prey to the "bush-meat" trade. The latter refers to wild meat, such as, non-domestic mammals, birds, reptiles, and amphibians. But, in August of 2017, National Geographic now confirms that the Lion's population declined 90 per-cent in the last 75 years. Even though the lion is not officially considered by some countries an endangered species, lions are still hunted illegally, often after being lured outside protected areas. This is what happened to a famous Zimbabwean lion called Cecil, when a dentist from the United States, Walter James Palmer, shot him dead on July 1, 2015. The government of Zimbabwe has started a legal process to extradite Palmer, but the Minnesota dentist has maintained that, if he had known the lion "had a name and was important to the country or a study, obviously, I wouldn't have taken it. Nobody in our hunting party knew, before or after, the name of this lion."

In my view, and that of millions of other people, Dr. Palmer had no right to end the life of an animal for game, for fun, and for his own distorted ego and satisfaction. As I have said before, give him a knife, a sword, or a machete and drop him in the middle of the African Savannah and let him go and hunt anything. Let's see if he comes back alive. In fact, it is said that he wounded Cecil with an arrow and that it was only about 40 hours later, after the animal had continually suffered, that Cecil was finally tracked down and killed. Such things often happen in trophy hunting. Cecil lived in Zimbabwe's Hwange National Park (also known as Hwange Game Reserve), but the dentist's guides lured it out of the sanctuary so that they could shoot it "legally." Apparently, the lion was not just a major attraction for tourists, but also part of a study being done by the University of Oxford. For more information, visit:

metro.co.uk/2015/09/07/dentist-who-killed-cecil-the-lion-defends-his-actions-and-says-hes-going-back-to-work-in-days-5378919/

When will the killing stop? Only a month later, on August 3, 2015, Alix Culbertson, writing in The Express, reported on "another American accused of illegally hunting in [the] same safari park [where] Cecil was killed." Culberston pulls no punches in his report:

> The second American, Jan Casimir Seski of Murrysville, Pennsylvania, was allegedly involved in an illegal lion hunt in April in Zimbabwe's Hwange National Park, the same park where the world's most famous lion was killed last month, resulting in a global outcry.

To many, the "cold-blooded killer" is a gynecological oncologist and director of the Centre for Bloodless Medicine and Surgery at Allegheny General Hospital – and is also a highly active big-game hunter. Please visit:

(express.co.uk/news/world/595537/second-American-arrested-illegal-lion-hunting-Hwange-Park-Zimbabwe-Cecil-lion).

Should all big game hunting be banned? The sport of killing animals with powerful weaponry in the form of rifles or crossbows is, to my mind, a cowardly way of conducting oneself when it is just for sport, trophies, or "fun." Such is the case of huntress Rebecca Francis (and others) who has hunted zebras, giraffes, and many other animals. What have those innocent animals, which are not even carnivores, done to justify a cruel, cold-blooded assassination? The animals are ambushed while minding their own business on the savannah and never see their end coming.

Yet animals mourn – it has been proven scientifically – so what happens to the rest of the herd that has just lost a member of their group and, in my opinion, to an insensitive, egocentric, and quasi-retarded hunter? Again, in my personal opinion, if Rebecca Francis does not want (or dare) to go outdoors with a knife and a spear to hunt, then just try going out there ten minutes ahead of another hunter carrying his or her high-tech crossbow or rifle, and let him or her hunt you down. How would that feel, and what odds would you really have for survival with just a spear and a knife?

Source: iStock

A friend of mine told me once: "Hunters should be thrown into the biggest game reserve in Africa, and let them hunt each other down until the last man (or woman) stands, so they understand what being hunted is all about." After careful thought, I personally think that is not such a bad idea!

Animals in danger of extinction

Many organizations publish lists of endangered species. After reviewing many lists, I summarize below, in addition to the ten-species listed previously, the others that, in my view, are most endangered and whose extinction, if it is allowed, will most seriously affect the ecosystem. These species together form an integral part of a natural chain that helps maintain the balance of the ecosystem along with the beauty of the surrounding environment:

Snow Leopard and Amur Leopard:
The first is affected by climate change, the second by illegal hunting.

Borneo Orangutan:
Threatened mainly by loss of habitat and relentless hunting.

Humphead Wrasse:
These fish live around coral reefs, which are being polluted throughout the world, causing loss of habitat. They are also being fished extensively.

Northern Hairy-Nosed Wombat:
Australian marsupial. Borrows tunnels underground with powerful claws. It is a short, strong, stocky animal that can weigh up to 40 kilograms and grow to a metre in length. Also being hunted indiscriminately.

Northern Caribou:
It is hunted in great number by humans, but wolves and climate change are also threatening the Caribou. It is a very well-adapted animal for northern winters, with a dense winter

coat for perfect insulation. An absolutely beautiful animal.

Source: iStock

Sharks:
They are being hunted by the millions every year and die a slow, painful death. The Chinese and Asian markets also have a keen taste for shark fins and do not mind how these beautiful, important ocean creatures are caught or killed. Finning is a very inhumane way of slicing and hacking the shark's fins. But even worse, they throw them back into the ocean with amputated fins, so the sharks just sink to the bottom like a rock and lie in agony, waiting for death.

Dense-Flowered Lupine:
A species from the flora category native to Canada and specifically to Victoria, BC. According to the Canada Wildlife Federation, they grow on clay cliffs, grassy seashores, and eroded grassy banks. They are losing habitat to erosion, trampling by people, oil spills, and invasive species.

Polar Bears:
The main reason for their danger is climate change, which is warming their polar territory. Canada's largest carnivore (after the Grizzly bear), with male adults capable of weighing close to 800 kilograms.

Source: iStock

Spotted Owl:
Mainly threatened by non-stop logging that is destroying their habitat. Canada exploits its natural resources regardless of the repercussions on the ecosystem and overall environment. Various species are being pushed to the brink of extinction, along with the natural resources themselves.

Wood Poppy:
This Canadian yellow flower is restricted to small, scattered sites in southwestern Ontario. The main threats are invasive species and human recreational activities.

Sea Lions:
These are wonderful swimmers that feed on fish and hang out on beaches and rocks. Their main threats are hunting, diseases, and lack of the fish they feed on due to climate change warming their waters.

Galapagos Penguin:
The WWF confirms that this is the only penguin found north of the equator and that their main threats are pollution, climate change, and bycatch. Some penguins that have been

exposed to domestic animals are now carrying diseases from them as well. The Southern Rockhopper penguin is another penguin species in danger of extinction for the same reasons.

The Pigmy Sloth:
One of the slowest mammals on planet Earth. Originally from Central and South America, they move at a rate of only about 40 yards per day. They depend on leaves, buds and twigs and are slow on earth but agile, quick, and smooth swimmers. Deforestation and illegal hunting are their biggest threats.

Poison Dart Frog:
Habitat loss and climate change are the main factors threatening this species. According to WWF, there are more than 100 species of poison dart frogs, including those that live in the Amazon, which are endangered mainly by deforestation.

Falcons:
According to a professor of biology at Yukon College's Yukon Research Centre in Whitehorse, both of the falcon species (the Ptarmigan and the Gyrfalcons) that live in the circumpolar ecosystems appear to be decreasing in quantities in the Yukon. In Canadian Geographic (July/August 2013) Genesee Keevil reports a correlation between decreasing falcon numbers and "declines in other species in the territory, including the snowshoe hare and Dall sheep – important prey for bigger predators such as Lynx," which suggests that "changes in climate here may be happening faster than species can adapt."

Catfish:
The catfish population is disappearing at an alarming rate. In the rainforest of Alabama, a catfish has not been seen since 2004, according to Jesse Greenspan in an article from March 2014 (page 18) in Scientific American entitled "The Rain Forest of Alabama – An extinction crisis is quietly unfolding in

the southeastern US." The Alabama rainforest receives fresh water from various isolated river basins, which should greatly assist in the biodiversity of aquatic life, but Greenspan says that the catfish (known as the chucky madtom) and over a dozen other species there are now on the brink of going extinct. The causes are familiar: "Species are being devastated by agricultural chemicals, dams, and invasive species. Sediment-laden runoff has also taken a toll, particularly on filter feeders." Greenspan quotes Ms. Tierra Curry (a biologist at The Center For Biological Diversity): "If water conditions never improve, then they'll just die."

Greenspan notes that water withdrawal for human consumption is also affecting the survival of many species in the area. He adds that a conservation crisis is taking place that almost nobody hears about; mountain-top removal mining, which is causing contamination and extinction crises in other parts of the US as well. Also, known as "mountain mining," this involves the total removal of the mountain tops or ridges of mountain chains in order to extract minerals, most commonly coal, which is in increasing demand in North America. Mountain mining has a severe ecological impact, especially since the mining companies usually do not clean up the mess they leave behind. The exposed rocks leach unwanted toxins and heavy metals that end up in our rivers and lakes, threatening animals, plants, and humans.

Source: iStock

Mountain removals such as the ones pictured here have taken place extensively in the Appalachian region of the US as well, seriously affecting the ecosystem and biodiversity of the area and beyond. Unfortunately, very few people know what is really taking place, so not enough action has been taken to try to put a stop to this destructive practice. We urgently need to start looking for cleaner sources of energy instead of our good old but decrepit friend Mr. Coal.

According to Encyclopedia Britannica, the Appalachian region "extends for almost 2,000 miles (3,200 km) from the Canadian province of Newfoundland and Labrador to central Alabama in the United States … [and forms] a natural barrier between the eastern Coastal Plain and the vast Interior Lowlands of North America."

In the US, it includes large parts of Virginia, Kentucky, Maryland, and North Carolina and extends into South Carolina, Pennsylvania, Georgia, Alabama and southern Ohio. It is a vital part of our geography that more people should know about, so we can join forces and do something about its ongoing degradation through mountain mining and other harmful practices. Recommendations on how the average person can assist are in the conclusions section of this book.

Source: iStock

Source: iStock

Majestic sight shattered by whale hunters!

Source: iStock

APPENDIX 2:

Brief Biography of the Author

Born and raised in Mexico City (D.F.) from 1958 to 1987. He studied his undergraduate degree in Economics (Mexico City) followed by a Master of Business Administration (MBA) in a joint programme between Notre Dame University (USA) and the London Graduate School of Business (England).

His professional career started as a professor and researcher in economics and finance in the Mexican banking system. He immigrated to Canada in 1987 where he concentrated on the creation and promotion of businesses under the 'turn-key-operation' concept. He assisted the Ministry of Economic Development at that time and created a database for businesses in the service industry for the provincial government.

In conjunction with government and banking programs, he worked to assist foreign business investors and local entrepreneurs establish and run a successful business. He assisted his various clients throughout their business start-up stage in trying to achieve their break-even point in the shortest and most efficient time possible, while trying to minimize their risks and expand their potential.

Carreras has acquired extensive professional experience in North America (Mexico, United States and Canada) and has travelled considerably for business and research throughout Europe, Asia and the American continent. As a researcher and writer, he is detailed and always tries to apply a logical and critical thinking to his overall framework and presentation.

<u>As an Author</u>:

His passion for writing is fuelled by the desire to open people's eyes to what is happening around them. He trusts this will improve their life style and bring harmony to their lives. Throughout his "Runaway Trilogy", an important goal is to bring awareness regarding the delicate situation Planet Earth is going through. He wants to share his experience and points of view for others to learn and benefit from the way he perceives this world and its progressive changes. As an author, he does not try to change people's views. Backed by real life experience and scientific evidence, his main goal is to create awareness of the real situation our societies and surroundings are going through. It is up to the readers to make an informed decision and act wisely. Always motivated by trust and hard work, the author hopes his readers see their reality in a different light, and perhaps, motivate them to protect their society, environment, and ecosystem above and beyond the search for money and power.

Carreras does his best to experience life from a realistic, responsible, and pragmatic perspective. This trilogy has been written with a down-to-earth and rational approach for anyone to understand and apply to improve their lifestyle if they choose to do so. All his groundwork, structure and conclusions are based on existing research platforms of well-known authors, scientists, book and magazine publications, newspapers, and the web. All this is backed by extensive travel experience and systematic evaluation. He is observant and detailed-oriented, trying always to uncover the truth, with a humble and respectful approach in spirit and to the best of his abilities.

INDEX

www.ingramcontent.com/pod-product-compliance
Lightning Source LLC
Chambersburg PA
CBHW061956280526
45787CB00005B/1889